The NFL's Pivotal Years

ALSO BY BRAD SCHULTZ

The NFL's Greatest Day: Roger Staubach, Franco Harris and the Story of Immaculate Saturday (McFarland, 2019)

The NFL's Pivotal Years
Remaking Pro Football, 1957–1962

BRAD SCHULTZ

McFarland & Company, Inc., Publishers
Jefferson, North Carolina

ISBN (print) 978-1-4766-8439-0
ISBN (ebook) 978-1-4766-4296-3

LIBRARY OF CONGRESS AND BRITISH LIBRARY
CATALOGUING DATA ARE AVAILABLE

Library of Congress Control Number 2021012491

© 2021 Brad Schultz. All rights reserved

*No part of this book may be reproduced or transmitted in any form
or by any means, electronic or mechanical, including photocopying
or recording, or by any information storage and retrieval system,
without permission in writing from the publisher.*

New York Giants assistant coaches Vince Lombardi (left) and
Tom Landry reviewing game plans on November 15, 1958 (Library of Congress)

Printed in the United States of America

*McFarland & Company, Inc., Publishers
Box 611, Jefferson, North Carolina 28640
www.mcfarlandpub.com*

Contents

Preface	1
Introduction	5
One. Innocence Lost	17
Two. Growing Up, Growing Old	33
Three. The Greatest Game Ever Televised	47
Four. The Ruthian Moment	63
Five. The Power of Myth	79
Six. Alphabet Soup	94
Seven. Oh, Canada!—And Beyond	113
Eight. Man with a Vision	129
Nine. By the Numbers	145
Ten. The Door Opens Wider	161
Eleven. Heir Coryell	173
Twelve. Time and Place	186
Chapter Notes	203
Bibliography	229
Index	235

Preface

Once ESPN began to get its feet on the ground in the 1980s and '90s, it launched a series of spinoff networks to capitalize on its success. One of those was ESPN Classic, which debuted in 1995 and primarily featured old game footage and other historic programming. The channel was a modest success, but was eventually phased out in favor of ESPNews, ESPN2 and ESPNU.

But the spirit of ESPN Classic returned in the spring of 2020 during the coronavirus pandemic. With no live sports programming to offer other than talk shows, outlets like ESPN, MLB Network, NFL Network and others had no choice but to air old sporting events. Even broadcast networks like Fox and ABC, now with empty slots to fill on weekends that had been reserved for baseball and playoff hockey, followed suit. Suddenly, every network was ESPN Classic. Some of the offerings strained the definition of "classic." Most of the programming was from the 2010s, suggesting that "classic" really meant something recent that looked aesthetically good on television and for which the network owned the rights. A true classic should bring to mind an all-time event that made an imprint on the sporting consciousness and not a 2008 regular season basketball game between Cal and UCLA that aired as a "classic" on ESPNU one Saturday afternoon.

By any definition or standard, the 1958 NFL Championship game between the Baltimore Colts and New York Giants is a classic, but you won't see it on ESPN or any other sports history channel. Yes, edited compilations exist, cobbled together using radio broadcasts and film footage, but even those are incomplete and miss important parts of the game. It's hard to believe that someone would not have recognized the importance of the game and preserved a copy, but television networks and the NFL did not do a good job of curating their history until the 1960s. Perhaps some copy of the game exists somewhere, but along with Super Bowl I, the 1958 title game is the Holy Grail of classic sports broadcasts.[1]

Yet, even without benefit of a television copy, many fans and experts consider the 1958 championship game the seminal moment in league history. Before it, the NFL was simply a mom-and-pop outfit trying to survive; after it, football soon became the most popular sport in America and the NFL evolved into one of the most powerful sports organizations in the world. More than sixty years later, "The Greatest Game Ever Played" still has the same magic and mystique among sports fans, in part because television so perfectly captured the drama of the Baltimore Colts 23–17 overtime win over the New York Giants.

This perspective seems to divide the NFL into two distinct time periods: before the game and after. But that is overly simplistic and misses out on some equally important events in league history. Just a month after the game, Giants assistant Vince Lombardi left New York to become head coach of the Packers and launch a new dynasty in Green Bay. In fact, the 1959 calendar year was monumental in NFL history.

- January: Lombardi takes over Packers
- August: NFL plays exhibition game in a foreign country
- August: Lamar Hunt announces formation of American Football League
- October: NFL Commissioner Bert Bell dies of a heart attack at an Eagles game
- December: Tom Landry agrees to become coach of the expansion Dallas Cowboys

Expand the circle a little more to 1957 and 1960 and you get even more. In 1957, the U.S. Supreme Court made a decision in a case against the NFL that eventually paved the way for players to form a union. In 1960, after a long and contentious meeting, NFL owners announced Pete Rozelle as their new commissioner. Rozelle did nothing less than transform the league and become the model for the successful CEO commissioners of today. Move the circle out to 1962 and you get the formation of NFL Films, which played just as an important role in the success of the league as Lombardi, Landry or the 1958 Colts.

Has there ever been a five-year period so essential to the growth of the NFL as this one? Some might argue the early days of the NFL in the 1920s, but that period was marked more by chaos and unpredictability rather than success. The years between 1965 and 1970 saw a merger between the NFL and AFL and the birth of the Super Bowl, but the groundwork for those events was laid in 1957–1962 when the AFL was formed and the NFL started a costly war to drive the newcomers out of business. Between 1982 and 1987 the NFL suffered through two work stoppages that threatened to destroy the game, but again, the genesis of those struggles came in 1957 with the Supreme Court decision in *Radovich v. National Football League.*

Pick almost any important event in the NFL in the last fifty years and you can draw a line from it back to 1957–1962. The Raiders moving from Oakland to Los Angeles back to Oakland and then to Las Vegas? That all goes back to the feud between Rozelle and Raiders owner Al Davis and the early AFL–NFL wars. The growth of free agency and contracts that have made NFL players multi-millionaires? Draw the line back to 1957 and a player named Bill Radovich. Social protests such as Colin Kaepernick taking a knee during the national anthem at games? The early American Football League was a breeding ground for minority athletes unwilling to accept the status quo.

All of the football events of 1957–1962 took place within a powerful historical and cultural context. The climate of the times included the Cold War, Cuban Missile Crisis, Civil Rights struggle, desegregation of schools, and a host of other issues. The transition from the seemingly banal Eisenhower years to the excitement of the Kennedy era had profound consequences for the trajectory of the NFL and its players, coaches and fans.

I did not set out to write a book about 1958, the Colts–Giants, or that particular era of the NFL. Like many ideas, it simply came to me one morning in the shower. The 1958 title game was running through my mind for some reason, and then I started connecting the dots— Lombardi and Landry, Bell and Rozelle, the AFL and the NFL. They all seemed to fit into that narrow slice of NFL history. As I started looking further, I found the NFL exhibition games in Canada, Bill Radovich, and Ed Sabol.

NFL history is filled with important events that often times seem completely unrelated. For some reason, many of those events directly or indirectly point back to 1957–1962. It is one of the most fascinating time periods in league history and I hope you get as much out of reliving it as I did in writing about it.

Introduction

There has been no bigger story in the 2020s than the coronavirus pandemic. It has affected almost every area of the globe and every facet of life. As deaths rose into the hundreds of thousands, the virus forced people to reexamine the daily habits they had always taken for granted—going to work, gathering food, and simply congregating with other people.

One of the earliest casualties was sports, as leagues cancelled games and sent their athletes, coaches and staff into isolation. The pandemic hit in the spring, right at the start of the major league baseball season, raising questions as to whether there would be any games at all in 2020. And while football had a few months before its season started, the National Football League was in similar danger. The first step was a modified college draft, which went totally online so as not to bring large crowds together. Then came the serious questions about how to start games in the fall, whether to hold games without fans, and even whether to have games at all. "As long as we're still in a place where a single individual tests positive for the virus that you have to quarantine every single person who was in contact with them in any shape, form or fashion, then I don't think you can begin to think about reopening a team sport," said Dr. Allan Sills, the NFL's chief medical officer, in May 2020. "Because we're going to have positive cases for a very long time."[1]

The coronavirus cloud that hung over the league was just the latest in a long list of issues that have put the NFL on the defensive and challenged its role as the most powerful and popular sport in the U.S.

The league as a whole can seem quite tone deaf to current cultural issues, including domestic violence among NFL players. Several players have been fined or suspended for allegations of domestic abuse, but there appears to be no standards in terms of NFL discipline. The league badly mishandled the Ray Rice incident in 2014 when the Baltimore Ravens running back was indicted by a grand jury, and Commissioner Roger Goodell showed little interest in obtaining or even looking at the damning evidence—video from a casino elevator that showed Rice punching his fiancée. Only when a media outlet released the video did the league move to suspend Rice indefinitely and he never played again in the NFL.

"The NFL took an uncharacteristically passive approach when it came to gathering evidence," said ESPN, which conducted an investigation for its *Outside the Lines* program, "opening itself up to widespread criticism, allegations of inconsistent approaches to player discipline and questions about whether Goodell gave Rice—the corporate face of the Baltimore franchise—a light punishment." ESPN went on to call the incident "the biggest crisis confronting a commissioner in the NFL's 94-year history."[2]

The biggest, that is, until the arrival of Colin Kaepernick. Until 2016, Kaepernick was known as a successful and versatile quarterback for the San Francisco 49ers, and he took the team to the Super Bowl after the 2012 season. During the preseason games of 2016, Kaepernick began kneeling during the national anthem instead of standing as a means of protesting social injustice and police brutality against blacks. "I am not going to stand up to show pride in a flag for a country that oppresses black people and people of color," Kaepernick said after his first protest. "To me, this is bigger than football and it would be selfish on my part to look the other way."[3]

The move created a firestorm of controversy that split the league into two camps, ignited similar protests by athletes in other sports, and essentially ended Kaepernick's career after that season as no team wanted the potential public relations fallout. Through it all, the NFL waffled and hedged, insisting that Kaepernick had the right to protest, but allegedly working behind the scenes to keep him out of work. When Kaepernick and another protestor, defensive back Eric Reid, sued the league for collusion, Roger Goodell rather weakly insisted, "Our clubs are the ones that make decisions on players. They make that individually. They make that in the best interests of their teams. I think if a team decides that Colin Kaepernick or any other player can help their team win, that's what they'll do." Such statements seemed to contradict comments from NFL owners, like the Ravens Steve Bisciotti, who said adding Kaepernick to the team "might hurt" its brand.[4]

The lawsuit was eventually settled out of court and contained a confidentiality clause, so only Kaepernick, Reid and the NFL know the final numbers. "Kneeling for the anthem started a movement that the league, which prides itself in keeping protests under control, simply could not control," observed longtime sportswriter Hal Bock. "Kaepernick's 'take a knee' statement spread like wildfire."[5]

Introduction

While the Kaepernick issue and domestic violence have somewhat ebbed and flowed in recent years, one problem that has shown staying power is the growing danger of concussions. The number of former players with CTE (chronic traumatic encephalopathy) has risen dramatically in recent years. A 2016 study by Boston University of 94 brains donated by former NFL players found evidence of the disease in 90 cases. The list of former players with CTE reads like a "Who's Who" of the Hall of Fame—Kenny Stabler, John Mackey, and Mike Webster, to name just a few.

"You're supposed to be tough and invincible," said another Hall of Famer, Rayfield Wright. "If something's wrong with you, you try to hide it. Which is exactly what I did." The former Cowboys lineman suffered from dementia, headaches, and memory loss. "I'm scared," he admitted. "I don't want this to happen. You don't want people to look at you any differently. You don't want people to know."[6]

It was the death of former Steelers great Webster in 2002 that first drew attention to CTE and Dr. Bennet Omalu who made the diagnosis. At first, the NFL denied and then attacked Omalu's findings. "These statements are based on a complete misunderstanding of the relevant medical literature on chronic traumatic encephalopathy ... [and] demonstrate the flaws in Omalu's assertions," the league and its supporters claimed.[7] The NFL did not publicly acknowledge a link between concussions and CTE until 2009, which the NFL confirmed in testimony before Congress in 2016.

For his part, Omalu, who wrote a book and became the subject of a movie called *Concussion*, has remained steadfast. "I don't attack the NFL," he said. "The NFL is a corporation. What do corporations do? They try to make money by selling a product or service. The NFL is not in the business of healthcare."[8]

That's why nearly 5,000 former players sued the league in 2011, claiming that for years the NFL was aware of the dangers of concussions but hid that information from its players. The suit was settled in 2013 for $765 million, but the judge overseeing the case was concerned that the amount was insufficient to cover the cost of adequate treatment. In 2015, Judge Anita Brody removed the $765 million cap and the final total was put at one billion dollars. When finally approved in 2016, it meant that 20,000 retired NFL players would receive payments for medical treatments for the next 65 years.

It's not just the NFL that has a concussion problem; it's football on all levels. Participation in high school football, which peaked in 2008, began to slow down and then decline through 2019. "This decline is associated with media attention focused on concussions or brain injuries among football players," said Dr. Chris Feudtner of the Children's Hospital of Philadelphia.[9] In 2018, 48 percent of parents said they would discourage their children from playing football because of concussion fears—an 8 percent rise in just four years.[10]

Taken together, these issues and controversies have dealt some serious blows to the power and prestige of the NFL. "And it's not just the national anthem issue that has turned off the public," writes Phil Mushnick of the *New York Post*. "It's the overall rotten comportment of players ... driving on suspended licenses, tweeting semi-literate boasts, and far worse. To deny the NFL is growing increasingly insufferable would be an exercise in polite, intentional ignorance."[11] Financially, fans could once identify with the players, who often made so little in salary that they were required to have off-season jobs. Identification is harder to come by when Seahawks quarterback Russell Wilson signs a five-year deal for $157 million, and the average NFL salary is more than two million dollars per year. NFL players often seem insensitive to the disparity, many of them holding out to renegotiate for even bigger paydays.

Thus, there has been no lack of doomsayers that predict that football in general, and the NFL in particular, is in deep trouble. In 2014, sport historian and scholar Michael Oriard published a treatise titled "Chronicle of a (Football) Death Foretold: The Imminent Demise of a National Pastime?" Oriard looked at safety issues and their affect on the decline in youth football and observed, "One grim scenario is easy to imagine for the not-too-distant future: a game known to be horribly self-destructive, played at the highest level only by the under privileged, as literal, not just metaphorical, gladiators."[12]

Six years later, *Forbes* magazine said that Oriard's nightmare scenario was coming true. Roger Pielke looked at not only the decline in youth football, but also the continuing regionalization of the sport, now concentrated most fully in the South and especially the Southeast. "More broadly," write Pielke, "gridiron football is in an era of rapid decline, and evidence suggests that the decline is accelerating."[13]

But football has been on its deathbed several times and always managed to survive. In 1905, the game was so brutal and led to so many deaths that a public outcry called for its abolition. President Theodore Roosevelt called a special meeting of football leaders, which included the legendary Walter Camp, to discuss how to save the game. Even Roosevelt, long a proponent of vigorous exercise and manly activity, was alarmed. "Brutality playing a game should awaken the heartiest and most plainly shown contempt for the player guilty of it. I hope to see both graduate and undergraduate opinion come to scorn such a man as one guilty of base and dishonorable action."[14] Roosevelt and football's leaders quieted the critics by bringing about rule changes that made the sport safer.

The NFL was in constant danger during its early chaotic years of the 1920s, the Great Depression of the 1930s, the exigencies of World War II in the 1940s, and the dominance of baseball in the 1950s. Yet each time it not only survived, it thrived, and grew bigger, better and more powerful. The league has constantly reinvented itself to meet new situations, and has shown a remarkable ability to transform in the face of crisis.

As the NFL celebrated its 100th season in 2019, it did so as the unquestioned behemoth of sports organizations in the United States, and even the world. Depending on what list one uses, the NFL ranks either first or second in the world in terms of economic power, with revenues in the hundreds of billions of dollars.[15] In *Forbes*' annual ranking of the world's most valuable sports franchises, the Dallas Cowboys ranked first for the fourth straight year, with profits at $365 million. More than half of the Forbes Top 50 were teams from the NFL.[16]

Such numbers are unsurprising given how football has so long dominated the American sports culture, years ago surpassing baseball in popularity among all ages, races and backgrounds of fans and non-fans alike. Where baseball once seemed to fit America's slower pace and rural roots as the "national pastime," it now seems slow and outdated in a fast-paced, digital world. Baseball, with its long stretches of inactivity, doesn't seem to work on television, where football, with its almost constant action and emotion, fits perfectly.

"The National Football League is more than a game or a sports league," writes Alison Kanski. "It's so ingrained in American culture, that even its missteps or major safety concerns about the game itself are quickly forgotten. Tens of millions of fans have stuck by the NFL … and the NFL's presence in Americans' lives goes beyond the game."[17] That presence is built on the marriage between the NFL and Sunday afternoons. "The league has staked a claim to a day of the week where friends, family, and neighbors get together to forget everything else and enjoy each other's company." Shawn McBride of Ketchum Sports goes even further—"[the NFL] really becomes part of a person's identity."[18]

That was a place once reserved for baseball, and also to an extent, boxing. Television may have doomed both, but for different reasons. Baseball, with its long lulls of inactivity, weather delays, and indeterminate length of games, never really translated well to the constraints of the small screen. In 2019, baseball executives changed some long-standing rules in order to help speed things up—limiting mound visits, timed inning breaks, and even timed pitching changes—all for the sake of television. Yet, the length of games still continues to rise, and television ratings as a whole, including for the World Series, continue to fall.[19]

Boxing, once "American's second favorite sport after baseball, now [is] a niche sport, on its way to near extinction."[20] Unlike baseball, boxing fit neatly into a television screen, and in the 1950s events were televised almost every night of the week. But many argue that overexposure on television caused the neighborhood gym to wither, leading to fewer boxers with lesser abilities. "While a good case can be made that skill levels in other spectator sports that engage us have increased," writes Larry Thornberry, "skills in the boxing game have eroded badly."[21] When NFL Commissioner Pete Rozelle went to Congress in 1972 to argue for the league's television blackout policy, he viewed boxing as the cautionary tale. "We all remember the Friday Night Fights, but how about the Wednesday Night Fights, the Saturday and the two Mondays," he warned. "The sport simply ate itself with overexposure."[22]

The NFL seems almost immune to these problems, and television is not the league's albatross, but rather its lifeline. What started out as just a game or two on Sunday afternoons has mushroomed into games on Sunday night, Monday night, Thursday night, and occasional Saturdays. And fans can't seem to get enough. In 2018, NFL television ratings rose 5 percent from the previous year, with games averaging 15.8 million viewers. Digital streaming rose 86 percent, and the NFL claimed 46 of the top 50 telecasts during the regular season.[23]

In 1937, George Gallup began polling people on the question, "What is your favorite sport to watch?" In that first poll, baseball easily beat football, 34 percent to 23 percent, with basketball a distant third at 8 percent. But in the 1950s, football began to trend up and baseball down in the poll, and by the mid-sixties football passed baseball for the first time. In 2017 Gallup polling, football ranked first at 37 percent, while baseball plummeted to 9 percent, behind even basketball (11 percent) and almost below soccer (7 percent). Football ranks first among the four sports for all age groups, political ideologies, and gender.[24]

While it's tempting to credit television for football's ascendancy, it cannot explain all the dominance. When the World Cup soccer competition takes place every four years, it draws huge television audiences, including in the U.S. The 2019 Women's World Cup, for example, shattered all previous viewership records, as more than eight million Americans watched the quarterfinal between the U.S. and France.[25]

But popularity on television for a quadrennial event like the Olympics or World Cup has not translated into popularity as a whole, at least in the U.S. In fact, after experiencing a surge in the 1980s and 1990s,

Introduction 11

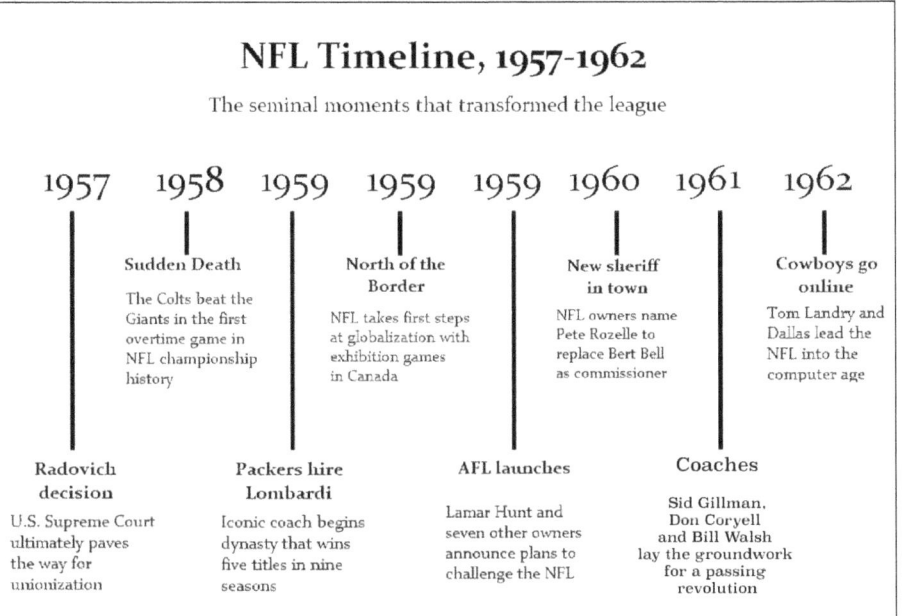

A timeline of important events in the NFL from 1957 to 1962. No other five-year period in league history had so many seminal events or was as important to the growth of the league.

participation in American youth soccer has now declined drastically, with much of the blame going to the high cost and burnout associated with traveling teams. "The decline has been felt everywhere," read a report from the Sports & Fitness Industry Association. "The number of children who touched a soccer ball even once during the year, in organized play or otherwise, also has fallen significantly."[26]

Clearly, forces and patterns beyond television have been at work to make, and keep, the NFL as the dominant force in American sports culture. Something, or some combination of events, seemed to come together in the 1950s or 1960s, to catapult the league past baseball and to its present position. "Any cultural practice must be functional or it will disappear," wrote anthropologist Clyde Kuckhohn. "That is, it must somehow contribute to the survival of the society or to the adjustment of the individual."[27] While baseball struggles to remain socially relevant and seems to be slowly disappearing from the cultural consciousness, "as it happens, and without having read Kuckhohn, the National Football League has come along at the right time in the right places with the right contribution."[28]

That is what this book is all about—to look at the forces that worked together to create the modern NFL. More specifically, it is believed that these changes can be pinpointed to a narrow, five-year window of time in which the NFL transitioned from a ragtag league just trying to survive to an all-powerful conglomerate that dominates the American sports landscape. The NFL, as we know and understand it today, changed most drastically from 1957 to 1962.

To become truly powerful, any organization needs to grow economically. Certainly, the growth of television in the 1950s was instrumental to the NFL's success. But at roughly the same time, other important forces were also at work. The seeds of economic growth took root in December 1957 with a Supreme Court decision (*Radovich v. NFL*) that tilted the balance of power toward players and away from the owners. The balance further shifted when the owners recognized the fledgling NFL Players Association that same month. Such recognition helped the NFL chart a course for economic success, even as major league baseball owners were digging in their heels to resist just such efforts. This is not to say that such recognition would never have come at any other time, or that it would have prevented future labor troubles (which it certainly did not), but only that it gave the NFL a leg up in trailblazing what became common ground for all other major sports.

The next milestone event came about a year later in December 1958, and this time it was on the field, not in a courtroom. The Giants and Colts played in the league's first-ever overtime championship game, won by Baltimore, 23–17. It was perhaps the most important game ever played in the NFL for a variety of reasons, including that it showcased the drama and excitement of the game to a national television audience.

But other NFL title games had been nationally televised and had not created anywhere near the excitement of the Colts and Giants. More significantly, it created a "Ruthian Moment," where man, moment, and media all combined in perfect harmony. Just as newspapers and radio made a hero of baseball's Babe Ruth, television now did the same for the Colts' Johnny Unitas.

Exactly a month after Unitas led Baltimore to the championship, the sad-sack Packers announced the hiring of a new coach. Green Bay had not had a winning season since 1947, and in 1958 had won only one game. On January 28, 1959, the team hired Giants assistant Vince Lombardi, who had never been a head coach in college or the pros. His impact was immediate, as the Packers had a winning record the following season, and the year after that played for the NFL title. Green Bay and Lombardi won the championship in 1961 and then seemed like they would never stop winning—five league titles and two Super Bowl wins before Lombardi stepped down in 1968. It was perhaps the greatest decade of dominance in NFL history.

But it was not just the winning that made Lombardi a legend, but *how* he won. It was Lombardi's emphasis on discipline, family, and pride that gave the NFL a mythic quality that transformed the games from mere athletic contests into dramatic battles of manhood and honor. "Because of Lombardi, our teams had a sense of closeness that enabled us to beat teams with more raw talent," said running back Paul Hornung. "We loved each other. It's as simple as that."[29]

As Lombardi convened his first Packers training camp in August 1959, a former third-team end on the Southern Methodist University football team was hatching a plan. Millionaire Lamar Hunt had watched the Colts–Giants game on television and saw the incredible reaction. He believed America wanted more football, so he went to the league seeking an expansion franchise. When the NFL turned him down, Hunt decided to start a new league to begin play in 1960.

At first, NFL owners laughed at Hunt and his American Football League, but the birth and development of the AFL turned out to be one of the most significant events in the growth of pro football. The ultimate success of the AFL proved Hunt right about the demand for football, and the merger of the two leagues in 1966 created the modern NFL. If not for the AFL, the old guard owners of the NFL might have continued down their path of tradition and conservatism, and the league might have developed much differently.

While the AFL saw the future of football in providing more opportunities at home, NFL owners and executives looked northward. In August 1959, the Chicago Cardinals played an exhibition game against the Canadian league Toronto Argonauts, and won handily, 55–26. While the hosts were disappointed in the outcome, and perhaps even more than a bit embarrassed to lose to one of the worst teams in the NFL, everyone seemed to agree that, "artistically, the game was a success."[30] NFL teams played in Canada for three straight years, winning all three games before sizable crowds. The success of the games, both on the field and at the gate, helped plant the seeds for what would later become the NFL's global expansion into Mexico, Europe and Japan.

Just two months after the Cardinals demonstrated the superiority of NFL football, the league lost one of its stalwarts. Commissioner Bert Bell died in October 1959 while watching a game at Franklin Field between the Eagles and Steelers. Bell had guided the league through some difficult times, including the war years, and had been a forceful leader who was unafraid to make tough decisions. With his death, and the threat of the AFL looming, NFL owners wondered who would now guide them through this tumultuous period.

The choice of a new commissioner ultimately fell to an unknown 33-year-old public relations specialist and general manager for the Los Angeles Rams. Despite his lack of experience, Alvin "Pete" Rozelle was the man perfectly suited to navigate the NFL through the 1960s. No caretaker commissioner, Rozelle vastly expanded the imprint of the league on the American sports scene, and is perhaps the single individual most responsible for the modern NFL. Bell's death, as tragic as it was, signaled the end of one era in the league and the beginning of another. "Rozelle may have been the rocket when [the league] took off," said longtime NFL executive Pete Hadhazy.[31] Rozelle successfully negotiated a merger with the AFL, and used television to turn the NFL from spectator sport into national obsession.

Rozelle was also unafraid to make tough decisions, such as his suspension of stars Paul Hornung and Alex Karras for the entire 1963 season. Hornung had just led the Packers to a second straight NFL title with a 16–7 win over the Giants in Yankee Stadium. It was a bone-chilling 17 degrees for the game, and seemed much colder because of a howling wind that made passing and kicking almost impossible.

The cold also made it difficult for television and movie cameras to operate, and some cameramen used makeshift bonfires to thaw out their equipment. That included a little-known group from Blair Pictures, documenting the game with approval from the NFL. The group shot reels of film, but afterwards had to throw much of it away because it simply broke in the cold. Blair Pictures had spent $3,000 for the rights to the game, and now it all seemed wasted.

But company president Ed Sabol pieced together enough usable film to show the game in a different way—not with distant shots from the press box accompanied by marching band music, but up-close and personal action accentuated with a dramatic musical score. The film became a big success, and Blair Pictures became NFL Films—the megaphone the NFL needed to spread its gospel. Yes, television could broadcast the action, but it could not as easily transform that action into heroism. Ed Sabol and his son Steve were storytellers and filmmakers, and their vision—with Lombardi front and center—was to build an NFL mythology. "It turned every game into Waterloo and every player into an epic hero. It taught American how to watch football."[32]

While Vince Lombardi and the Packers stood unchallenged atop the NFL in 1962, the expansion Dallas Cowboys made another modest leap forward by winning five games. The Cowboys went winless in the first season in 1960, and then won four games in 1961. Their coach was Tom

Landry, a man well acquainted with Vince Lombardi from their time together as assistant coaches with the New York Giants. While Lombardi coached the Giants offense, Landry ran the defense, and his groundbreaking ideas helped the team win an NFL title in 1956. The Giants came within an eyelash of beating the Colts in 1958, and Landry helped them return to the title game in 1959, again losing to Baltimore, 31–16.

Like Lombardi, Landry was organized and supremely confident. Both men could spend hours in front of a chalkboard diagramming and breaking down plays. Like Lombardi, Landry believed his time in New York prepared him to become a head coach. And like Lombardi, Landry received several opportunities, finally deciding to join the Cowboys in 1960.

But in many elemental ways, the two men were polar opposites. While Lombardi brought passion and pride to Green Bay, Landry introduced precision and programming in Dallas. Lombardi created the myth, while Landry celebrated the method. Under Landry, the Cowboys introduced sophistication, computerization, and calculation. He brought the NFL from diagramming plays in the dirt of the huddle, to building them out of an opponent's charted tendencies and weaknesses. If Lombardi became the league's soul, Landry became its brain, and their battles in the 1960s defined the entire league.

The road to computerization led Landry, general manager Tex Schramm and scouting director Gil Brandt to A. Salam Qureishi. A native of India, Qureishi had come to America to study computers and statistical analysis. The Cowboys hired him in 1962, thinking he could help them streamline the process of evaluating and drafting college talent. "We had an Indian who knew absolutely nothing about football," said Schramm, "and coaches who knew nothing about computers and less about Indians. Luckily, Landry is always looking for a better way to do things."[33]

The approach transformed Dallas from doormat to dominance in just a few years, and other teams began to take notice. Qureishi and computers would go on to revolutionize the league, and what at first started as a gimmicky novel has now become standard operating procedure for every organization in the NFL and other sports as well. "Until I was called to Dallas," said Qureishi, "I knew nothing about American football. I had learned to enjoy baseball because of its similarity to cricket. Now I think American football is easily the most scientific game ever invented."[34]

Radovich and Unitas, Lombardi and Sabol, Bell and Rozelle, and Landry and Qureishi. They all made their mark in the seminal period in NFL history between 1957 and 1962. In some cases, their stay in the sporting spotlight was brief. For others, it lasted decades. But all of them left a lasting imprint on the NFL that is still being felt today.

One

Innocence Lost

To new generations of NFL fans, the picture of the game they have in their heads is one of crystal-clear high definition. Digital technology has made the broadcast version of the game just as real as seeing it in person, and in some cases even better. After all, most fans in the stadium can't see beads of sweat rolling down a player's neck, listen in on sideline conversations or hear a quarterback as he changes a play at the line of scrimmage.

The picture of the game in the 1950s is much different—grainy, black and white and many times out of focus, which seems to perfectly fit the simplicity of that bygone era. It was a time, noted NFL Films, when "football grabbed headlines, yet still retained the innocence and charming awkwardness of the last dance at a high school sock hop. The style of the era was typified by goofy gimmicks ... one might find in the slapstick comedy of TV stars such as Milton Berle and Sid Caesar."[1]

Many NFL players of the era shared the attitude of Rams running back Paul "Tank" Younger. "We had a lot of fun playing football," Younger said. "We didn't make much money, so consequently we had to subsidize it by having fun."[2] Fun, goofy and awkward described not only the NFL of the 1950s, but in many ways America itself.

There is a common belief, sharpened by the passage of time, that America, and by extension American sport, enjoyed an age of innocence in the 1950s. Eager to put the brutality of World War II behind them, Americans retreated into an era of traditional values, normalcy (to borrow a word from Warren Harding), and simplicity.

Instead of throwing themselves into European bunkers, Americans now crammed themselves into phone booths, just one of the silly activities of young people that became a national craze, along with swallowing goldfish, eating TV dinners, and twirling Hula Hoops. It is fondly remembered as a time of dungarees, bobby socks, and malts at the local drug store. "It would be impossible for today's youth to imagine, or understand, the innocence of the 1950s," notes author Robert Ringer, who grew up in Columbus, Ohio, a town considered the most middle of middle America. "My parents, my friends, my house, my school, Ohio State football—nothing was ever going to change. Life was static."[3]

"As almost any general history of the 1950s points out," observed biographer Stephen Ambrose, "it was a decade characterized by complacency. Americans could find little to worry about, and much to praise, in their assessment of the nation. The fifties were unique and blessed, or so people thought."[4]

This romantic version of life also carried over to American sport. In this monochromatic view there were good guys and bad guys, white hats and black hats. Athletes were heroes—the Lone Ranger riding to the rescue—or in the language of the newspapers at the time, gladiators. They never smoked, swore or got drunk, but instead played hard and clean; not for money, but for the love of the game. Like the fictional Frank Merriwell from the turn of the century, they "could run like a deer, make a touchdown almost any time it was needed to win the game, row, swim, [and] outshoot the boldest of bad men. [They] never did anything that could possibly be out of keeping with the highest standards of gentlemanly conduct."[5]

The places they played were cathedrals, as if to recognize the religious devotion of both player and fan. "In the old parks there was always the feeling that you were at home," said baseball author and historian Robert Creamer, "that you knew the players and the other spectators, that in a sense you were living in the same neighborhood."[6] And in no place was this sense of neighborhood more powerful, and no citizenry more religious about its sports team, than Brooklyn. Still upset over ceding independence to become part of New York City in 1898, Brooklynites turned to sports, and especially the baseball Dodgers, as a means of civic pride.

"People just constantly talked baseball, arguing," said Joe Flaherty, who grew up in Brooklyn. "They lived and breathed with the Dodgers. The thought of walking through Prospect Park to see a rare night game at Ebbets Field—you felt like F. Scott Fitzgerald first seeing the ivory towers of New York. My God, it was like the Emerald City."[7] "Years ago," wrote baseball historian Harold Seymour, "Identification was easier, the bond between players and fans more plausible, because people retained a surer confidence in traditional American beliefs, and the players themselves more nearly personified them."[8]

But Seymour also notes that "profound changes ... were corroding this comfortable creed."[9] To be sure, there were great changes indeed taking place in the 1950s, including the upheaval associated with civil rights and integration. Just a few years before, Jackie Robinson had integrated major league baseball at tremendous personal cost. "Everywhere, men and women talked about the Jackie Robinson Dodgers," said sportswriter Roger Kahn, who covered those teams as a sportswriter, "and as they talked they confronted themselves and American racism. That confrontation was, I believe, as important as *Brown vs. Board of Education of Topeka*."[10]

The NFL actually beat baseball in integration, as Woody Strode and Kenny Washington played for the Los Angeles Rams in 1946. Going back even farther, Fritz Pollard led the Akron Pros to the 1920 pro championship, despite the fact that he was ignored by teammates and often had to practice by himself in a corner of the field. "The thing I most remember," he said, "was the humiliation."[11] In 1933, when Ray Kemp played with Pittsburgh and Joe Lillard with the Chicago Cardinals, things had changed little. All experienced much of what Robinson went through. "A pioneer has to suffer the consequences," Kemp said years later. "You have to start someplace. And as little as it's known, I did open the door. I was a pioneer."[12]

Things had not drastically improved by the 1950s, either for baseball or football, but Seymour's "profound changes" were coming: *Brown vs. Board of Education*, Rosa Parks, Dr. Martin Luther King. When Jackie Robinson began to make such an impact upon baseball and Brooklyn, black fans began flocking to Ebbets Field, not necessarily to cheer the Dodgers, but to support Robinson. "When blacks started coming to the games, a lot of whites stopped coming," said Dodgers fan Herb Ross. "As long as they went home at night to wherever they lived, it was okay. But once they started to live in the neighborhood, then the neighborhood started to change; it was time to move out."[13]

In reality, there was very little innocence in 1950s America, even as some wished to pretend otherwise by sticking their heads in the sand. "Diversity is a commodity that was in short supply in the fifties," says Ringer, "and, as a result, America was a pretty peaceful place."[14] Peaceful, of course, except for a war in southeast Asia, lynchings and Jim Crow laws in the South, Cold War espionage and executions, and multiple strikes by organized labor, especially in the steel industry.

Hovering over it all was McCarthyism and the Red Scare—the terrifying notion that Communists were hiding everywhere in the country, actively working with foreign agents for the destruction of the American way of life, if not America itself. "Every decade of the nuclear age has been full of tension," wrote Ambrose, "but the fifties felt it most. The men of the fifties were the first to have to live with long-range bombers, ICBMs, and Polaris submarines. Most frightening of all, the weapons these delivery systems carried were H-bombs, big enough ... to take out a city. Any city."[15]

Whether reactionary elements wanted to hold back such events or simply ignore them, it was impossible to do either, in large part because of the growth of media. Americans knew more than ever before about their neighborhood, their country and their world, and they could know it instantly through radio and the emergence of television. These media were still sanitized, to be sure, but they still afforded an often unvarnished look at cultural change, and in some cases created the change themselves.

Sports reporters and writers had been reluctant to contradict the Merriwell myth, even when they knew first-hand the seamier side of games and athletes. That changed in the 1950s with the emergence of what came to be known as the "New Journalism," where writers would find a player's weakness, pick at it, and then expose it for all to see. Its most noted practitioner was Dick Young, who covered New York sports for fifty years, almost right up to his death in 1987. "His writing probably could be called strident or tempestuous and always fearless," wrote Shirley Povich, another sportswriting icon of the era. "No mercy for those miscreants lousing up the world of his special interest. The sinners should be exposed and held to account. He knew no demigods."[16]

It was the work of men like Dick Young that eventually led to the salacious reporting styles of the 1970s, ushered in by former pitcher turned diarist Jim Bouton. If there was any hesitancy left in reporting on the dark side of sports—drugs, sex, alcohol and adolescent behavior on the part of athletes—Bouton removed it forever with his tell-all account of the 1969 baseball season, admitting that afterwards it was impossible to ever return to "the milk and cookies image."[17]

To the extent that social and external forces created unrest in sports, it is tempting to look at money as the main culprit. "No one should be misled here into any feeling of sentimentality about professional football," Thomas Morgan wrote in 1959. "The game is being sold to the American people just as baseball was sold in the Twenties—by men with a substantial capital investment."[18]

Frank Merriwell may have played for the love and honor of the game, but in the real world athletes were trying to get their slice of the financial pie, legally or illegally. "We live in a materialistic society," said former 49ers receiver Clifton McNeil, "and let's face it—it's economics that count."[19] "I've played sports my entire life because I liked them," echoed another receiver, Carroll Dale, "but now football is a profession to me like any other."[20]

This attitude is certainly not new. Professional baseball in America traces its origins to the Cincinnati Red Stockings of 1869; by 1885—years before Merriwell won glory for Yale—players formed the first union, the Brotherhood of Professional Base Ball Players. Even though the union was eventually destroyed by ownership, it planted seeds (and court challenges) that eventually led to the formation of the modern Major League Baseball Players Association.

Nor were such attitudes limited to professional players who were ostensibly playing only for the money. Between 1945 and 1951, college basketball had suffered through five scandals where gamblers and players conspired to fix games by shaving points. The most serious came in 1951 when seven schools and 32 players from around the country were implicated in a scheme masterminded by gamblers. Those indicted included players from the City College of New York, the defending NCAA and NIT Tournament champions. Newspaper reports suggested, "The itchy fingers of gamblers have been active in other sports," including baseball, hockey and boxing.[21]

That list includes professional football. Shady elements had always lurked in the fringes of the sport, but they were exposed to the light in the 1946 championship game. Fixers approached Frank Filchock and Merle Hapes of the Giants with offers of $2,500 apiece to take it easy in the game against Chicago. Both men denied accepting the offers, but NFL Commissioner Bert Bell suspended both of them, essentially for the rest of their careers. "Professional football cannot continue to exist unless it is based upon absolute honesty," Bell said when the suspensions were announced. "The players must be not only absolutely honest, they must be above suspicion."[22] It was starkly reminiscent of the ruling made by baseball commissioner Kenesaw Mountain Landis in banning for life eight players from the Chicago "Black Sox" in 1920.

Part of the reason athletes were tempted by gamblers is the absolute control team owners had over players. As long as owners had monopoly power over their employees, either through restrictive rules or lack of competition, they could keep salaries and costs artificially low. "A monetary frustration hung over them all," wrote Eliot Asinof of the Black Sox, although he could have been referring to any professional athlete at the time. "If the public looked up to them, admired them, chased after them, this very prominence served to exacerbate their sense of helplessness."[23]

In baseball, periodic challenges to the established major leagues forced salaries to increase. The most notable example was the Federal League, which debuted in 1914 and immediately began raiding National and American League teams for talent. Major league owners raised salaries accordingly, but dropped them back down when the Federal League folded after two seasons.

The death of the Federal League prompted its disgruntled owners to file a lawsuit against the major leagues for violation of federal anti-trust laws, in effect, charging that baseball had a monopoly. The majors survived that threat, and another in the 1970s when outfielder Curt Flood directly challenged the reserve clause, which bound players to one particular team for the entirety of their playing careers. The reserve clause finally died at the hands of an arbitration panel in 1976, and the ensuing period of free agency and player movement caused salaries to skyrocket.

If owners could not control salaries, they would find other ways to maintain economic power. Team relocation became the norm in the 1950s, as owners left quickly changing and decaying inner-city circumstances for the greener pastures of the suburbs, parking lots, and new stadiums. The Boston Braves moved to Milwaukee in 1953, the first major franchise shift in major league baseball in fifty years. "The Braves, attendance champions of the major leagues since they moved to Milwaukee from Boston ... [went] over the two million mark for the fourth straight season" in 1957.[24]

The unqualified success the Braves found in Wisconsin prompted the Giants to leave New York for San Francisco in 1957, accompanied by—gasp!—the Dodgers abandoning Brooklyn for Los Angeles. The Polo Grounds and Ebbets Field—still thought of as cathedrals by their fans—were now seen as inadequate relics by the men who owned them. Dodgers owner Walter O'Malley wrangled with New York City Commissioner Robert Moses over the building of a new stadium, but when finances and location could be not worked out, O'Malley picked up his club and headed west, where local officials gave him a package that included a new stadium and part of downtown Los Angeles. "Greed was the whole thing," said Dodgers fan Bill Reddy. "O'Malley feathered his nest. They gave him half of Los Angeles for nothing, and the bum, he got the money, but what did he do to us?"[25]

NFL owners had the same kind of leverage, and franchise relocations were even more pronounced than they were in baseball as the league struggled to find sure footing. Many of today's familiar teams actually began in some unfamiliar places—the Redskins left Boston in 1937 and landed in Washington, and not long after winning the NFL title in 1945, the Cleveland Rams bolted town for Los Angeles.

By far, the strangest case was that of the Dallas Texans. The team started as the New York Yanks, but moved to Dallas in 1952 when Texas millionaires Giles and Connell Miller bought the team. High school and college football was still king in Texas, and the 76,000-seat Cotton Bowl often looked like a ghost town on game days. After nine straight losses the Millers gave up and returned the team to the league, which forced the Texans to play the rest of their games on the road. Somehow, the team managed to upset the Bears on Thanksgiving for their only win of the season. The last team in NFL history to fail financially, the Texans became a "dog-and-pony show, following geek shows and carnivals and playing exhibitions in out-of-the-way hamlets all over the country just to pick up a new fan or two."[26]

How the NFL treated the Texans, forcing them to work out of Hershey, Pennsylvania, and then playing on the road to end the season, was not an isolated incident. For a brief period from 1946–1950, the All-America Football Conference challenged the NFL. The AAFC, which included such powerful teams as the Cleveland Browns, began outbidding the NFL for player talent and salaries rose accordingly. But when the AAFC folded in 1950, and three teams were absorbed into the NFL, salaries went down accordingly. Power returned to the owners and they wielded it harshly.

In 1948, the Buffalo Bisons of the AAFC offered Art Donovan of Boston College a $15,000 contract, a $5,000 signing bonus and a new car. Donovan turned down the offer to stay in school and graduated in 1950. He was now property of the Baltimore Colts, and with no competition from the defunct AAFC, the Colts offered Donovan $4,500, conditional on him making the team.

All the players had off-season jobs, and in many cases went to work directly from games or practices. Donovan sold liquor, Lou Groza sold insurance, and Paul Warfield co-owned a tire shop. "Gentlemen," Paul Brown told his players, "you're going to be off Mondays and Tuesdays. Get a job." "So I did," said linebacker Jim Houston, who opened an insurance agency. "You needed money; you had to go to work."[27]

Actually, salaries were not the only issue, and in fact, a salary of $4,500 in 1950 was higher than the average *family* income for that year of $3,300.[28] NFL players were also concerned about working conditions, minimum salaries, and getting paid for exhibition games. Working conditions were especially troubling, as each team set its own policy for training camp and practices. "All we did was scrimmage," said Donovan of his first Colts training camp in 1950. "No drills. No chalk talk. No run-throughs of plays. Just hot, humid, bone-breaking, full-pad scrimmages. We began at nine-thirty in the morning and didn't stop until quarter to twelve. So this was pro ball!"[29]

The seeds of discontent were germinating, and had indeed, already been sown.

In 1946, defensive lineman Bill Radovich of the Detroit Lions went to team owner Fred Madel and asked to be traded to the Los Angeles Rams in order to be closer to his ailing father. When Madel, Jr., refused, Radovich found an opportunity with the Los Angeles Dons of the new AAFC, where he played for two seasons. "The little creep said I'd either play in Detroit or I wouldn't play anywhere," Radovich said of Madel. "He also told me if I tried to play in the new league, he would put me on the blacklist for five years,"[30] which Madel and NFL Commissioner Bert Bell apparently enforced.

Radovich fought back through the courts, challenging that the NFL was in violation of federal anti-trust law by attempting to destroy the rival AAFC and eliminate player options. Two lower courts found for the NFL, but in 1957 the Supreme Court reversed those opinions and ordered the case back for retrial. In a curious case of logic, the high court said that among professional sports only baseball qualified for protection from anti-trust legislation, and accordingly "under the Sherman Act's general prohibition of unreasonable restraints of trade ... the petitioner has thereby suffered injury."[31]

Radovich settled out of court, claiming the NFL pressured his lawyer to drop the case. While Radovich's lawyer denied such claims, it's certainly understandable why the league would want to settle. Had the case gone back to the lower courts it could have been a devastating legal blow. "The suit is part of NFL history, whether it's good or not," Radovich said years later. "It's the first time that any professional sport was ever taken to court and beaten. What I did was open doors."[32]

Radovich opened the door and soon others followed, including Creighton Miller.

Miller was both the son and grandson of Notre Dame football stars, and his father Don Miller was a member of the famous Four Horsemen backfield. Creighton also played at Notre Dame, leading the nation in rushing in 1943 and helping the Irish to a national championship, but health issues prevented him from playing professionally. Miller instead worked as an assistant coach for Paul Brown in Cleveland, and used part of his salary to help pay for law school. After graduation, he returned to Cleveland as a practicing attorney and legal counsel for the Browns.

Sometime in 1954 Miller was approached by Browns players Dante Lavelli, Abe Gibron, and George Ratterman about forming a players association. Over the course of the next two years, Miller met individually with players, trying to build up enough support to create an organization. By 1956, he had 370 of the league's 420 players on board, as only the Chicago Bears refused to take part. "Baseball players now have an organization that makes known the ideas of the players," Miller said at the time, "but football has not reached that stage yet. All we can say now is that an organization is established and I am the authorized representative."[33]

But it would be a toothless organization unless recognized by NFL owners, and those owners had an obvious interest in keeping their players in line. Part of the reason the Bears refused to take part was fear of retaliation by Chicago owner George Halas, who had enough influence to have them blacklisted around the league. When asked by the Chicago Cardinals to publicly deny such chicanery, one player claimed anonymity and refused to take the bait. "Although it wasn't compulsory for us to reply, our chances of staying with the team would probably be very slim. I don't feel I can sign my name to this letter because it will definitely hurt my chances of staying with the Cardinals."[34]

There was also some reluctance to the basic idea of a union, with the negative connotations of strikes and union bosses, and many players instead wanted something more like a grievance committee. "[Commissioner Bert] Bell thinks we're organizing a union," said Rams quarterback Norm Van Brocklin. "We are not. I don't believe in unions."[35]

Bell and NFL owners had little reason to recognize Miller's organization, and they stonewalled, refusing even to meet with players. Some owners, like Brown in Cleveland, Dan Reeves in Los Angeles, and Carroll Rosenbloom in Baltimore, appeared to see the handwriting on the wall and made overtures to Miller and the players. But the old guard, headed by Bell, George Halas in Chicago and George Preston Marshall in Washington, dug in their heels. Bell declared, "The contract used in the NFL is, in our opinion, the best in any sport from the player's standpoint." Miller countered, calling the contract a "monstrosity" and the NFL draft system "medieval." The graduating college player "is able to determine what club 'owns' him by reading the newspaper the morning after the NFL draft meeting."[36]

Two events finally convinced Bell and the holdout owners to change their minds. The first was an ongoing investigation into unfair labor practices by a U.S. Congressional subcommittee. The chairman of the subcommittee, Emanuel Celler of New York, was particularly sympathetic to the plight of the players and willing to take legislative action. At first, Bell took a hard stance, telling the subcommittee that the players were "careless, because 80 percent of them don't even read their contracts outside of what they are getting paid."[37]

Committee members were incredulous. Eagles linebacker Chuck Bednarik, who had a degree in business from the University of Pennsylvania, told them, "I feel that I am fairly intelligent, but I never read the fine print. I just look at the amount of money they are going to pay me."[38]

Miller also testified, saying the players didn't read their contracts because they couldn't do anything about them. He also threatened to petition the National Labor Relations Board to order the owners to deal with the players. Seemingly cornered by both Celler and Miller, Bell appeared to soften, and on August 1, 1957, he formally recognized the

Players Association during testimony, and told reporters he was willing to open negotiations immediately on minimum pay and working conditions.

But Bell could not act unilaterally, and any recognition of a players association would require votes from ten of the 12 owners at their meeting in December. Such approval would not come easy. "Bert is supposed to carry out the wishes of the owners," said George Preston Marshall. "We never gave him the authority to change the contractual arrangements between the players and the clubs."[39]

In his talks with Bell, Miller also recognized the commissioner was having trouble. "In the last two months Commissioner Bell and I have been discussing our difficulties," Miller said in November. "But we've made no progress in negotiations with the owners."[40] Even Bell admitted his hands were tied.

The other shoe dropped on November 21 when Miller and the players filed a $4.2 million anti-trust lawsuit against the NFL. Miller said the suit would not have been filed if owners had recognized the association, and based the figure on the difference between what "the players are getting now and what they would be able to get if they were able to offer their services on an open market."[41] Miller said in addition to recognition, the players wanted the right to negotiate with their teams on even footing.

Certainly, $4.2 million caught the attention of the owners, especially in light of the Supreme Court finding in favor of the Radovich anti-trust case. Bell apparently got wind of the lawsuit two weeks prior, and on November 13 telephoned owners to twist a few arms, most especially those of Marshall and Halas. "I told [Miller] that things were going along very well and that Rome wasn't built in a day," Bell said.[42]

At a contentious meeting on December 2, 1957, in Philadelphia, the NFL waved the white flag. As expected, Halas and Marshall remained firm, but were finally convinced by Steelers owner Art Rooney. "If you don't do this," Rooney told the holdouts, "[Bell's] effectiveness as commissioner is finished. Bert went before Congress and told them he was going to get that done."[43]

Bell got the ten votes he needed, and the league formally and officially recognized the players association. The lawsuit, combined with the threat of congressional action, ultimately put the NFL in a pincer grip it from which it could not escape. "That's the way Congress wants it," said Bell after the smoke cleared. "I talked with any number of congressmen and senators, along with attorneys, in Washington last summer. I followed their recommendations in what I presented to the owners."[44]

Miller and the players dropped their lawsuit in exchange for a host of concessions, including:

- recognition of the Players Association;
- a minimum salary of $5,000;
- set pay of $50 per exhibition games;
- coverage of medical expenses for players; and
- the right to bargain for salary to play in all-star games.

Left in place was the NFL draft and football's version of the reserve clause, which bound a player in perpetuity to the team that owned his rights. The willingness of Bell, and ultimately the NFL owners, to give in to the players made Congress much more amenable on those issues. Celler's subcommittee recommended that a professional sports antitrust bill, which would have eliminated the draft and reserve clause, should not be passed and it was not.

Creighton Miller and Bert Bell were the leading figures in the entire drama, but their legacies remain cloudy to this day. Bell is often credited for his recognition of the players association, even against the wishes of the owners. "I recognized the Association before Congress and the owners approved my action," he said with no small amount of pride.[45] But Bell did so only at gunpoint. In 1959, when players came to Bell and the owners with plans to create a pension, they again tried to stall. Only when the players, led by Billy Howton, presented the owners with the ultimatum of another multi-million-dollar lawsuit in Federal court, did the owners capitulate. "It was thrilling how fast the owners responded when Billy threatened to hit them in the pocketbook," said defensive back Bernie Parrish, who was the Browns' player representative and later became NFLPA vice president. "Within thirty minutes Bert Bell called and set up a meeting for that afternoon and the pension plan was established."[46]

That Howton, Parrish, and other player representatives had eclipsed Miller's authority is not accidental. Even though he stayed with the association for eleven years, Miller never really wanted it to become a union, and the players would not win the right to collective bargaining until he left in 1968. "Miller steered the Association off the course of orthodox unionization," claims Parrish. "This attitude cost the players at least $30 million in salaries and fringe benefits since the inception of the organization."[47] Collective bargaining was achieved only when Parrish led the players in at attempt to join the Teamsters union, a possibility that so frightened the owners that they reversed a longstanding pledge never to collectively bargain with the players.

The players never did get rid of the draft, which would have given them complete freedom of movement and choice of employment, but they came very close. In 1970, a player named James "Yazoo" Smith sued the NFL, claiming that if not for the draft he would have been able to sign a much more lucrative contract. In 1976, U.S. District Court judge William B. Bryant ruled in Smith's favor, awarded him $276,000 in damages, and called the draft system "absolutely the most restrictive one imaginable. It utterly strips [the players] of control over the marketing of their talents."[48]

When the U.S. Court of Appeals for the D.C. Circuit upheld the decision, the NFL draft was suddenly in great danger. But in 1977, NFL lawyers cut a backroom deal with players that explicitly allowed the draft to continue. Yazoo Smith's lawyer, Stuart H. Johnson, warned against a deal, saying, "NFL players [should] stop, look and listen before voting on the proposed agreement,"[49] but players ratified it anyway as part of a collective bargaining package.

Smith's case showed just how dramatically the game was tilting from the owners to the players. Also in 1976, quarterback Joe Kapp sued the league for $12 million in back pay and damages related to the lack of free agency. While Kapp lost the case, the presiding judge noted that the league's ability to perpetually restrain a player's movement was both unreasonable and illegal. What eventually played out over the course of several more years was complete free agency for the players.

The growing power of the players was never more evidenced than in two work stoppages in the 1980s. In 1982, the Players Association voted to strike on a variety of issues, most notably to receive 55 percent of the league's gross revenues. "We hadn't seen the owners' books," said Giants lineman Gary Jeter, "and when we were finally able to see them, we were upset at the percentage we were receiving. It wasn't fair."[50] The two sides finally reached an agreement after 57 days, but when the players struck again in 1987, owners decided to take a harder line. "This time the owners were loaded for bear," admitted Eagles tight end John Spagnola.[51]

Teams recruited replacement players, called scabs by the players and many fans, and played three regular season games with a group of mostly anonymous faces. "You guys are cattle and we're the ranchers," Dallas general manager Tex Schramm reportedly told a group of striking players. "And ranchers can always get more cattle."[52] The replacement games were certainly not NFL-caliber, and while attendance and television ratings declined, the owners saw enough interest to stand firm. When several high-profile players began to cross the picket lines, the Players Association decertified, and the owners appeared to have a huge victory.

But decertification, meaning the union could no longer represent players, also meant the players could now take their chances in court under anti-trust law, just as Bill Radovich had done. Those lawsuits went through federal court in Minnesota, where over a period of years Judge David Doty often found in favor of the players, and threatened to impose his own version of free agency if the owners and players could not agree on one.

"At the end of the day, it's about control and money," said Cameron Jordan of the New Orleans Saints. "Those are the two things that really resonate with the NFL."[53]

Control and money—both have shifted to the players. From what began in 1957, the NFL has become a player's league, not an owner's league.

That is not to say that owners are somehow impoverished or ineffectual. Dallas owner Jerry Jones bought the Cowboys in 1989 for $140 million. Thirty years later, through shrewd management and good fortune, Jones turned the franchise into the most valuable in the world, worth an estimated five billion dollars. The value of other NFL franchises has similarly increased, with revenue growing from $3.8 million per team in 1967 to $261 million in 2010. Much of that windfall comes from television, which supplanted ticket sales as the primary economic engine of the league, and pumps billions of dollars into NFL coffers.[54]

But a league once defined by its coaches (Brown, Lombardi, Shula), and to a lesser extent its owners (Halas), is now clearly defined by its stars, in great part because of the leverage won through the courts and the players association. At one time, players were very much like Tex Schramm's cattle—bought, sold and traded with almost total impunity on the part of ownership.

In 1964, Jim Ringo was a seven-time Pro Bowl center who had helped Green Bay win two NFL titles. He went in to see Vince Lombardi, general manager as well as coach, and asked for a raise from $12,000 a year to $15,000. "Actually, I talked to him by phone and told him what I was looking for," Ringo said later. "He said, 'I'll get back to you.' The next thing I know he's on the phone. 'Jim,' he says, 'you can negotiate with Philadelphia now. I just traded you.'"[55]

Certainly, modern NFL general managers and owners have the right to trade players, but such heavy-handed approaches have disappeared. In light of increased salaries and free agency, trading has become much more difficult. Players are also empowered with no-trade clauses that essentially give them final say in where they want to play. "Nary a single athlete in the history of Western civilization would find not having the ability to put the kibosh on a trade preferable to having that choice," writes Alex Rubenstein. "Seriously, who's saying 'thanks, but no thanks' to the idea of having the control to prevent a life-changing event?"[56]

And seriously, what owner would willingly give up that kind of authority if he or she didn't have to?

The year before Vince Lombardi traded Jim Ringo to Philadelphia, the Packers coach suffered through a difficult season without star running back Paul Hornung. Hornung had played a starring role on two championship teams, leading the league in scoring for three straight years. But Hornung, along with Detroit Lions defensive lineman Alex Karras, had violated the league's prohibition against gambling by placing bets on his own team. And not just nickel and dime wagers on the front nine of the local golf course. "The violations of Hornung and Karras were continuing, not casual," said NFL Commissioner Pete Rozelle. "They were continuing, flagrant and increasing. I could only exact from them the most severe penalty short of banishment for life."[57]

Rozelle suspended Hornung and Karras for the entire 1963 season. "I made a terrible mistake," Hornung admitted after the sentence was handed down. "I am truly sorry."[58] Karras kicked up a storm and threatened legal action, but finally accepted the penalty and sat out the season. Six years later, Rozelle again flexed his disciplinary muscles with quarterback Joe Namath, who was nowhere near as contrite as Hornung. The commissioner wanted Namath to divest his interest in a New York bar thought to be frequented by gamblers and shady characters. Namath, fresh off a historic Super Bowl win, thought he had the star power to challenge Rozelle and tearfully announced his retirement. Upon more sober reflection, Namath eventually backed down and sold out.

Rozelle was widely applauded for such action and viewed as a "model for commissioners"[59] of other sports for acting as his own judge, jury and executioner. To be sure, he instigated and followed a rigorous investigatory process, especially in the cases of Hornung and Karras. But the final decision was his and his alone, as were many fiats that affected NFL players in that era. When the NFL was challenged by the American Football League in 1960 (see Chapter Six), Rozelle quickly moved with NFL owners to approve a new 14-game schedule for 1961. The move was made without consultation of the players, "in order to generate additional revenue with which to pay salaries commensurate with those offered by the AFL, which already played 14 games."[60]

Flash forward to 2019 as the NFL mulled the possibility of expanding the regular season to 18 games. Commissioner Roger Goodell simply can't do what Rozelle did because he doesn't have the power to make it happen. Instead, Goodell and the owners must include the NFL Players Association in any such discussion, which is one reason the idea has floated around so long without any movement. "I don't see how a collective bargaining agreement is negotiated without it," says football writer Andrew Brandt of the proposal. "With the NFLPA giving up many concessions in 2011, this is the only paved path to the new CBA."[61] In 2020, the league settled instead for a new 17-game regular season and even that was barely approved by the NFLPA, 1,019 votes to 959. The new schedule will take effect sometime after 2021.

Goodell is similarly handcuffed in many disciplinary matters. Where once the commissioner had absolute authority, that power has been weakened by not only by a players association but by the courts as well. Players have no reservations about using the judicial system to lessen or reverse league sanctions, such as when Ray Rice went to a U.S. District Judge to get his 2014 suspension for domestic violence reduced. Goodell originally suspended the Ravens running back two games, but when public opinion demanded a stiffer sentence, he upped it to an indefinite suspension. Judge Barbara Jones overturned the suspension, criticizing Goodell for not being "fair and consistent" in his discipline.[62]

For such difficulties, Goodell has been portrayed as incompetent, ineffective, and worst of all, inconsistent and indecisive. When Goodell appeared at Gillette Stadium after announcing a four-game suspension for Patriots quarterback Tom Brady for his part in the Deflategate incident, thousands of fans waved towels that featured the commissioner with a clown nose. T-shirts were also printed with the same image and included "the biggest clown on Earth #FireGoodell."[63] Michael Gee of the *Boston Globe* noted of Goodell, "Nothing is more dangerous to an organization than a bungler hell bent on doing the right thing, unless it's a weak leader trying to make a show of strength. His improvisational acts of player discipline have exposed the NFL to scorn, ridicule and worst of all, possible financial damage."[64]

Gee went on to note that Rozelle faced far worse crises than Goodell, "but always appeared unflappable. He picked a course and stuck to it."[65] But even Rozelle seemed weak and ineffectual later in his tenure as the power of the players union increased. Under Rozelle, there were two strikes and three other work stoppages, and he wasn't even involved in negotiations with the union; that was left in the hands of the NFL's management council, which included hardliners such as Tex Schramm and Hugh Culverhouse of Tampa Bay. "It's hard to remember a time in the '70s and early '80s when there was good feeling between management and labor," said Joe Browne, a longtime NFL executive. "We fought more in the courts than we negotiated at the bargaining table."[66]

In fact, Browne believes it was labor trouble, especially the 1987 strike, that caused Rozelle to step down as commissioner in 1989. "The decade of the '80s was tough on Pete because the league was playing defense on so many fronts. There was a general malaise in the league for almost the entire decade."[67] Paul Tagliabue took over from Rozelle and restored some sense of peace, in part because the 1993 collective bargaining agreement finally allowed player free agency in exchange for a salary cap.

There has been relative peace on the NFL labor front since a short lockout in 2011 that lasted over the course of the summer but did not cancel any games. The issue then was a new collective bargaining agreement, which is up for reconsideration after the 2020 season, and there are once again the rumblings of labor discontent. In 2019, the union provided its players with a "Work Stoppage Guide" that included advice on how to prepare for a strike or lockout. "Ownership's nuclear option is to shut down the operation until labor gives in. Labor's nuclear option is to walk out the door."[68]

Whether or not a work stoppage will take place is not the issue, but rather the very fact that NFL players *can* shut down the season because they have the power to do so. Commenting on the 2014 reversal of his suspension, Ray Rice said, "I am thankful that there was a process in place to address this issue."[69]

It was a process that took root from the seeds that were sown in 1957 by Bill Radovich, Creighton Miller, and a host of NFL pioneers. Those pioneers "cast giant shadows upon the landscape of pro football, and today these shadows loom even larger in the memories and imaginations of those who love the game. [They] have transcended time and place to make the Fabulous Fifties an unforgettable part of the magic and myth of pro football."[70] Even if this age of innocence was more myth than reality, it played an essential part in the growth of the NFL. No more so than in the transformative period starting in 1957.

Two

Growing Up, Growing Old

It did not seem obvious at the time, but several eras of NFL football were coming to a close on December 29, 1957. On a brilliant, sunny day at Briggs Stadium in Detroit, before a capacity crowd of 55,263, the Detroit Lions and Cleveland Browns met for the NFL championship game. This would be the fourth meeting in the NFL title game for these two teams in the past six seasons, with the Lions winning close games in 1952 and 1953, while Cleveland blasted Detroit, 56–10, in 1954.

While having the same two teams in the championship game again may have seemed monotonous to some, it was a good kind of monotony for NFL owners and fans. When the Lions and Browns met in 1957 for the 25th championship game, the league had moved past its shaky beginnings to become an established presence in American sports culture. To be sure, baseball, boxing and college football still commanded center stage in the sporting landscape, but pro football was waiting in the wings, no longer in danger of getting kicked out of the theater.

No one could have envisioned that in 1920 when a light-hitting outfielder on the New York Yankees decided to walk away from professional baseball. George Halas hit just .091 in twelve games with New York, injured a hip, and was sent down to the minors. Just the year before Halas had won MVP honors in the Rose Bowl, and he now decided his future was in football. Halas got together with other interested football men to create the American Professional Football Association, the forerunner of the NFL. Representatives from a dozen teams, all from the Midwest, met in the showroom of an automobile dealership in Canton, Ohio, and decided to grant membership for $100. "There wasn't one hundred dollars in the room," said Halas, "but still each of us put up one hundred dollars for the privilege of losing money."[1]

For the next thirty years the new professional league would be defined by a fight for survival. Teams appeared and then disappeared seemingly overnight. Schedules and rules were haphazard, characterized by almost constant changes and uncertainty. The 1925 Pottsville Maroons ended the season with the best record in the league and decisively beat the second-place Chicago Cardinals to apparently win the league title. After the season ended, Pottsville scheduled a game against Notre Dame in hopes of making some extra money, and the Maroons beat the Irish, 9–7. But league president Joe Carr had warned the team not to schedule the game. Carr fined Pottsville $500, took away the championship, and kicked the Maroons out of the league. The Cardinals were declared the winner of their first, and so far only, championship.[2]

At the time, college football was considered far superior to the fledgling pro league, and Notre Dame was usually the best in the college ranks. Coached by the legendary Knute Rockne, and featuring such players as the Four Horseman backfield, the Irish went undefeated four times in the 1920s and won three national championships. Rockne's last title came in 1930 when Notre Dame crushed USC, 27–0, to clinch an unbeaten season.

As the Great Depression began to deepen that fall, a special exhibition game was scheduled in New York to aid the city's unemployment fund. It would match Notre Dame against the New York Giants, a team that had finished second in the league to the Green Bay Packers. Rockne not only had his championship team, he also brought with him the Horsemen, who last played in 1924. "Fellows, these Giants are heavy but slow," Rockne told his team before the game. "Go out there, score two or three touchdowns on passes in the first quarter, and then defend and don't get hurt."[3]

More than 55,000 fans jammed the Polo Grounds on December 14, 1930, expecting to see Notre Dame dominate, but by halftime the Giants led 15–0, and Rockne's opinion of the pros had changed drastically. "I came here to help a charity," he told Giants president Harry March as he walked to the locker room. "You are making us look bad. Slow up, will you? I don't want to go home and be laughed at."[4] The Giants did let up, eventually winning 22–0, and afterwards Rockne called it the greatest football machine he had ever faced.[5] Perhaps more importantly, the game raised some $115,000 for relief efforts.

Despite such successes, the NFL could never quite capture the attention of the sporting public in the same way of baseball, boxing and college football. One thing those sports had that the NFL needed desperately was a marquee attraction that baseball had with Babe Ruth and college football had with Rockne and the Four Horsemen. It was the performance of the Horsemen in a 1924 win over Army that led Grantland Rice to pen his famous opening in the *New York Herald-Tribune*:

Two. Growing Up, Growing Old

Outlined against a blue, gray October sky, the Four Horsemen rode again. In dramatic lore, they were known as Famine, Pestilence, Destruction, and Death. These are only aliases. Their real names are Stuhldreher, Miller, Crowley, and Layden. They formed the crest of the South Bend cyclone before which another fighting Army team was swept over the precipice of the Polo Grounds this afternoon....[6]

The same day that the Horseman stampeded Army, Red Grange thrilled a homecoming crowd at the University of Illinois by running for three touchdowns, returning a kick 95 yards for a score, and passing for another. In the 39–14 win over a stout Michigan team, Grange was the "flashing red-haired youngster, running and dodging with the speed of a deer.... Grange doubled and redoubled his football glory in the most remarkable exhibition of running, dodging and passing seen on any gridiron in years."[7]

The following year, Grange then did something even more amazing—he skipped his senior season to play for the Bears in the NFL. Grange was the first college player to leave school early, the first to hire an agent, and the first to capitalize on the financial potential of pro football. In an era where most players made $100 per game, Grange was guaranteed thousands and a percentage of ticket sales. As the Bears barnstormed the country with Grange as the headliner, that alone earned him $40,000 in just two games against the Eagles and Giants in 1925. He earned thousands more by appearing in two movies ("One Minute to Play" and "Racing Romeo") and lending his name to a candy bar.

The tour not only made Grange rich, it may have saved several shaky franchises in the process. An estimated 200,000 came out to see him play his first eight games, including 70,000 in New York. The game at the Polo Grounds was significant for the Giants in that it helped the team dig out of a $45,000 debt.

But the Bears may have shortened Grange's career with a barnstorming schedule that some called suicidal. He appeared in 19 games in a little more than two months in the winter of 1925-26. On one part of the tour Grange played on a Wednesday in St. Louis, Saturday in Philadelphia (followed by a banquet that night), Sunday in New York, Tuesday in Washington and Wednesday in Boston. "If he doesn't slow up, he'll blow up," said Harry March, an early promoter of pro football. "This isn't baseball."[8]

It was perhaps overwork that led to a knee injury, which reduced the speed and effectiveness of the "Galloping Ghost." "I had my cleats dug into the ground and somebody fell over my knee," Grange said. After that, "I was just another halfback."[9] Even so, noted *Sports Illustrated*, "his simple decision to get paid to run the ball had a colossal impact on the evolution of the sport."[10]

Even as Grange was touring the country with the Bears and drawing big crowds, there was still skepticism. When Grange left Illinois and signed his pro contract, the *Chicago Tribune* observed that "pro football as a sport has not entirely warmed the cockles of our heart."[11] Other newspaper outlets and radio stations felt the same, and treated the NFL "like pro wrestling" according to Giants owner Wellington Mara. "We were looked at askance in the press," he said. "Major league baseball and college football dominated."[12] The sanctioning body of college football, upset over Grange leaving for the pros, wanted nothing to do with the NFL.

The league would grow in the 1930s, adding a formal championship game in 1933, but for every step forward there seemed two steps back. As the Redskins and Eagles played an afternoon game at Griffith Stadium in 1941, announcements began trickling in over the P.A. system asking for servicemen to report to their posts. "We didn't know what the hell was going on," said Redskins quarterback Sammy Baugh. "I never heard that many announcements one right after another. We felt something was up, but we just kept playing."[13] What was happening was that the Japanese had bombed Pearl Harbor, but Redskins owner George Preston Marshall wouldn't allow an announcement during the game figuring it would distract the fans.

The war soon became a major distraction for the NFL, which saw many of its players and coaches headed for the service.[14] Player shortages forced the Cleveland Rams to suspend play for the 1943 season, while other teams were forced to merge. The Chicago Cardinals and Pittsburgh Steelers went 0–10 in their only year together and became known as the "Carpets." The Steelers also briefly merged with the Philadelphia Eagles and were known as the "Steagles." "I guess it sounds like an advantage, putting two teams together," said Al Wistert, a tackle with the Eagles. "But all it meant was we had twice as many lousy players."[15]

No sooner had the league barely survived the war years, a rival league presented a serious challenge. The All-America Football Conference (AAFC) started play in 1946 with eight teams, and in the inaugural game 60,135 fans showed up in Cleveland to watch the Browns beat the Miami Seahawks, 44–0. Later that year, the Browns set a new record by drawing 71,134 to a game against Los Angeles.

Cleveland, coached by Paul Brown and featuring a roster laden with Hall of Fame talent, almost killed the AAFC through its dominance. The Browns won all four league titles, going unbeaten in 1948 and piling up a record of 47–4–3. The Browns certainly could have played with the best in the NFL and there were talks about a "World Series of Pro Football" between the champions of each league. It never happened, primarily because of the NFL's arrogance. "The worst team in our league could beat the best team in theirs," sneered George Preston Marshall.[16]

While the two leagues never met on the field, the most immediate impact of the AAFC was to create a bidding war for college players, returning veterans and even established stars. Chicago Bears lineman Lee Artoe became the first of roughly 100 NFL players to jump leagues, signing with the Los Angeles Dons for $15,000. The conflict ultimately cost the two leagues more than five million dollars, and it became clear both leagues could not survive.

After the 1949 season, Cleveland, San Francisco and Baltimore were taken from the AAFC into the NFL to begin play in 1950. The NFL scheduled its 1950 season opener to feature the two-time league champion Philadelphia Eagles against the AAFC champion Browns. Here was another opportunity for the NFL to establish its credibility with the public, just as it tried to do in 1930 when the Giants beat Notre Dame.

Instead, the upstart Browns destroyed the Eagles, 35–10 in a game not even as close as the score. Cleveland, with Otto Graham, Marion Motley, Lou Groza and Dante Lavelli, gave a black eye to the league it had just joined. "They didn't upset us," said Eagles lineman Bucko Kilroy after the game. "Man for man, they were just a better team."[17] Three months later, the Browns concluded their first season in the NFL by beating the Rams for the league title.

Graham, Motley and other NFL standouts became stars during the decade of the 1950s, but the league still needed that one standout it had lacked since Grange retired. One appeared on the horizon in 1957, a rookie from Syracuse University who was just as much a star in lacrosse as he was in football. Jim Brown led the league in rushing in 1957, and for seven of the next eight seasons after that until his retirement in 1965. "These people pay to see perfection," *Sports Illustrated* wrote in 1958 of the record crowds coming to watch the Browns, "or the closest thing to it, and in Cleveland the man who comes nearest to giving it to them is James Brown."[18]

Yet fans could not give themselves over wholly to Brown because he never gave himself over completely to them, or to football. He was quiet and introspective, and never believed that football was the defining part of his life. His premature retirement in 1965 at the age of 29 was shocking, but not surprising to those who knew him best. "I want more mental stimulation that I would have playing football," he said at the time. "I want to have a hand in the struggle that is taking place in our country, and I have the opportunity to do that now."[19]

Brown also happened to be black in an age still battling with Jim Crow and overt racism. Stories about him often focused on his animalistic physical attributes, such as his "shoulders of a Miura bull and 30-inch waist," and likening him to a "great hunting cat asleep in the sun."[20] Brown's growing involvement in civil rights later in his career seemed to further estrange him from the public. "Jim Brown is heroic, but he's no hero," wrote his biographer, Dave Zirin. "I think that's the best way to look at his life."[21]

Even if Brown could seemingly never be the hero the public wanted, his ascendancy nevertheless helped redefine the NFL. Brown was a model of consistency, always productive yet never vulnerable. He made the Pro Bowl and All-Pro team every season except for one, and finished his career as the NFL's all-time leading rusher. For a league desperate to move beyond its chaotic beginnings, Brown represented stability.

If the NFL couldn't find heroes, it certainly could find characters. The brawling, rowdy early years of the league seemed to attract an odd assortment of fly-by-night personalities. Johnny "Blood" McNally, a Hall of Famer halfback who won four titles with the Packers in the 1930s, was said to be the inspiration for the character Dodge Connolly in the 2008 movie *Leatherheads*. McNally once climbed to the top of a moving train, walked to the engineer's car, dropped through the ceiling, and spent the trip entertaining the drivers.[22] Even into the 1950s, said Colts defensive tackle Art Donovan, "there were wild teams stocked with wild guys playing during wild times. The NFL was not always the corporate entity it evolved into today. At one point, the NFL was about as sophisticated as a tong war."[23]

The 1957 NFL season was a microcosm of the league's first 37 seasons—uncertain, unpredictable, and wildly entertaining. In started in August when Lions coach Buddy Parker addressed fans at the team's eighth annual "Meet the Lions" banquet. Instead of delivering a pep talk, Parker shocked his audience by announcing his immediate resignation. "I can't handle this team," he said. "It's the worst team I've ever seen in training camp. We've got good boys here, but there's been no life. It's a completely dead team."[24]

Parker had issues with the board of directors running the Lions and some of his players believe that too much drinking that night led to the announcement. "It was like, 'What did he just say?'" said receiver Jerry Reichow. "We didn't know what to say or do, so we went out and got beat the first game."[25] That first game seemed to justify Parker's pessimism, as the Colts routed the Lions, 34–14.

Detroit quarterback Bobby Layne did not play well at all in the loss, throwing no touchdowns and three interceptions. In his tenth year in the league, and eighth in Detroit, Layne had forged a reputation as one of the game's most versatile players and greatest leaders. Layne quarterbacked, kicked, and played defense; just the year before he led the league in scoring and field goal percentage.

He was unafraid of berating opponents or teammates, and on many occasions chased his own players out of the huddle for poor play. "Just once," he told center Ed Beatty, "take out your man and we'll all declare a damned holiday."[26] Opposing linebacker Sam Huff of the Giants said of Layne, "Most quarterbacks are quiet, kind of laid back and easy going. Bobby had the competitive spirit of a linebacker."[27]

But Layne's competitive fire was tempered by his love of a good time. So notorious was his drinking and hell-raising that often times Layne was either hung over or still drunk in the huddle. One time he was sacked by Art Donovan of the Colts, who asked him, "You all right, Bob?" Layne replied, "I'm all right, Fatso. But don't do it again because I'm going to meet you afterward. I'm having a big party and you're all invited."[28] If there was a party, Layne's teammate Dorne Dibble was likely there, not to carouse, but to try and keep Bobby in check. "I went out with him to make sure he went to bed," Dibble said.[29]

Layne never let his good times interfere with his play, and in his Hall of Fame career he led Detroit to a pair of NFL titles. Before one of the rare games he lost, to Cleveland in the 1954 championship, Layne and his teammates went to bed early the night before. Layne blamed that for the 56–10 rout suffered at the hands of the Browns.

The Lions avenged the opening loss to Baltimore a few weeks later and as the season progressed found themselves in a dogfight with the San Francisco 49ers in the Western Conference. The 49ers had enjoyed little success since coming over from the AAFC, but after a win over Chicago on October 27 they had taken over first place. Owner Tony Morabito, urged by doctors to stay away from the games after a heart attack in 1952, had another while watching the Bears game at Kezar Stadium. He died a short while later at a San Francisco hospital. "He had lived for the day when the 49ers would hold first place," read newspaper reports, "then missed seeing it by less than an hour."[30]

The Lions and 49ers split their two meetings during the regular season, and with two games to play the teams stood tied for first place at 6–4. On December 8 both teams won as San Francisco beat Baltimore and Detroit topped Cleveland. But in the second quarter of the Browns game, Layne suffered a serious break of his right ankle. Teammate Gene Cronin went to see him in the hospital. "He's laying there [with] his football pants on," said Cronin. "A Marlboro cigarette in his mouth. He's watching a game involving the 49ers. The doctor comes in [and] Layne tells him, 'You get out of here! I told you not to bother me until this game is over!' Toughest old guy I ever saw."[31]

Because of Layne's history of injuries, the Lions had acquired veteran Tobin Rote from the Packers the year before. Rote had split time with Layne all season and now took over full-time, leading Detroit to a win over Chicago in the last game of the season. Since the 49ers also won, beating the Packers, the teams would meet in San Francisco on December 22 for a special playoff game to determine the Western Conference champion.

The 49ers, who had never won so much as a division title before, bombarded the Lions in the first half, much like the army of seagulls who perpetually inhabited Kezar Stadium managed to target visiting players. The first score came on a play that seemed to perfectly capture the zaniness of pro football up to that point—an "alley-oop" pass from quarterback Y.A. Tittle to end R.C. Owens.

Owens came to the 49ers from the College of Idaho where he was an outstanding basketball player; so good, in fact, that he was drafted by the Minneapolis Lakers of the NBA. Owens demonstrated his jumping ability in an October game against the Rams when he and Tittle improvised two touchdown passes. Tittle essentially threw the ball straight up in the air and Owens out jumped his defender for the scores. In his account of the game, Bill Leiser of the *San Francisco Chronicle* called them "two of the most dumbfounding, astonishing, impossible catches ever wrought on any gridiron."[32]

Whether named for a popular comic strip character at the time, as Tittle later claimed, or for the traditional phrase trapeze artists yell as they begin their routine, the alley-oop soon became a sensation. A month later against Detroit, Tittle and Owens did it again, this time connecting on an alley-oop to beat the Lions on the last play of the game. Owens out jumped two defenders this time, as San Francisco won, 35–31. "I decided to go for the alley-oop pass," Tittle said afterwards. "I knew I had to lay it in the end zone, high, and I just reared back and threw it as hard as I could."[33]

Y.A. Tittle played 17 years in the NFL, made the Pro Bowl seven times, and eventually the Hall of Fame. But he is perhaps best known for a gimmick play that was born by accident and seemingly drawn up in the dirt of the early NFL. "You could do it, I could do it, my wife could do it," he said years later of the pass. "Just throw the ball up high in the air and let R.C. jump for it."[34]

San Francisco led at the half 24–7, and the Lions trudged back to the locker room. A thin wall separated the two locker rooms and the Lions could clearly hear the 49ers celebrating on the other side. "They were very confident that they were going to be opening the champagne," said Lions defensive back Jack Christiansen, "and their wives had already spent the championship money for fur coats and houses."[35]

"They're beating on the wall and '(expletive) you,'" said Detroit defensive end Gene Cronin. "And [coach] George Wilson got up and said, 'I was going to say something, but that's what they think of you,' and he sat down."[36]

The 49ers kept up the chirping as the teams walked back to the field, and then opened the third quarter with Hugh McElhenny racing 71 yards down to the Lions' nine-yard line. The game looked to be over.

Instead, Detroit held the 49ers to a field goal, and even trailing 27–7, the Lions had flipped momentum. "If there was a turning point it was when San Francisco failed to score seven points after McElhenny's long run," said Detroit coach George Wilson. "We knew we then could come back."[37] Although Wilson did admit he would have done the same thing, kicking the field goal instead of trying for the touchdown.

The Lions then scored 24 unanswered points, and at the time the 31–27 win was the largest come-from-behind effort in league history. "Who knows how?" the 49ers blew the game asked Ron Fimrite, then a young fan growing up in San Francisco and later a writer for *Sports Illustrated*. "We were all too stunned to remember. All over the stadium beer cans dropped from the hands of disbelieving fans. It all seemed to happen with a terrible inevitability."[38]

Layne, watching the game on crutches from the sidelines, shook hands with Rote as the game ended. Rote played solidly, through unspectacularly, completing 16 of 30 passes with one touchdown. "I guess you'd have to say I was having a bad day in the first half," Rote told reporters. "But we sure went to work in the second half. I didn't give up. None of our players did."[39]

The jubilant Lions headed for home and a date the following week in the NFL title game against Cleveland. Many considered the Browns, with a week off to rest, as the favorite, even though the game would be played at Briggs Stadium in Detroit. Behind the rushing of rookie Jim Brown, who led the league with 942 yards, Cleveland rebounded from a losing record the year before to win the Eastern Conference title.

Brown became the centerpiece of a Cleveland offense that was still struggling to replace Hall of Famer Otto Graham at quarterback. In his ten-year pro career, Graham never missed a game and led the Browns to the championship game every year, winning seven times, a streak of consistency that earned him the nickname "Automatic Otto." "The test of a quarterback is where his team finishes," said his coach, Paul Brown. "By that standard, Otto was the best of them all."[40]

But the "Automatic Otto" nickname may also have referred to Graham's less than colorful personality. He played the oboe, sold insurance in the off-season, and lived a quiet life in the suburb of Bay Village,

Ohio, married to the same woman for 57 years. In an era of hell raisers and beer drinkers like Layne and Art Donovan, Graham marked a transitional point to what would become the norm in the NFL. When the Browns destroyed the Eagles in that 1950 season opener, it was Graham who noted, "We were so fired up, we would've played them anywhere, anytime—for a keg of beer, or in my case, a chocolate milk shake."[41]

Graham's retirement in 1955 left a gigantic hole in the Browns offense. The team tried George Ratterman and Babe Parilli, but they lasted only the 1956 season. So in 1957, the Browns turned to veteran Tommy O'Connell and rookie Milt Plum. Neither set the world on fire—they combined for just eleven touchdown passes all season—and it was very much Jim Brown's offense that carried the load all season and into the championship game.

The prospect of a championship matchup between Rote and O'Connell, two career backups who would play for seven teams in the pro careers, did not exactly set hearts aflutter, as would a Layne-Graham meeting. But it thrilled the fans in Detroit, who would not be able to see NBC's national television coverage because of blackout rules. More than 3,000 camped out outside Briggs Stadium to stand in line for tickets. The line lasted for three days, and Lions officials passed out coffee to those who braved the sub-freezing temperatures.

Weather forecasters predicted more of the same for the game, but it was sunny and mild on December 29 when the teams kicked off. What followed shocked the capacity crowd of 55,263, the Browns, and even the Lions themselves. Three-point underdogs, Detroit went out and handed Cleveland the worst loss in its history, 59–14. "The championship game was kind of like, 'Well, the hard game we just passed up,'" said Reichow of the win in San Francisco. "Right away, we started scoring touchdowns, and it was one of those games where we couldn't do anything wrong and the Browns couldn't do anything right."[42]

The game was still in doubt in the first half with Detroit leading, 17–7, when the Lions lined up for a field goal. Instead, Rote changed the play in the huddle and called for a fake, hitting a wide-open Steve Junker for the touchdown that essentially ended the game. Rote finished with four touchdown passes, two to Junker, and rushed for another. The Lions intercepted five passes and held Jim Brown to 69 yards rushing on 20 carries. "Don't mention that," Rote laughed afterwards when asked about changing the play. "I'd be in the doghouse. George [Wilson] is a gambler, too. He would have gone along."[43]

Cleveland coach Paul Brown hated to lose, and sometimes even hated it when his team won but didn't play the right way. After one loss in 1949, Brown told his team, "I'm telling you this and it's cold turkey. If those of you who fell down on the job don't bounce back, I'll sell you."[44] Before that defeat, the Browns had won 29 games in a row.

This time, there was little Brown could say. "I'm philosophical about it," Brown said with a faint smile and shrug of the shoulders. "The ball was just going to bound that way and it did. I told the boys, 'Just go home and forget.' These things happen sometimes and there's nothing you can do about it."[45]

Cleveland quarterback Tommy O'Connell completed only four of eight passes, with two interceptions, and admitted afterwards that he played the game on a broken leg. When he injured the leg a month earlier, it was first diagnosed as a sprained ankle. "My leg didn't bother me as much," he said. "I just had a lousy day. My timing was way off."[46] Brown said he would have played backup Milt Plum, but Plum had pulled a hamstring that week in practice.

The fans carried the victorious Lions off the field and the players made plans to continue the party at an area hotel. Bill Ford, a part owner of the team, came up to Gene Cronin in the locker room and said, "I hear you and [linebacker] Joe [Schmidt] are having a party later. Can [my wife] Martha and I come?" Years later, Cronin laughed telling the story. "I wasn't going to tell him no. And we had to carry him out of there [drunk]."[47]

The whole city partied like there was no tomorrow, and so far for the Lions championship dreams, there hasn't been. Up to 1957, the Lions were one of the most successful teams in the league, winning four NFL titles and playing for another. "You were the most inspirational team in the history of the game," NFL Commissioner Bert Bell told the Lions before the 1958 season started. "Let's see you play that way this season."[48] They did not. Instead, in the sixty-plus years since that win over Cleveland, the record reads: twelve playoff appearances, one playoff win, and no Super Bowls.

It's called "The Curse of Bobby Layne," as in 1958 Detroit shockingly traded its star quarterback to lowly Pittsburgh. There were several explanations for the move: Layne was 31 and coming off an injury; there was a power struggle between Layne and coach George Wilson for control of the team; Layne was allegedly rumored to be betting on games and when the Lions found out they dumped him. Layne always denied the gambling, but Paul Hornung of the Packers, who himself was suspended for the entire 1963 season for betting on games, said, "Bobby gambled more than anybody who ever played football, period. How did the league go all those years without ever getting him?"[49]

For whatever reason, Layne was off to Pittsburgh for a reunion with Buddy Parker, while the Lions got quarterback Earl Morrall and two draft picks. Legend has it that on his way out of town, Layne cursed the Lions and said it would be fifty years before the team ever won another title. In 2008, the year the curse was supposed to end, the Lions became the first team ever to go 0–16 in a season.

Whether Layne actually cursed the Lions depends on who one talks to. There's no actual record of Layne ever uttering the words, and he was non-committal about it up to his death in 1989. "I think he was pretty bitter," said Lions teammate Joe Schmidt. "I think he had that attitude, which is, hey, I brought all these championships to you and now you're going to broom me?"[50]

Layne's banishment to the NFL's Siberia at the time meant that a lot of fun left the Lions, and the league as a whole in a way. The league had moved past its ragtag early years, which was both blessing and curse. Certainly, the league no longer had to worry about survival, and gone was the chaos of players and teams hopscotching to new towns almost every week. Gone were the days when a player would play three games in a week for three different teams using three different names.

Corporatization had begun to take hold, reflective of a growing trend in America itself. A war of rationing, service, and self-sacrifice had ended, and the economy boomed to such a degree that consumerism grew to heights never before imagined. "By early 1955," noted Stephen Ambrose, "a boom was on [and] the result was a buying spree."[51] The assembly lines that only recently produced airplanes, tanks and guns, now churned out cars, television sets, and refrigerators. "The good purchaser devoted to 'more, newer and better' was the good citizen," explained historian Lizabeth Cohen, "since economic recovery after a decade and a half of depression and war depended on a dynamic mass consumption economy."[52]

It was an economic boom not unlike the one in the 1920s following World War I. In 1925, President Calvin Coolidge took note of the country's growth and famously remarked, "The chief business of the American people is business."[53] While those words have been long remembered (and often misquoted), what has somehow become lost are Coolidge's next words from the same speech: "Of course, the accumulation of wealth cannot be justified as the chief end of existence. The chief ideal of the American people is idealism. I cannot repeat too often that America is a nation of idealists."[54]

But in the 1950s, idealism seemed to get lost in cultural retrenchment. The decade is often remembered as an idyllic, care-free time in American life, filled with drive-in movies, college panty raids, and perfect home life as expressed in the television sitcom *Leave It to Beaver*. Towering over all of it was President Dwight Eisenhower, a grandfatherly figure who projected an aura of calmness and serenity. "Eisenhower," wrote one biographer, "seemingly, was quite content to preside over a fat, happy, satisfied nation that devoted itself to enjoying life, and especially the material benefits available in the greatest industrial power in the world."[55]

The main image many Americans have of Eisenhower in the fifties is not him in the Oval Office, but rather on a golf course. Ike golfed on the White House lawn, played nearly 800 rounds while in office, and put in what Democrats called "a 36-hole workweek."[56] How bad could things be if the leader of the free world was leisurely hacking on the back nine?

Plenty bad, as it turned out. On the same October weekend that saw the Lions beat Green Bay for their first win of the 1957, the Soviet Union launched Sputnik, the world's first man-made orbiting satellite. An announcement from Moscow noted, "The present generation will witness how the freed and conscious labor of the people of the new Socialist society turns even the most daring of man's dreams into reality."[57] American recoiled in shock, not just at the achievement itself, but because how "Sputnik swept away certain basic American assumptions and caused a crisis in self-confidence."[58]

The Friday before that weekend, demonstrations at Central High School in Little Rock, Arkansas, finally began to die down. For ten days white students had threatened violence to prevent black students from attending. Eisenhower finally had to send out the National Guard to allow integration to take place. The reality of the fifties—the Cold War, the Red Scare, McCarythism, Civil Rights unrest—was a harsh underbelly of the decade that could not be raked away as easily as one of the golfing sand traps that Eisenhower frequented.

This fear and uncertainty was perhaps best expressed in Sloan Wilson's 1955 novel *The Man in the Gray Flannel Suit*, which tells the story of a young American couple searching for meaning in a world dominated by business. "The novel does succeed in capturing the spirit of the fifties," says Jonathan Franzen, who wrote an introduction for a 2002 reprint of the book. "The uneasy conformity, the flight from conflict, the political quietism, the cult of the nuclear family, the embrace of class privileges."[59]

Eisenhower critics, afraid to speak out because of his enduring popularity, became bolder after Eisenhower's death in 1968. Author Norman Mailer wrote, "Eisenhower's eight years have been the triumph of the corporation—tasteless, sexless, odorless sanctity."[60] Conservative icon William F. Buckley, no fan of Mailer or Eisenhower, observed that the criticism usually referred to Eisenhower's tenure as "boring, lacking in ideals, and styleless."⁶¹ An article in *Esquire* magazine in November 1959 bemoaned "the decline of exuberance in daily life."⁶²

All of this had begun to play out in the NFL, which had been making incremental steps toward corporatization. The 1950s saw the development of televised games, recognition of a players' union, and a standardized schedule. But as it did for the character Tom Rath in *The Man in the Gray Flannel Suit*, progress may have come at a high price. The soul of the game started to change, and the characters that defined the early years of the league—men like Blood McNally, Art Donovan and Bobby Layne—were now as passé as leather helmets and the single wing offense. "The money side of the game has almost become more important than what goes on between the white lines," said Donovan after his playing days ended. "Today's players are all goddam businessmen. They certainly don't hang around together in the bars like we did in the old days. Whether this is good or bad is for you to decide."⁶³

For good or for bad, for better or for worse, the NFL was a growing corporate concern heading into the 1958 season. Television was beginning to make the game more accessible, but somehow blander at the same time. What the NFL needed was to regain some of that lost soul. The league had plenty of great players. What it needed was a man and a moment.

Three

The Greatest Game Ever Televised

In the 2016 NFL season, the Indianapolis Colts, still fighting a hangover in the post–Peyton Manning era, finished at 8–8 and missed the playoffs for a second consecutive year. Andrew Luck filled in capably for the departed Manning, throwing 31 touchdown passes against just 13 interceptions. It was Manning's first year of retirement after a 17-year career that saw him win Super Bowls for both the Colts and Broncos.

It went largely unnoticed at the time, but 2016 marked an interesting milestone for the Colts. It was their 32nd season in Indianapolis as compared to the 31 they played in Baltimore, meaning they now had a longer history in Indiana than they did in Maryland. That still seems hard to believe for many who grew up with the tradition of the Baltimore Colts in the 1950s, many of whom refuse to forgive Robert Irsay and the Irsay family for sneaking the team out of town in 1984 and relocating it to the Midwest. "You just cried and cried and couldn't believe it," said Colts fans Antoinette Duda of the team leaving Baltimore. "It was very hard. You cuss out Irsay, and you go through all of that."[1]

The first iteration of the Colts, when the team came to Baltimore, began just as badly, if not worse. The team began play in 1947 in the All-America Football Conference, and in three seasons managed to win only 11 of 42 games. After the 1949 season, the NFL absorbed three AAFC teams, including the Colts.

The 1950 Baltimore Colts set NFL records for futility that still stand today. The team went 1–11 on the season, gave up 70 points in one game against the Rams, and became the only team in NFL history to give up more than 50 points four times. They allowed the most points per game (38.5) in NFL history, and gave up 462 total points—an NFL record broken by, wait for it: the 1981 Baltimore Colts. John Steadman, who covered sports in Baltimore for seven decades, including every Colts game from 1947 to 2000, called the 1950 Colts "a comic book season—the most mixed-up, confused, disorganized, chaotic, and bizarre series of events any team or city ever had to endure."[2]

Yet, even in the wreckage there were positive signs. On November 5, the Colts won their only game of the season, beating Green Bay, 41–21, behind three touchdowns and 176 yards rushing from fullback Jim Spavital. When the game ended, fans jumped out of the stands and carried Spavital off the field. True, there weren't a whole lot of fans at the game—the Colts finished last in attendance in the NFL averaging about 16,000 per game—but the few who did come showed a passion that remained even after the team folded.

The Colts pep club kept going, as did the Baltimore Colts Marching Band, even though they had no team to support. "The relationship between the team and our city was one of love at first sight," said Art Donovan, who was a rookie in 1950. "And like a good marriage, the love affair grew stronger with each passing year."[3]

But like some marriages, there would be a brief separation. Owner Abe Watner gave the Colts back to the NFL for $50,000, which covered rights to the players, uniforms and equipment. But there was a significant problem in that Watner didn't own the team outright. There were stockholders, including Baltimore scion and philanthropist Zanvyl Krieger, who wanted to keep the team in town. When they filed a lawsuit against the NFL, the league settled by relocating the defunct Dallas Texans—a team just as bad as the 1950 Colts—to Baltimore in 1953.

The first Baltimore Colts had simply vanished into the NFL history books, and the second version was the offspring of the last league team to go bankrupt. Clearly, pro football in Baltimore was off to an inauspicious start.

The 1953 and 1954 Colts finished with a record of 3–9, due mainly to lack of talent. Quarterbacking those teams were men such as Fred Enke, Jack Del Bello, and Gary Kerkorian. But the team did take some significant strides toward respectability, first in 1953 by hiring Don Kellett as general manager. It was Kellett who solved the talent problem by drafting receiver Raymond Berry (20th round, 1954), running back and Heisman winner Alan Ameche (first round, 1955), and running back Lenny Moore (first round, 1956). And it was Kellett who also brought in quarterback Johnny Unitas after he washed out with the Steelers (see Chapter Four).

Kellett's other main contribution was the hiring of Wilbur "Weeb" Ewbank as head coach in 1954. Ewbank had spent his entire life in coaching, and came from Cleveland where he served as an assistant to Paul Brown and helped the team win an NFL title in 1950. Ewbank brought to Baltimore Brown's "keying" system, which had players reacting to opposing tendencies rather than trying to stop someone through brute force. If a defensive player saw the offensive guards pulling to the right, he would read that "key," assume the play was a sweep, and react accordingly.

"When Weeb [and defensive coach Joe Thomas] came in and introduced the keying defense," said Art Donovan, "man, I was in hog heaven. Weeb Ewbank made [me] a Hall of Fame football player. I loved him for that; I will always love him for that."[4]

As he would prove later with Joe Namath, Ewbank had a talent for working with quarterbacks, and he certainly had a diamond in the rough in Unitas. Ewbank worked tirelessly with Unitas to improve his technique, including his footwork, drop back, and follow through. The coach had detailed diagrams of how Unitas should move on every play—his steps, his fakes, and his positioning. "I think he was one of the greatest quarterback coaches of all time, based on his results with Unitas and Namath," said newspaper sports editor Steve Stout, "taking two guys from scratch to NFL champions. Especially with Unitas, who nobody wanted, and he became maybe the greatest quarterback of all time."[5]

Ewbank also watched the way Unitas threw, the tremendous torque he put on his arm, and wondered how he didn't hurt himself after every pass. But he didn't change his motion, and for the most part left the youngster alone. In many ways, Ewbank succeeded as a coach by knowing when not to coach. "The most important thing about Unitas," Ewbank once said, "is that he had a real hunger. This was a kid who wanted success and didn't have it so long that he wasn't about to waste it when it came."[6]

Some may consider Ewbank's hands-off approach genius, but to others it suggested a weakness in game-day strategy. Weeb did his work during the week in terms of preparation, and then essentially turned things over to Unitas. During one close game against the 49ers in 1958, the quarterback came over to his coach for advice.

"Weeb, what've you got?" Unitas asked.

"What have you got?" Ewbank replied, staring straight ahead.

Unitas answered, "Well, I'm not sure, so what've you got? What do you think I should do?"

"Well, John," Ewbank answered, "what do *you* think you should do?"

The conversation continued in the vein for some time before Unitas, finally exasperated, said, "Aw, this is bullshit, Weeb." He want back to the huddle, drew up a play in the dirt, and threw a touchdown pass.[7] Years later, Namath and Jets receiver Don Maynard experienced much the same thing. After Ewbank sent in two plays during a game that resulted in interceptions, Maynard told Namath, "Joseph, don't listen to him anymore. On game day, he needs to be home."[8]

In today's era of radio communication with players, instant photo analysis, and ongoing coaching adjustments, Unitas had a level of control that's almost hard to believe. "[Ewbank] never called the plays," Unitas said. "He turned the game plan over to me. The guys up in the press box would ask me, 'What do you want to know?' I said, 'If you can find any kind of tendency on them as far as their rushing linebackers, let me know. Otherwise, just sit there and enjoy the game.'"[9]

None of Ewbank's first three Colts teams had a winning record, and there were whispers that his job was in jeopardy. When Kellett went to the players to get their opinion, they defended the coach and believed the team was close to turning the corner. Ewbank stayed, and in 1957 with Unitas, Moore, and Ameche firmly established as stars, the Colts had the first winning season in their history, finishing at 7–5. The offense finally caught up with what had always been a pretty good defense, featuring Hall of Famers Art Donovan and Gino Marchetti.

In 1958, the Colts started like a house afire, winning all six exhibition games and then opening the regular season by dominating the defending NFL champion Lions, 28–15. They scored 51 points on the Bears, came back to put 40 on Detroit in another win over the Lions, and won their first six games of the season.

"Hey, Fatso, just how goddamn good, are we?" Marchetti asked Donovan after Baltimore destroyed Green Bay, 56–0.

"If everybody pulls together," said Donovan, "shit, nobody's gonna stop us."[10]

Nobody really did, although the team had a bit of a letdown at the end of the season, losing meaningless games on the West coast to the Rams and 49ers. Baltimore still finished at 9–3, won the Western Conference title, and would play in its first NFL championship game.

The Colts other loss came against the Giants in New York, 24–21, a game Unitas missed because of injuries. The Giants and Browns tied for the Eastern Conference title, also at 9–3, and a special playoff game was held in New York on December 21 to see who would advance to play the Colts. In an incredible display of defensive football, the Giants shut out Cleveland, 10–0, and held the Browns to 86 yards of total offense. Jim Brown, who led the NFL in rushing with 1,527 yards, had just eight yards in seven carries, while the Browns also lost 52 yards on six sacks.

Beginning play in 1925, the Giants had always been one of the bedrock franchises of the NFL. Under innovative coach Steve Owen, the team won two league titles and played in the championship game another six times. But the last championship had come in 1938, and

Three. The Greatest Game Ever Televised

when the Giants fell to fifth place in 1953, Owen was unceremoniously replaced by Jim Lee Howell.

Many wondered why one of the league's glamour teams would take a chance on Howell. He played eight solid, if unspectacular, seasons with the Giants as a receiver and caught a grand total of seven touchdown passes. His coaching resume consisted only of assistant jobs at the University of Arkansas and Manhattan College, and three years as the head coach of Wagner College, where his teams went 24–30–3. Army assistant Vince Lombardi was widely considered the favorite to get the job, and one newspaper, the *New York Daily News*, trumpeted a headline, "Giants Boot Owen Upstairs, Lombardi Seen New Coach."[11]

Lombardi would indeed join the Giants, but as an assistant to run the offense under Howell. The defensive assistant was Tom Landry, who transitioned into coaching after a seven-year career as a defensive back of underwhelming physical skills, but one who succeeded on intellect and preparation. With two future Hall of Fame coaches on his staff, Howell was often portrayed as a figurehead. There are stories of reporters wandering the halls at the Giants offices, passing one room with Lombardi watching offensive game films, another room with Landry watching defensive films, and yet another room with Howell reading a newspaper. Howell himself admitted that with two such talented coaches, his job was simply to "blow up the footballs and keep order."[12]

There may be an element of truth in that, but Howell made some important moves that restored the Giants to contention. He made key trades for Andy Robustelli and Dick Modzelewski, and talked veteran quarterback Charlie Conerly out of retirement. Howell also drafted well, finding defensive lineman Rosey Grier in 1955, and in 1956, defensive end Jim Katcavage and Hall of Fame linebacker Sam Huff. "No one on that team had any doubt who held the ultimate authority," said kicker Pat Summerall, "and that was Jim Lee Howell. He was the glue that held the entire team together."[13]

Howell never had a losing season in his seven years in New York and in 1956 guided the Giants to the NFL championship. New York went 8–3–1 on the season, and in the championship game avenged a tie against Chicago by dominating the Bears, 47–7. It was a game every bit as lopsided as the score would suggest. "We didn't have to try to fire up the boys for this one," Howell said after the game. "In fact, we tried to play it down to keep them from getting keyed up too much. I knew they wanted to win this more than anything else."[14]

The Giants regressed a bit in 1957, finishing behind Cleveland, but in 1958 beat the Browns three times. On the last Sunday of the season the Giants had to beat Cleveland to force a playoff, and did so, 13–10, when Summerall booted a 49-yard field goal through the snow. The next week the teams met again in the playoff and the Giants dominated. "I never saw anyone play Cleveland so defensively like we did," said Howell after the shutout in the playoff. "In fact, I never saw any club defend against a good club the way they did."[15]

Even though there was a newspaper strike in New York at the time, there was little trouble in attracting interest in the Colts–Giants championship. The Colts led the NFL in both yards and points, while the Giants had that stifling defense that had suffocated the Browns and led the league in fewest yards allowed. Given that the Giants had to play an extra game and the Colts were coming in fresh, odds makers installed Baltimore as a 3.5-point favorite.

The game on December 28, 1958, in New York became one of the most discussed, most analyzed, and most talked about games in NFL history. An almost untold number of books and documentaries are dedicated to what became to be known as "The Greatest Game Ever Played." Many have given it that name because it was the first NFL championship game to go into overtime and was not decided until an Alan Ameche touchdown won it for the Colts, 23–17. "Never has there been a game like this one," gushed *Sports Illustrated*. "When there are so many high points, it is not easy to pick the highest. It was a game that had everything."[16]

That included some very un-championship-like play. The teams combined for seven turnovers, seven sacks, and some questionable play calling. "The Greatest Game Ever Played," laughed Art Donovan, "what a load of crap. We were thirty times better than the Giants and we should have kicked the living shit out of them. We weren't feeling ecstasy; we were feeling relief."[17]

As a *game*, the championship left a lot to be desired. As *theater*, it exceeded beyond any expectation. And what made it compelling theater was television.

The broadcast media has always had a complicated relationship with sports. For years, newspapers dominated coverage because they were the only game in town. With most sports revenue coming from ticket sales, teams viewed newspapers as valuable promotional outlets, and worked to get coverage in local outlets. That was a lot easier for baseball than for the fledgling NFL. Back in the 1940s, "Papers didn't staff our training camps," said Rams public relations director Tex Schramm. "I wrote stories for the papers and sent them via Western Union. In the offseason, I got in my car, drove to four or five papers, and wrote stories. Not only that, I wrote the headline and helped ship the copy to the composing room."[18]

Three. The Greatest Game Ever Televised

When radio emerged and offered the possibility of live broadcasts of games, there was reservation and skepticism. The idea was that broadcasting games live was essentially giving away the product and would hurt attendance. Why come to the game if you can stay home and listen for free? Baseball faced that same issue, and in 1932 the three teams in New York agreed to ban local broadcasts for five years. But those teams that ignored the ban and broadcast their games—such as the Chicago Cubs—found out that live broadcasts not only increased attendance, but also became another source of revenue, both in rights fees and advertising.

The NFL took its initial step into broadcasting in 1934 when the Thanksgiving Day game between the Lions and Bears became the first game broadcast nationally on radio. Just five years later, in a game between the Eagles and Brooklyn Dodgers, NBC aired the first game on television to people in New York, but only 500 of them had sets at the time. In 1953, the fledgling Dumont network put the NFL on for a full season, coast to coast. "Our ratings beat all three major networks," said Ray Scott, who announced the games. "That was the first example that National Football League football on television was a great advertising buy for major U.S. corporations."[19]

But when the Dumont network ceased operations in 1956, NFL teams were left to come up with their own television contracts. That created a disparity in which teams in big markets, such as the Giants and Bears, could cut more lucrative television deals, while small market teams like Green Bay got left out. Realizing this would eventually lead to a competitive imbalance on the field, the NFL wanted to negotiate a single television deal for all its teams, which would then split the revenue.

The problem was that such cooperative negotiations violated federal anti-trust laws. So the NFL went to Congress, which in the Sports Broadcasting Act of 1961 made an exception for football (as well as baseball, basketball, and hockey) and allowed the revenue sharing plan. It was a ruling that did nothing less than transform the entire landscape of the NFL. "You can't predict what would have happened," said Giants owner Wellington Mara, "but we certainly would not have the league we have today. That was the most important decision ever made in the league."[20]

It was a decision that eventually changed the NFL revenue structure from one dependent on ticket sales to one driven primarily by television revenue. After passage of the Sports Broadcasting Act, the NFL signed a two-year deal with CBS television for $9.1 million. By 1964, the figure had jumped to $28.2 million. In 2011, the NFL signed a nine-year contract with CBS, Fox, and NBC, with each paying the league around a billion dollars per year. As it has with every television contract since 1961, the NFL divides up that revenue equally between its teams.

As it had for several years, NBC would nationally televise the championship game, but many fans in New York would not get to see the broadcast. The game was not a sellout, and in fact, more people had watched the same teams play in November. Still leery of how television would affect the gate, NFL Commissioner Bert Bell mandated a broadcast blackout within 75 miles of New York. "If we ever start valuing the TV audience more than the paying public," Bell warned, "we'll be in trouble."[21] Eventually, 64,185 fans made their way to Yankee Stadium for the game, including some 20,000 Baltimore fans who came north on special trains and buses.

As the teams waited in the locker rooms before the 2 p.m. kickoff, Ewbank went to his psychological bag of tricks. First, the plastered the room with signs that said "We Outgutted Them," a reference to a comment made in the newspapers by Giants quarterback Charlie Conerly after New York beat Baltimore in their first meeting in November. Then Ewbank gathered his team together and delivered a speech that Art Donovan called "a real three-hankie affair. He went down the roster one by one, telling every guy on the team how he had been rejected. 'Pittsburgh didn't want you,' he told Unitas, 'but we picked you up off the sandlots.' What a delivery! He should have won an Oscar."[22]

Over in the Giants locker room, Howell went over game strategy with Conerly and backup quarterback Don Heinrich. Heinrich would actually start the game and play a few series, so Howell and Conerly could look over the defense from the sidelines. It was an unusual arrangement, but not a surprising one, as Heinrich had started six times during the regular season.

Heinrich would play the first three series, completing two of four passes, and contributing a fumble when he tried to pull away from center too soon. It was part of a ragged first quarter that saw Unitas also fumble and throw an interception, and the Giants block a field goal attempt by Steve Myhra. A bigger problem for Baltimore was an injury to running back Lenny Moore, who thought he had broken a rib after catching a long pass. "I can't turn, I can't bend," he told Ewbank on the sidelines. "Does John [Unitas] know?" Ewbank asked him. "Hell, Weeb, John knows everything," Moore replied. "Well," said Ewbank, "tell him he's going to have to use you as a decoy."[23] Moore stayed in the game as a receiver, but Ameche and L.G. Dupre took over most of the rushing duties.

With Conerly finally in the game, he led a drive that ended with a Summerall field goal for a 3–0 Giants lead. But the next New York drive

Three. The Greatest Game Ever Televised

ended in another fumble and after a Colts drive, Ameche powered over from two yards out to put Baltimore on top, 7–3. After an exchange of fumbles, Unitas led the Colts on a 90-yard drive that culminated with a touchdown pass to Raymond Berry. On the day, the future Hall of Famer would catch 12 passes—a playoff game record what would last for 24 years—good for 178 yards and a touchdown. Baltimore led at the half, 14–3, and "the Giants, now 11 points behind, looked well-whipped."[24]

As the teams traded punts to open the second half, there was an amusing near-fight on the Baltimore sidelines after a late hit on Colts receiver Raymond Berry. Amusing because it involved the 6'1", 230-pound Huff and the diminutive Ewbank, who was 5'7" and weighed barely 150 pounds. Many believed that Ewbank took a swing at Huff and actually hit him. "We all pushed him," said Weeb. "Huff kneed one of my men out of bounds. He should have been kicked out of the game."[25] Art Donovan called it one of the funniest things he had ever seen in his playing career. "Here came Weeb," laughed Donovan, "raising his dukes like he was going to throw a haymaker at Huff. But while he was staring down Huff, the whole team had backed away. Weeb turned beet red and made a beeline behind a group of us."[26]

It wasn't so funny for the Giants when Baltimore threatened to break open the game. Unitas led a drive that put the ball on the New York three-yard line with a first and goal, and a Colts touchdown would give them an insurmountable 21–3 lead. Three times Baltimore plunged into the Giants line, and three times the defense turned them back. With it now fourth and goal, Ewbank passed on a field goal and kept the offense on the field.

Unitas called for Ameche to sweep to the right and throw a half-back pass to Jim Mutscheller. But Ameche missed the call and thought it was a simple sweep. With Mutscheller in the end zone instead of blocking, Ameche was quickly tackled for a four-yard loss and the Colts opportunity was gone. "I'm standing there by myself," said Mutscheller. "Alan couldn't throw at all; he threw like a girl. But even Alan could have completed that one."[27]

Given new life, the Giants roared back. Conerly completed a long pass to Kyle Rote, who fumbled, but teammate Alex Webster picked up the loose ball and carried it to the Colts one-yard line. "I really didn't fumble," Rote insisted. "The guy pulled the ball away, and I just went numb. Thank God for Alex Webster."[28] Fullback Mel Triplett punched it over two plays later, and New York had cut the lead to 14–10 at the end of the third quarter.

After a Baltimore punt, Conerly moved the Giants back downfield again. Two big completions to Bob Schnelker, for 15 and then 46 yards, put the ball on the 15-yard line. From there, Conerly passed to Frank Gifford, who shook off a tackle and scored the touchdown that put the Giants ahead, 17–14. As the fourth quarter wound down, and the New York defense succeeded in keeping the Colts off the scoreboard, the Giants seemed content with running out the clock.

With less than three minutes to play, the Giants had the ball on their own 40-yard line, facing a third and four. A first down would just about kill the remaining time and the Colts. In the huddle, Conerly called for Gifford to carry off tackle behind Triplett, but Gifford suggested a sweep would work better. So Conerly changed the play to "Brown right, over, 49 sweep." It was the same power sweep, with both guards pulling, that offensive coach Vince Lombardi would make famous in the coming years in Green Bay. "I just wanted the ball," Gifford said. "I knew I'd get it. The Colts knew I'd get it, and I didn't care. I knew I'd make the first down."[29]

Gifford raced around right end and was met by defensive lineman Art Donovan and Gino Marchetti. They dragged him down at the 44-yard line, where Gifford was convinced he had the first down. But when the officials came out to measure, the ball was about a foot short. The game hung in limbo for what seemed like an eternity, not only for the measurement, but to get Marchetti off the field. After the tackle, his teammate Gene "Big Daddy" Lipscomb, a behemoth at the time at 6'6" and 285 pounds, piled on and broke Marchetti's ankle. Instead of seeking medical treatment, Marchetti insisted on watching the rest of the game from a stretcher on the Colts sideline. It was all that confusion and delay, said Gifford, which caused referee Ron Gibbs to mark the ball short. "It turned out to be the best play Big Daddy made that day," he said, "was a late hit on his own man."[30]

Marchetti stopping Gifford proved to be the decisive play of the game. To his dying day, Gifford always insisted he made the yardage. Just as obviously, the Colts maintained he didn't. "We dragged him down well short of a first down," said Donovan. "Giants fans swear the officials spotted the ball wrong, but don't let them kid you. We nailed him well behind the line."[31]

Both Lombardi and Tom Landry urged Howell to go for it, but having seen the Colts fourth-down gamble fail earlier in the game, and knowing his defense had shut out Unitas in the second half, Howell decided to play it safe. Don Chandler punted to the 14-yard line where Carl Tassef called for a fair catch. The Giants were 86 yards from the goal line as the Yankee Stadium clock showed 2:20 to play. "The goal posts looked a million miles away," thought Colts receiver Raymond Berry.[32]

Three. The Greatest Game Ever Televised

Berry played a pivotal role in those final minutes, catching four passes despite double coverage from Giants defenders. "The hero of the sequence was the most unlikely," *Sports Illustrated* wrote of Berry. "He had a bad back and one leg is shorter than the other ... his eyes are so bad he must wear contact lenses when he plays. [But] without him the Colts would surely have lost."[33]

But the real hero was John Unitas, who displayed a cool under fire and a willingness to improvise that made him perfectly suited for the two-minute drill. If his past two seasons in the NFL had made Unitas a star, then this drive, and the one to come in overtime, made him a legend. When asked about the difference between the teams after the game, Howell credited the Colts linemen, but quickly added, "Too much Unitas."[34]

The final pass to Berry put the ball at the Giants 13-yard line with seven seconds left. Today, a 20-yard field goal attempt would be considered a "gimme," but it was anything but certain in 1958. Linebacker Steve Myhra would attempt the kick, and he had made only four of ten field goals during the regular season and also missed three extra points. Like every other NFL kicker, Myhra used the squared-toe, straight-ahead style that gradually vanished when soccer-style kickers arrived in the late 1960s. The most accurate kicker in the league in 1958 was the Rams' Paige Cothren, who hit only 56 percent of his chances. The Colts had another kicker on the roster, Bert Rechichar, but he was their long distance specialist and had already missed a 46-yarder. Myhra was used on the close kicks, but he had played almost the entire game on defense and had also missed a field goal.

Add to this the pressure of having the entire season ride on a single kick, and the cold, frozen condition of the field. As Myhra and his holder, backup quarterback George Shaw, rushed on to the field, Shaw kept repeating to himself, "Don't drop the ball, don't drop the ball. When the ball reached my hands it felt like a heavy hunk of ice."[35] He was not the only nervous Colt. "I saw that the Giants were trying to block it," said Donovan, "and that they were going to come right over me. They had done it on an earlier extra point [and] it had almost worked. I was scared shitless it was going to work now."[36]

The Giants did come over Donovan, but Myhra got the kick up and it sailed through the uprights, tying the game, 17–17. Bill McColgan turned to his partner Joe Bolan in the NBC radio booth. "Joe," McColgan told his listeners, "with just seconds to go if the Giants don't run back this kickoff for a touchdown, for the first time in history we're going to say, 'And now [we're] going into the fifth period of a football game.'"[37] The Giants did not, and the game headed into overtime.

Going into uncharted territory meant a lot of confusion for coaches, players, and fans. Some of the players thought the game would end in a tie and that the teams would split the proceeds. New York captains Kyle Rote and Bill Svoboda weren't sure what to do until an official led them to the 50-yard line for the overtime coin toss. Fans in the stands and those at home were similarly bewildered. When the television announcers introduced overtime by calling it a "game we'll never forget," a housewife in Milwaukee turned to her husband. "Why did he say that?" she asked. "Because of the sudden death," he replied. "Sudden death," she said. "Who died?"[38]

The Colts' chances seem to have died when the Giants won the coin toss and took the ball on offense, but after the Unitas drive and Myhra's kick, all the momentum was with Baltimore. The defense held the Giants to three plays, and Chandler punted down to the Colts 20-yard line. When Unitas got in the huddle and told his teammates that they were going to go down the field and score, no one doubted him.

The big play in the drive was another Unitas pass to Berry for 21 yards on third and 14. Unitas then audibled a quick trap for Ameche that gained 23 yards, hit Berry again inside the ten, and then with everyone on the defense expecting run, he hit Mutscheller with a pass down to the two. The play was originally designed as an Ameche run, but Unitas changed it at the line. It was pure Unitas: bold and daring, but at the same time cold and analytical. When some criticized him afterwards, saying that an interception in that spot could have cost the Colts the championship, he replied simply, "When you know what you're doing, you don't get intercepted."[39]

The catch made the ending a foregone conclusion. On the next play, with 6:45 left in the overtime period, Ameche barreled through a gaping hole in the Giants line and into the end zone for the winning score. Photographs of the famous play show Ameche lowering his shoulder to brace for contact, but there was no one there. "Unitas takes, he gives to Ameche," said McColgan on NBC radio, "and the game is over! Alan Ameche has scored the touchdown and the Baltimore Colts are the professional football champions of the world!"[40]

No extra point was attempted or even possible. Fans rushed the field and tore down the goalposts, and then carried Ameche off the field. With a few minutes left in regulation, writers had prematurely named Conerly the game's most valuable player. Now, the award, and with it a new Corvette, went to Unitas. "For months afterwards," said Conerly's wife Perian, "I had nightmares about Dorothy Unitas driving gaily around Baltimore in 'my' Corvette."[41]

The rest of the nation seemed just as stunned as Mrs. Conerly, not

Three. The Greatest Game Ever Televised

Alan Ameche scores the winning touchdown in the 1958 NFL championship game as the Colts beat the Giants, 23–17. Because the game went to overtime and was televised nationally, many people credit this as the exact moment the NFL came of age in the sporting consciousness. *AP Photo/File.*

quite sure what to make of what they had seen. The victorious Colts rejoiced in their championship locker room, led by Weeb Ewbank. "I miscalculated," he told team owner Carroll Rosenbloom. "I predicted it would take five years to build a champion. It took me an extra quarter."[42]

"We outgutted them,"[43] guard Art Spinney shouted above the din, a taunting reminder to the Giants of Conerly's words after the first meeting between the teams. Ameche appeared on that week's *Ed Sullivan Show*, and when the team returned to Baltimore a crowd of 30,000 greeted them at the airport. Reporters called it "an unruly mob of victory-frenzied fans [that] caused a near panic."[44]

Even in defeat, the Giants and their fans seemed to realize the enormity of what had happened. The next day, Howell invited reporters to watch the game film with his assistant coaches. One of the reporters, Joe Trimble of the *New York Daily News* said of the session, "It was almost as exciting as the game itself."[45] From that point forward, according to Gifford, "a nation began to recognize the unique appeal of a sport in which any one play could bring extraordinary athletic feats. On December 28, 1958, everything changed."[46]

And it changed primarily because of television.

Television perfectly captured the drama of the NFL, but gave it something more. It legitimized pro football, making it palatable to a nation that had in years past had barely recognized its existence. If football was on television, with *Lassie* and *Dr. Kildare*, then it must be worth watching. "Pro football is the Lawrence Welk kind of thing," said motivational researcher Dr. Ernest Dichter. "Football is law and order in playful fashion. People are watching fair play. The good guys are rewarded and the offenders penalized."[47] It was *Gunsmoke* on a football field, with Marshal Dillon beating the bad guys every week.

It wasn't so much that more people were watching football, which certainly was the case, but that the watching itself changed American cultural habits. Fall Sundays became reserved for football, and specifically for consuming it on television, upending long standing traditional patterns. Sunday drives in the car and family dinners went by the wayside, while many churches changed the times of their services so as not to conflict with the NFL. "Yes, it is Sunday," observed *Sports Illustrated*, "for hear the thunder of drums, the stir of martial music; there is the anticipation ... the National Football League is on the air! For three, five, maybe even eight hours Sunday is consumed."[48]

No one was more successful at exploiting this dynamic than television executive Roone Arledge. It was Arledge who first understood how to package the drama of football and deliver it through a television camera lens. While most early football telecasts settled on simply reporting the action from a distance, Arledge wanted close-ups and behind-the-scenes shots. He wanted viewers to see the players behind the facemasks and helmets; to humanize them as part of his "up close and personal" approach to television sports. "He alone moved American sports from daytime to prime time, from small time to big time," said fellow television sports producer Dick Ebersol of NBC.[49]

It was Arledge who convinced the NFL and ABC television, in last place among the three networks and shut out of pro football coverage, that his approach would work on Monday nights. With nothing to lose, ABC began televising *Monday Night Football* in 1970 and it became an instant cultural sensation. The announcer interplay between the unctuous Howard Cosell and folksy Don Meredith became instant must-see television that transformed not only Monday nights, but also American habits in general. "Anytime 35 million people suddenly start spending three hours of a hitherto normal weekday evening watching a pro football game on TV," wrote William Johnson, "they are bound to significantly influence mass culture, business trends and possibly the birthrate."[50]

As America embraced pro football on television, and pro football on television changed America, the money logically followed. With a ready-made audience of tens of millions every weekend, advertisers poured money into the networks. The networks, in turn, poured money into the NFL for the right and privilege of showing NFL games. In 1958 at the time of the Colts–Giants championship game, there was no national television contract and each team cut its own deal. Just six years later, each of the three networks submitted sealed bids to the NFL for the television rights package. The contract with CBS, for 4.65 million a year, was expiring. "I was starting to up my hopes," said NFL Commissioner Pete Rozelle. "The rumors were fantastic; I thought we might get $10 million a year."[51] When the bids came in, CBS held on to the rights by bidding $14.1 million per year for two years—triple the amount of the previous contract.

The money today, of course, is much greater, in the billions of dollars. The amounts have changed, as have the networks, as in 1993 the upstart Fox network came in and stole the rights package from CBS. Out of the NFL game for four years, CBS was desperate to get back in, and did so in 1998. According to Neil Pilson, the former president of CBS Sports, "The negative impact was so severe that CBS went to the NFL and said, 'Name your price and we'll pay whatever to get a package.' We lost affiliates, ratings, the male audience and a lot of sports sponsorships. But when CBS got the NFL back, everything picked up again."[52]

The money has changed, the networks have changed, the players have changed, the announcers have changed, and most certainly the technology has changed. Today's digital technologies have made it much easier to consume the televised product on computers and phone screens, expanding the audience far beyond the living room, and far beyond America. By 2019, viewership in Europe had grown steadily in terms of both hours of content viewed and live hours viewed.[53] That kind of exposure had led to several NFL regular season games played overseas, and talk of expansion teams in London and elsewhere (see Chapter Seven).

But what has not changed is America's almost insatiable desire to watch pro football on television. Sunday afternoons have now mushroomed into Sunday nights, Monday nights, Thursday nights and the occasional Saturday game after the college season ends. There are more new leagues popping up, such as the XFL, which began play in 2020, all based on the premise that Americans simply can't get enough football.

Ultimately, the XFL failed, driven out of business not by lack of television ratings but rather by stay-at-home orders issued as part of the coronavirus pandemic. Whether it might have succeeded under different circumstances is arguable. What cannot be argued is that much of the success of the NFL, certainly from a television standpoint, can be traced back to December 28, 1958.

It was, Arledge said of the Colts–Giants game, "a defining moment in the growth of pro football. [After that] the networks all of a sudden woke up and saw that they had to have football."[54]

Four

The Ruthian Moment

To understand what was happening to pro football in the 1950s, it's helpful to look at the evolution of other professional sports in North America. Baseball, of course, has the longest history, predating the NFL by fifty years. By the time pro football came around in the 1920s, baseball was already a successful, established business. Yet it went through many of the same growing pains as football, including a fight for survival in its formative years.

One of those consistent pains was gambling, a particular threat to the game in the early years when players made little salary and looked for ways to supplement their income. One of the best at fixing games, or worst depending on the point of view, was a talented first basemen named Hal Chase. Chase played for four teams in the early part of the 1900s and his athletic skill was exceeded only by his ability to manipulate baseball games. Not waiting for gamblers to approach him, Chase often arranged his own action, often bribing his own teammates to help him throw games. "He became adept at making faulty plays around first base so that everyone would look bad but himself. In the process, the outcome of the game would be altered."[1]

While Chase had a deserved reputation as baseball's "malignant genius"[2] he was by no means alone. It was common for players to ease up in certain situations depending on the whims of odds makers and gamblers. Sometimes, players would take plays off to help friends on other teams when a game was not in doubt, such as third baseman playing deep and allowing a hitter to get an easy bunt single. Such doings were well known inside baseball's fraternity, but shielded from the public. Baseball's "official, if unspoken policy, was to let the rottenness grow rather than risk the dangers involved in exposure and cleanup."[3]

But the rottenness of the Black Sox scandal in 1919 could not be ignored. Eight members of the heavily favored Chicago White Sox allegedly accepted bribes to throw World Series games against the

Cincinnati Reds. Some accounts suggest that the players themselves instigated the fix, which led to the Reds eventual championship.

When the scandal came to light a year later, baseball hired Kenesaw Mountain Landis as commissioner to clean up the game and he banned the suspected players for life, even after they were declared not guilty in a jury trial. The trial showed baseball not as the wholesome game it claimed to be, but rather an unseemly enterprise populated with shadowy figures. "The Black Sox scandal of 1919 may be remembered as having hit baseball out of the blue, but the truth is that it was simply the largest and ugliest blight on a game that had been mired in scandal and infighting for several years."[4]

All of this came at a time when the game was still stuck in the dead ball era. It was a style favored by such giants of the game as managers John McGraw and Connie Mack—"inside baseball"—that meant lots of singles, bunts, stolen bases, and sacrifice flies. Shutouts and one-run games were common, as a single baseball was often kept in play throughout the course of an entire game.

With public resentment and suspicion growing, and the game still mired in defensive stalemate, baseball had very real concerns about its future. It needed something, or rather someone, to restore confidence and excitement.

Along came George Herman "Babe" Ruth.

Ruth started his career as a pitcher with the Boston Red Sox in 1914 and became perhaps the best left-hander in the game. In the six years he served primarily as a pitcher, Ruth won more than twenty games twice, led the league in ERA one season (1.75) and in complete games (35) in another. He helped the Red Sox to two championships, and decades after his retirement still owned the World Series record for consecutive scoreless innings pitched. It's no exaggeration to say that he could have made the Hall of Fame primarily for his pitching.

But when Ruth went from Boston to New York in 1920, and switched from pitching to outfielder full time, he began to transfix a nation. For the 1920 season, trick pitches like the spitball were outlawed, and the baseball was made livelier. Ruth, now employing his trademark uppercut for the Yankees, set major league records in a dozen categories, many of which lasted the rest of the century. His 54 home runs was an 86 percent increase over his record from the year before, and he outhomered every team in the American League. Philadelphia's Cy Williams led the National League in homers with fifteen.

Before the season started, Ruth set his goal at an unthinkable 50 homers. As he smashed his old record on July 19, and 50 began to look reachable, fans flocked to ballparks to see him. When he hit the milestone on September 24, the *New York American* noted, "The crowd went quite mad. They had witnessed something no other people had ever seen before. Perhaps no one now living will ever see such a thing again."[5]

As the Babe kept hitting home runs, other players in both leagues began to copy his approach. Home runs, scoring, and attendance soared, but while other players hit a lot of home runs, no one hit them as often or as far as Babe Ruth. His emergence is credited with nothing less than saving the game of baseball. Echoing what many others have said, *The Smithsonian* stated simply that Ruth "changed the fortunes of a team, a city and a sport."[6]

Such transformation could not have taken place without the help of the media, which in Ruth's case was primarily newspapers and then radio. Media and reporting tend to reflect the cultural values of their time periods, such as with the idealized Frank Merriwell athlete of the late Victorian period, and the skepticism and cynicism in reporting associated with the Watergate era. In between came Ruth, who benefited greatly from the relaxed social mores of the 1920s.

Much has been written about the "Roaring Twenties," or "Jazz Age." Coming out of the horrors of World War I that killed 40 million, and a worldwide influenza pandemic that killed 50 million more, Americans were ready to enjoy life, or what President Harding called a "return to normalcy." Drinking flourished, even in the midst of Prohibition, and attitudes about fashion and sexual activity loosened. "Sex itself would come out in the open as never before," wrote historian Thomas Steissguth, "[and] popular culture responded: movies featured romance and scantily dressed vamps; spicy novels and confessional magazines uncovered the details of thousands of private lives; dancing moved to new venues where couples were unchaperoned and unsupervised."[7]

Ruth embodied all of these things, and more. He amazed teammates with his eating ability, frequented brothels in almost every American League city, and left $100 silk shirts in countless hotels, preferring to buy new ones rather than do laundry. Years after his death, Ruth's hometown *Baltimore Sun* wrote of his "supposed womanizing, gluttony and Prohibition-era imbibing. If Ruth had a boy's love for baseball, in popular memory, he also had an adolescent's passion for self-indulgence."[8]

But again, such stories came out only years later after Ruth had passed from the scene and American cultural values had shifted again. At the time he played, Ruth was lionized as perhaps no athlete before or since, in great part because the media were complicit in keeping his off-field activities a secret. There is a story, perhaps apocryphal, about reporters riding on the train to cover a Yankees road game. A naked

Babe Ruth suddenly ran through the car, followed closely by a woman chasing him with a knife. Supposedly, one reporter turned to another and said, "It's a good thing we didn't see that or we'd have to report on it."[9]

This is not to say that reporters weren't fascinated with Ruth's indiscretions. They followed him around like puppies, and the Babe, hungry for attention and validation, often included them among his growing number of hangers-on. On more than one occasion, newspapers reported Ruth had died after one of his many automobile mishaps. When Ruth's first wife Helen was in the hospital with a nervous breakdown, brought on in large part by the Babe's womanizing, he allowed reporters in the room to take photos of the anguished scene.

At a time when the country needed uplifting, the sporting media saw its role as to create heroes and perpetuate the heroic mythology. Men such as Grantland Rice used florid writing to turn an otherwise non-descript baseball game into a display of epic achievement. In 1927, Martin Haley of the *St. Louis Globe-Democrat* wrote of one of Ruth's home runs, "Homeric Herman careened the animated leather for a sky-scraping bull's eye into the distant center-field bleachers, the ball clattering up the icy seats at the point where the left-center and dead-center field sections conjoin."[10]

"The reason for the idolization of ball players lies in man's urge to create heroes," observed baseball historian Harold Seymour. "In ball players they see living evidence that certain values and assumptions deep in the American psyche still have validity."[11] According to Dr. Harry Scott at Columbia University, "More people appreciate the work that goes into a moment of heroism on the field. People feel it is good for an individual to achieve a great thing—a zenith—even if it does not change the world. The professional's accomplishment is being appreciated on its own terms."[12]

Charles Lindbergh, Jack Dempsey, Bobby Jones, and especially Babe Ruth became something even bigger than the hometown hero who wins the game for the local fans—they became global icons; known and admired the world over because of the reach of newspapers and radio, and the willingness of the media to contribute to the heroic mythology. "When a sportswriter stops making heroes," Rice once remarked, "it's time to get out of the business."[13]

The mythology business was very good to Babe Ruth in the 1920s. Newspaper reporters and later radio followed his every move. He was "The Bambino," "Herman the Great," "The Colossus of Clout," "The Sultan of Swat," and dozens of other nicknames that testified to his greatness. He was no ordinary man but a "superman" according to scientific tests that Ruth undertook in 1921. "His eye, his ear, his brain, his nerves all function more rapidly than do those of the average person," wrote Hugh Fullerton in *Popular Science*. "Further, the coordination between eye, ear, brain, and muscle is much nearer perfection than that of a normal, healthy man."[14]

Even today, a superlative performer in some field is often referred to as "the Babe Ruth of" music, or mathematics, or meatpacking, or whatever. When discussing the impact of Roone Arledge on television (see Chapter Three), Don Hewitt of CBS said, "There will never be another Roone Arledge because there will never be another Babe Ruth."[15] Not another Hank Aaron (who broke Babe's all-time home run mark), or Barry Bonds (who broke Aaron's record), or Roger Maris (who broke Ruth's single-season homer record), but another Babe Ruth.

There are dozens of biographies of Ruth, not including an autobiography he ghosted with two sportswriters, and more come out almost every year. Robert Creamer wrote perhaps the definitive Ruth biography, and noted, "More than any other man, Babe Ruth transcended sport, moved far beyond the artificial limits of baselines and outfield fences and sports pages."[16]

It's almost impossible to describe Ruth's popularity, not only at the time he played, but even in the years following his death in 1948. Red Sox outfielder Harry Hooper played with Ruth in the 1910s, when Ruth was a successful pitcher who helped the Sox win two World Series titles. He later played against Ruth when the Bambino moved on to greater fame in New York. "I saw it all happen, from beginning to end," said Hooper. "But sometimes I still can't believe what I saw: This nineteen-year-old kid, only lightly brushed with the veneer we call civilization, gradually transformed into the idol of American youth and a symbol of baseball the world over—a man loved by more people and with an intensity of feeling that perhaps has never been equaled before or since. I saw a man transformed from a human being into something pretty close to a god."[17]

In short, Babe Ruth was the right person in the right place at the right time. That unusual combination of time, space and fortune that can be called the "Ruthian Moment." The Ruthian Moment can be defined as the perfect intersection of man (or woman, if you prefer), moment, and medium that shifts the trajectory of sport within a culture. When all three elements come together, the effect can push sport beyond the limits of cultural boundaries and engrain it in the national consciousness. Lacking any of these elements can cause a sport to miss a true transformational moment. One such missed opportunity came in the 1980 Winter Olympics with the U.S. men's hockey team.

Canadians have always thought of hockey as their game. They claim to have invented it, defined it, and perfected it to the point that is has become an integral part of their national consciousness. Hockey is who Canadians are. "The fact is that the game of hockey and the Canadians who play it at the highest level are our identity," writes Paul Henderson. "And no one wants to lose part of their identity."[18]

If anyone should know, it's Henderson. It was his goal on September 28, 1972, that is considered one of the most defining moments in the country's history. Henderson's goal in the waning moments of the eighth and final game against the Soviets in Moscow clinched the Summit Series for Team Canada.

Many Americans, notably those in such places as Minnesota and the northeast, follow hockey rabidly, but the majority of Americans simply don't pay attention until the Olympics roll around every fourth year. Even then, their anticipation usually ends in disappointment, as American teams typically don't fare well against the Canadians and teams from Europe. With the exception of a stunning gold medal showing at Squaw Valley, California, in 1960, U.S. teams had never had much success in Olympic hockey after the Soviets started competing in 1956.

That's why the success of the Americans at the 1980 Winter Olympics, held in Lake Placid, New York, was such a surprise. It came at a time when the Olympics still held to the amateur ideal and professionals were not allowed to play. At least, professionals as defined by the rigid standard of getting directly paid for competing. For years, the Soviets had skirted this issue by putting their best players on a Red Army team. While the players were not technically paid to play hockey, they lived and trained together, spending much more time on hockey than they did on maneuvers. "They skated three times a day, perfecting both their individual skills and their teamwork," said Alpo Suhonen, who coached Team Finland at the time. "They practiced around 1,200 hours a year. In Finland, we practiced a third of that."[19]

How good were the Soviets? In 66 games against the Finnish team during the 1970s they won 63, lost two and tied one. In the winter of 1979, the Soviets embarrassed an NHL All-Star team in a series of exhibition game, winning twice in what was called the Challenge Cup. It wasn't much of a challenge as the Soviets outscored the NHLers, 9–0, over the last game and a half. "This is a better team," said NHL center Bobby Clarke, who also faced the Russians in the Summit Series. "If they had a weakness, we never found it."[20]

It was practically the same cast of Soviet characters who came to Lake Placid, having not lost an Olympic game since 1968. No one talked of the medal chances of Team USA, which featured a group of college kids who had played together only a few weeks under coach Herb Brooks. In a tune-up game before the Olympics began, the Soviets crushed the Americans, 10–3, at Madison Square Garden in New York. "I don't mean to sound defeatist," said Brooks after the game, "but practically speaking, we don't have a chance to beat the Russians."[21]

As if to emphasize that point, the Soviets swept through the preliminary round, averaging ten goals a game. The U.S. started slowly, but surprisingly beat the Czechs, Norway and Romania to advance to the medal round and a showdown with the Soviets. Suddenly, Americans caught a case of Olympic hockey fever, as they began to think that maybe, just maybe, this group of ragtag collegians could compete with the Soviet machine.

The game was scheduled for Friday, February 22 at 5:00 p.m., but ABC television, which held the Olympic rights, asked permission to move the game to 8:00 p.m. to show to the country in prime time. The Soviets complained, arguing that the change would start the game at 4:00 a.m. back home, so the International Hockey Federation kept the game at its original time. ABC decided to show the game tape-delayed in prime time, meaning that the game was already over by the time the television airing began.

ABC and other outlets were careful to try and avoid passing along the final score before the game aired, but many people found out anyway through radio, word of mouth, or simply by watching the raucous scene behind ABC host Jim McKay as he introduced the game. Fans watching the game on ABC affiliate WJLA-TV in Washington, D.C., found out the score when sportscaster Renee Poussaint accidentally passed it along during a station break between the second and third periods.

Even as the drama of the game began to build, parts of it were edited out for time consideration, including the start of the third and decisive period when the Americans trailed by only a goal. "Your fondest hope was that the U.S. team would keep it close, not that they would win," said ABC's Dennis Lewin. "If I cut out too much, we'd be dead meat."[22]

Instead, ABC showed the two goals that put the U.S. ahead, and then the agonizing final ten minutes of play as the Americans protected their lead. The "Miracle on Ice" became a signature moment in television sports, punctuated by the call of ABC's Al Michaels, "Do You Believe in Miracles? Yes!" as Team USA pulled off perhaps the most stunning upset in Olympic history, 4–3. Two days later, the U.S. team beat Sweden—this time televised live—to win the gold medal.

But again, no one saw live what turned out to be perhaps the defining moment in the history of the Winter Olympics. In the end, it turned out to be a missed opportunity for a "Ruthian Moment."

In a similar way, the National Basketball Association missed its Ruthian Moment with its own Ruthian figure, Wilt Chamberlain. Like the Babe, Chamberlain was a man of large talents and large appetites that made him the Paul Bunyan of pro basketball. At 7'2" and 250 pounds, he literally towered over his competition, but also had the athletic grace to run track and succeed as a high jumper. When he joined the Philadelphia Warriors in 1959, his battles with Boston Celtics center Bill Russell became instant must-see viewing for NBA fans.

Playing third fiddle behind pro baseball and football in the early 1960s, the NBA still didn't have a national television deal and its revenues depended largely on attendance and ticket sales. Neutral site games were common as the league tried to build its fan base throughout the country. That's why the Warriors found themselves in Hershey, Pennsylvania, on the night of March 2, 1962, to face the New York Knicks.

With no television or video cameras in the arena, only local radio listeners and the 4,124 fans in attendance could attest to what happened that night. Chamberlain set an NBA record that may never be broken by scoring 100 points, the first and only player ever to reach triple digits in a single game, and just for the heck of it added 25 rebounds. Perhaps the most impressive statistic on the night was that Wilt, a notoriously bad foul shooter, hit 28 of 32 free throw attempts.

Yet the only visual proof of the most incredible moment in league history are a few still photos of the game, including one which showed Chamberlain in the locker room afterwards holding a handmade sign with the number "100" scrawled on it. The NBA would certainly grow and thrive in the coming years, but a golden opportunity slipped away. It had the man and the moment, but lacked the medium.

Like baseball in 1920 and Olympic hockey in 1980, the NFL faced its own transformational moment in the 1950s. Pro football needed something, or someone, to give it its own Ruthian Moment. Baseball was still king in American sports, thanks in great part to the lasting legacy of Babe Ruth. "Pro football was struggling," said broadcaster Bob Wolff. "In those days, pro football wasn't considered a major sport like college football or baseball or boxing."[23]

Riding to the rescue came Johnny U, NBC television, and the 1958 NFL championship game.

John Constantine Unitas did not look or act the part of a Babe Ruth, and in fact, looked very little like a professional athlete. "He looked so much like a Mississippi farmhand that I looked around for a mule," said Colts teammate Alex Hawkins. "He had stooped shoulders, a chicken breast, thin bowed legs and long, dangling arms with crooked, mangled fingers."[24]

Unitas grew up in Pittsburgh, the first of a long line of Hall of Fame quarterbacks from that region that came to include Joe Namath, Dan Marino, Jim Kelly and Joe Montana. Montana starred at Notre Dame before coming to the pros, and it was Unitas's dream to play for the Irish as well. But at 5'11" and only 137 pounds, he was considered too small for Notre Dame. "I like what you do, but God you're so small," Irish assistant Bernie Crimmins told him. "We're liable to be sued for manslaughter up here."[25] Not for the last time would someone badly underestimate John Unitas.

He went instead to the University of Louisville, playing offense, defense and returning kicks for a team that never had a winning record in his three varsity seasons. His hometown Pittsburgh Steelers drafted him in the ninth round of the 1955 draft, and in training camp he competed with three other quarterbacks. Coach Walt Kiesling never gave Unitas much of a chance, deciding "he was too dumb to remember the plays,"[26] and he was released before the season started.

Unitas returned home to Pittsburgh to support his family, worked in construction, and on weekends he played semi-pro ball with the Bloomfield Rams, earning six dollars per game. With nowhere else to go, Unitas got an invitation to tryout for the sad sack Baltimore Colts, a team that in four years in the league had never finished higher than fourth place. Unitas impressed coach Weeb Ewbank at the spring tryout, earning himself a chance to make the team in summer training camp. "You knew right away," said Ewbank. "We knew that as soon as he learned the offense he would be our quarterback."[27]

Until that time, Unitas would back up number-one draft pick George Shaw. When Shaw broke his leg early in the 1956 season against Chicago, Unitas came in and his first pass was intercepted and returned for a touchdown. On the next play, he mishandled the ball resulting in a fumble that led to another Chicago touchdown. "When we first saw this guy," said teammate Art Donovan, "we all thought he was a bum who was never going to make it. None of us had any idea we had found ourselves anything more than a quarterback who had a great knack for leading the opposition on tremendous touchdown drives."[28]

Instead, Unitas rebounded and led the Colts to wins over the Packers and Browns, and finished with nine touchdown passes on the season. The next year, 1957, he put it all together to lead the league in passing attempts, yards, touchdown passes, and quarterback rating to become the NFL's Most Valuable Player. More importantly, he led the Colts to their best ever record, 7–5, and a second-place finish in the conference.

Unitas dropped off statistically in 1958, but what he lacked in numbers he more than made up for in leadership. Soft spoken off the field, he took complete charge in the huddle, calling plays and changing them at the line of scrimmage as needed. Unitas never cared if his teammates liked him, and in fact, had a strained relationship with many of them. "He could be a trying person sometimes," said linebacker Mike Curtis, who played with Unitas in the 1960s. "I was going out for a pass one time [in practice], and when I crossed the line of scrimmage he hit me in the head with the ball from behind. I came back and told him if he ever does that again, I'll kill him."[29]

But Unitas demanded, and got, complete respect from his teammates. During one game in 1958, he had called for several running plays by Lenny Moore. In the huddle, Moore told Unitas, "Hey man, cool it. I'm getting tired." Unitas gave Moore a hard look and said, "Listen, asshole. Nobody tells me to cool it. I'll run your ass till you die."[30]

It was a part of the flinty Unitas personality that reflected his mental and physical toughness. He was never afraid to challenge defenders, either by running the ball or by holding on to it in the pocket waiting to pass. On one occasion against the Bears, Unitas and the Colts trailed with but seconds to play. Chicago's Doug Atkins buried Unitas on a rush that left his face mangled and bloody. "Well, kid," said Atkins. "That's about it for you today." Struggling to his feet, Unitas replied, "Not yet, it ain't." After heading to the sideline to get his nose packed with cotton to stop the bleeding, and with his eyes almost swollen shut, Unitas returned to throw the winning touchdown pass.[31]

Unitas put all of those qualities on display in the 1958 championship game against the Giants. He threw an early touchdown pass to Raymond Berry to give Baltimore a 14–3 lead, and when the Giants rallied in the second half to go ahead, it was Unitas who engineered a drive in the final seconds to earn and field goal and send the game to overtime. Then in the overtime, it was Unitas again, mixing plays expertly, and crossing up the Giants defense with an unexpected pass down to the goal line. Alan Ameche finished it off with his famous touchdown, and the Colts had won the first overtime game in the history of the NFL, 23–17.

The man and the moment had met, and they became legends thanks to the medium. NBC had the television rights to the game, which was not shown in New York because of the league's rule of blacking out games to local audiences. Two local announcers, Chris Schenkel, who called Giants games, and Chuck Thompson, who did the same for the Colts, would work the game. They flipped a coin to determine who would call which half; Schenkel won the flip and picked the second half, figuring if the game was close he would make the dramatic call. Thompson got the first half and ultimately the overtime period. The game was covered extensively on radio, with NBC providing national coverage and WBAL and WCBS doing the game locally for audiences in Baltimore and New York City, respectively.

As the drama grew throughout the game, so did the television audience, which by the end set a record with 45 million viewers. As the Colts got the ball in the overtime period, fans inched closer to their black-and-white sets. Unitas moved the ball down the field, setting up the Colts on the Giants' eight-yard line when he called time out. Suddenly, a technical problem with the NBC coverage caused the picture to change over to snow, a common occurrence in the early days of television. Millions of fans were in danger of missing the winning score.

That's when a drunken fan stumbled on to the field, causing police to chase him down, and delaying the game for several minutes. "Play will be halted now," said Bill McColgan on NBC radio. "A fan running out onto the field with three of New York's finest trying to corner him. And they get him around the 22-yard line."[32]

NBC television used the delay to get its signal repaired, luckily missing only one play, which was a short plunge into the line, and television viewers were able to see Ameche's dramatic touchdown to win the game. One account of the game said simply, "A deliriously happy Baltimore fan raced onto the field during a timeout and sailed 80 yards, bound for the Baltimore huddle, before the police secondary intercepted him and hauled him to the sideline."[33]

It was later learned that the "fan's" name was Stan Rotkiewicz, and he may not have been drunk at all. Rotkiewicz worked as a business manager for NBC, and it was widely believed that he went out on to the field to save the network from ultimate embarrassment. Watching the whole scene, Unitas found it hard to believe that anyone could act that drunk, but others were convinced. Broadcaster Lindsey Nelson, working for NBC at the time, said, "[Rotkiewicz] was capable of posing as an errant fan long enough to save the day for his network's national telecast of a big football game."[34]

Thanks to in great part to Rotkiewicz, as soon as Ameche crashed into the end zone the NFL had its Ruthian Moment. "This is the greatest day in the history of professional football," NFL Commissioner Bert Bell said tearfully after the game.[35]

It was Bell who helped create the moment with his suggestion of sudden death overtime for championship games, and this was the first in league history. Before 1958, there had been plenty of dramatic title games, including the very first one between the Bears and Giants in 1933. It was the first season the NFL had split into two divisions with the winners meeting for an undisputed championship, and the game had a little bit of everything, including a center-eligible pass and a primitive version of the hook-and-lateral play that accounted for the winning touchdown in the Bears 23–21 triumph. In 1945, the Cleveland Rams edged the Washington Redskins, 15–14, and the margin of victory was a safety awarded to Cleveland when Redskins quarterback Sammy Baugh hit the goal post with a pass out of his own end zone.

But no one had seen overtime and certainly no one had played through it. After the Colts tied the game on a field goal and the clock ran out, there was general confusion on the field as to what came next. The players were unsure exactly what would happen, although they certainly understood the tension of the moment. "After we tied the game," said Art Donovan, "I started screaming at [teammate Jim] Parker as we were coming off the field. And he was screaming back, 'Hey, don't bother me. Don't bother me. I'm nervous!' Listen, we were all nervous."[36]

Television provided the medium that perfectly captured that tension and the excitement of the winning score. It would be determined that the game had a Nielsen rating of 27.7 and share of 75, meaning that nearly 28 percent of all television households were tuned to the game, and of the sets that were actually on, 75 percent were watching NBC and the game. "Here come the Colts to the line of scrimmage," Thompson said on the telecast. "Unitas over the center. The ball is snapped, given to Ameche. He is over for a touchdown! The Colts are the world champions!"[37]

It was the equivalent of any Babe Ruth home run. The Ruthian Moment had been reached and the torch had passed from the Babe. "I'd have rather seen that game than Pearl Harbor,"[38] said a Giants fan who watched from Yankee Stadium. Those who saw the game on television were no less enthusiastic. According to author Ed Gruver, "The nation's number one spectator sport began at precisely 4:51 p.m. Eastern Standard Time."[39]

Some argue that the defining moment in the NFL came in 1969, when a brash Joe Namath led the underdog New York Jets to a stunning upset over heavily favored Baltimore in Super Bowl III. It was the first win for the American Football League in the Super Bowl, and gave the AFL credibility in the merger between the two leagues. Sportswriter and author Martin Ralbovsky said, "Super Bowl III changed the attitudes of an entire nation of fans toward a league and its showcase player. For that reason alone, it may have been the most important single professional football game ever played."[40]

Defensive back Johnny Sample disagrees. He played in both games, first for the Colts in 1958 and then for the Jets, getting revenge on the

The iconic image of Colts' quarterback Johnny Unitas passing in the 1958 NFL title game against the Giants. Unitas rallied the Colts to victory twice, the second coming in overtime, to give the NFL its "Ruthian Moment." *Getty Images/Robert Riger.*

team and the league that let him go. Talking about the Colts win in 1958, Sample said, "TV was born that day. Fans started to call their neighbors while the game was going on, telling them to turn on the TV and watch something special."[41]

It might be better to say that the NFL was born that day, or at least reborn, as it was quite likely the exact moment that professional football leaped passed baseball and burned itself in the American consciousness. When the 1959 NFL season began, crowds jammed into stadiums across the league—71,297 in Los Angeles for the Rams opener against the Giants, 41,697 in San Francisco to watch the 49ers and Eagles, a sellout in Green Bay to watch Vince Lombardi's first game coaching the Packers—and the 300,000 tickets sold guaranteed a profitable season for several teams.[42]

Football writer and historian Dan Daly makes the point that attendance figures immediately following the 1958 championship game are misleading. Yes, average attendance did go up, but it actually went up at a higher rate in 1953 (5.5 percent), 1955 (15.1 percent), 1957 (11.2 percent), and 1958 (6.0 percent) than it did in 1959 (4.5 percent), and actually went down in 1960 (−8.0 percent). Attendance increased in 1959 for eight teams in the league, but dropped for the other four, including perennial powers Detroit and Cleveland. The Rams, after their big opening night, had the highest attendance in the league (thanks to the cavernous Coliseum), but also lost the most fans from the year before.[43]

But lost in such observation is not the effect on live attendance, but rather the establishment of television as the primary means of consuming the NFL experience. As league television exposure increased and improved, it raised an important question for NFL fans—why go to the games and suffer through high ticket and food prices, battle crowds and traffic, and often endure terrible weather conditions, when you can stay home and get everything for free? In that scenario, it would be logical for attendance to decline. It's a battle the NFL is still fighting, especially in a modern era on the Internet, 4K picture quality, and social media.

Television had always been ideal for football in terms of the technology because the action fit so perfectly on the screen. What the 1958 championship game delivered, then and seemingly forevermore, was the audience needed to make it work financially. "On December 28, 1958, everything changed," said Giants running back Frank Gifford, who played in the championship game and later spent decades connected to the NFL as a television broadcaster. "The National Football League grew up from Madison Avenue to small-town living rooms where fans began to pay attention to our weekly battles on their small-screen televisions."[44]

In November 1959, Giants linebacker Sam Huff became the first NFL player to appear on the cover of *Time* magazine, and was described as a "confident, smiling fighter fired with a devout desire to sink a thick shoulder into every ballcarier." Huff admitted, "We try to hurt everybody. We hit each other as hard as we can. This is a man's game."[45] When CBS television and Walter Cronkite featured Huff in a documentary a year later—*The Violent World of Sam Huff*—he seemed to become the face of the new NFL.

But it was not Huff, Gifford or any other of the stars of the New York Giants who came to symbolize the growth of the NFL. It was rather a quiet, stoop-shouldered quarterback who wore high top shoes and when he ran a football looked like a gangly ostrich. It was Johnny Unitas "who changed the sport all by himself."[46]

"The men who brought beauty to brutality every week on a football field could be seen as a new breed of the old American frontier," wrote Gifford. "[The] idea of ruggedness, and individuality, and—above all—toughness and resilience."[47] Johnny Unitas represented all of that and more. For a nation of emerging NFL fans, he was Gary Cooper on the football field—when the outlaws had the town surrounded, the bullets started flying and the action was at its hottest, that's when Unitas was at his coolest and toughest. "Let me put it this way," said sportswriter Frank Deford, who grew up in Baltimore watching and idolizing Unitas, and was unabashedly prejudiced. "If there were one game scheduled, Earth versus the Klingons, with the fate of the universe on the line, any person with his wits about him would have Johnny U calling the signals in the huddle, up under center, back in the pocket."[48]

Unitas didn't look like a celebrity or act like one, but that's exactly what he became after the 1958 championship. He endorsed gasoline, cigarettes, hunting rifles, wristwatches, and even shampoo. He appeared so often in newspapers, radio and television, that his face became as familiar to the American public as presidents and movie stars. When Unitas and teammate Art Donovan went to the Pro Bowl in Los Angeles, they visited some Serbian neighborhoods with an ex-teammate named Paul Salata. "Salata took us from house to house in the Serbian community," remembered Donovan. "Nobody knew me, but every one of those Serbs knew John Unitas. Everywhere we went it was like the Second Coming of the Lord."[49]

Beyond its significance for the NFL, Super Bowl III was also viewed as a passing of the guard. The old pro, Unitas, at 35 years old, had spent much of the season on the sidelines with an arm injury. He played only the last quarter of the game in a desperate attempt to rally the Colts, leading them to their only touchdown in a 16–7 loss. In his close-cut hair and high-top black shoes, he seemed to belong to an age gone by.

By contrast, Namath at 25 fit perfectly in his times. Young and confident, he boldly predicted before the game that the Jets would beat favored Baltimore, and then he went out and backed it up. He was not shy about criticizing the man who replaced Unitas, Earl Morrall, nor was he reluctant to talk about his off-field adventures, especially with the young women of New York. "Namath ... looked tradition in its overbearing eye and poked a finger into it. Why, said Namath, can't an athlete admit publicly to drinking alcohol, smoking tobacco, making love to beautiful women—if, indeed, he does?"[50]

Even the Unitas records—and he retired with dozens of them seem like a relic of a distant age. His safest record of all, throwing a touchdown in 47 consecutive games, was broken by Peyton Manning, Tom Brady, and the current record holder, Drew Brees with 54. Those three, all of them products of the pass-happy NFL of the 2010s, are now generally considered the greatest quarterbacks of all-time. Joe Montana, John Elway, and Dan Marino comprise the next tier, and then there is some mention of Unitas.

But once again his critics have underestimated Johnny U. Considered washed up after Super Bowl III, he came back to lead the Colts to a win in Super Bowl V, his third NFL championship. He retired after the 1973 season, and while his records have not held up, his reputation absolutely has. There is something intangible about Unitas—his presence, his leadership, his toughness—that still commands attention in a sports culture becoming ever more obsessed with numbers and statistics. "You show me a quarterback today and I'll show you a surfer," said Art Donovan in 1987. "They all look like beach boys. These guys look like they would pass out at the sight of blood. Unitas dished out punishment when he ran. And he ran a lot."[51]

"What he conveyed to his teammates and to Baltimore and to a wider world was the utter faith that he could do it," wrote Deford. "He could make it work. Somehow, he could win. He would win. It almost didn't matter when he actually couldn't. The point was that with Johnny U, it always seemed possible. You so very seldom get that, even with the best of them. The belief he gave us was his gift."[52]

Five

The Power of Myth

In December 1958, as the Colts and Giants went to overtime to determine the very best team in the NFL, there was no debate as to the worst. The Green Bay Packers had just finished the most difficult season in their distinguished history, winning only one game while losing ten and tying one. Their only victory came against Philadelphia, a team that managed only two wins all year. Green Bay native and Pulitzer Prize–winning sportswriter Red Smith noted wryly, "Green Bay had one of the most soft-bitten teams in pro ball. In 12 games, the Packers underwhelmed 10 opponents, overwhelmed one and whelmed the other."[1]

The 1958 season was the nadir of a ten-year bottoming out that saw the Packers go from a perennial NFL power to league punching bag. Under the direction of founder, coach, general manager and halfback Earl "Curly" Lambeau, the Packers won six NFL titles and became a bedrock of the league, even in its smallest city. As owner, it was Lambeau, with the franchise on the verge of bankruptcy in 1923, who decided to incorporate and sell shares in the team, making the Packers the only publicly-owned professional team. As coach, Lambeau launched the NFL into the passing era with quarterback Arnie Herber and receiver Don Hutson, whose talents were so prodigious that his records lasted more than four decades after his retirement.

Curly's demise came in the late 1940s when he ran afoul of the Packers' executive committee, the group that now ran the team. Convinced of his own infallibility, Lambeau began making questionable decisions without consulting the committee, and the Packers began to struggle on the field and at the gate, going deep into debt. A tipping point came in 1946, when Lambeau convinced the executive committee to sink $32,000 the team didn't have into Rockwood Lodge, a state-of-the-art training facility located outside the city. Perhaps the only thing that saved the franchise from bankruptcy was Rockwood burning to the ground in 1950 and the team collecting on the insurance money. So damaged was Lambeau's reputation that George Calhoun, his friend and partner who helped him co-found the Packers in 1921, remarked bitterly, "I just want to live long enough to piss on Lambeau's grave."[2]

Lambeau eventually became an NFL icon with his name on Green Bay's stadium, but in 1950 he was essentially run out of town and took over the woeful Chicago Cardinals. His departure began a merry-go-round of coaches in a decade where the Packers would have only one winning season. Gene Ronzani lasted only three seasons and part of a fourth, and was replaced by Lisle Blackbourn. "He was a super guy as far as handling people and getting along with people," said Packer lineman Dave Hanner of Blackbourn. "Of course, we weren't loaded with talent at that time."[3]

Hanner was one of the few All-Pros on the roster, but Blackbourn did help with some terrific drafting. The list included future Hall of Famers Bart Starr, Forrest Gregg, and Paul Hornung. In 1958, Blackbourn hit another gold mine with three more Hall of Famers in Ray Nitschke, Jerry Kramer and Jim Taylor. But somehow, he never could get all that talent to jell, and was fired that same year after winning just 17 games in four seasons. Some players chafed under Blackbourn's discipline and found him hard to play for.

"He was slimy," lineman John Martinkovic said of Blackbourn. "He'd tell you something, then a half-hour later he'd say, 'Why'd you do it that way?' He was not well liked. If you told him off, he'd get rid of you, and I told him off a few times."[4]

Blackbourn's hard line also made it hard to get along with the Packers' executive committee, so in came Ray "Scooter" McLean. It was night and day going from the authoritarian Blackbourn to the easy-going McLean, who had few rules and hardly bothered to enforce those. "The guys on the team didn't give a shit about anything," said Hornung, who led the team in rushing with only 310 yards. "It was sad."[5]

"Scooter would play poker with the players the night before the game," said receiver Gary Knafelc, "and what's worse is that he wasn't even good at it. [Max] McGee would just take him to the cleaners."[6]

McLean also had trouble figuring out his quarterback situation. The 1958 Packers had three quarterbacks competing for playing time, although rookie Joe Francis also saw action at halfback. The veteran was five-year man Babe Parilli, who wound up leading the team with ten touchdown passes. Behind him was a former 17th-round draft choice from Alabama. Bart Starr played in all 12 games, but threw only three touchdowns compared to 12 interceptions. "I lost confidence in my passing," Starr admitted. "I wasn't sure about the plays I called. Every time I was intercepted, it would kill me. It worried me the rest of the game."[7]

Five. The Power of Myth 81

In three seasons, Starr had thrown twice as many interceptions as touchdowns and seemed on his way out of the league. The same could be said for McLean, who quit at the end of the miserable 1958 season and landed as an assistant coach in Detroit. The obvious question in Green Bay was not so much who would take over, but how in the world could he clean up the mess?

The answer walked in the door on January 28, 1959.

For a month the Green Bay executive committee had wrestled with the issue of a new coach. Power within the organization had greatly diffused since the time of Curly Lambeau, and with 45 directors on the committee, along with president Dominic Olejniczak and general manager Verne Lewellen, it had become increasingly difficult to steer the ship in the same direction. It was not uncommon at the time for players to bypass the coach and take their complaints directly to the executive committee. Oliver Kuechle of the *Milwaukee Journal* likened it to the Soviet politburo.[8]

Leery of ceding power, not everyone was on board with the man who emerged as the leading coaching candidate, especially when it was learned that he wanted the roles of both coach and general manager. Some on the committee remembered the final chaotic years under Lambeau and balked at giving another person that much power. Others worried that his head coaching experience consisted only of a few years at a New Jersey high school. "There was healthy discussion about it," Olejniczak said of the process. "No one tried to tear down the roof. It was just a healthy discussion, that's all."[9]

But facing bankruptcy off the field and humiliation on it, the Packers had little choice. "He was our man without a question of a doubt," said Olejniczak.[10]

Enter Vince Lombardi and enter the NFL into a new era.

He didn't even attend his introductory press conference, instead addressing reporters by telephone from New York where he was leaving his job as offensive assistant with the Giants to sign a five-year contract. The word "assistant" would never again be applied to Lombardi.

"My word will be final," Lombardi told the reporters. "I've never been connected with a losing team and I hope to instill a winning spirit in the Packers in a lot less than five years."[11]

"Spirit" and "winning" would be ideals the Packers would come to embrace in the coming years, but in the short term everyone immediately got the point that Lombardi was in complete command. "Under Blackbourn and McLean, I had drifted over to practice and talked to whatever players I wanted," said one reporter. "At the first practice I attended under Lombardi, a player turned his head every so slightly. 'Please don't speak to me,' he said. 'Coach Lombardi will kill me.'"[12]

There was a new sheriff in town.

At his first meeting with his new team, Lombardi told the assembled players, "Gentlemen, we are going to relentlessly chase perfection, knowing full well that we won't catch it. But we're going to relentlessly chase it, because in the process we will catch excellence." After the meeting, Bart Starr rushed to call his wife at home. "Honey," he said with excitement, "we're going to win again."[13]

Shortly after taking over, Lombardi had a visitor in his office innocently ask exactly what a football general manager did. Showing rare patience, Lombardi answered, "Today, they called me up from the stadium to ask whether they should water the field and could they buy a new sprinkler. The other day I had to let a fellow go, Howie Ferguson, and it hurt. He's been around a long time. I told him he shouldn't play on account of a shoulder he's got, and he said it was all he knew. It was tough. That's what a general manager does."[14]

Yes, Lombardi felt badly about fullback Howie Ferguson, who had played in the NFL for six seasons. But the bottom line was the bottom line, and for Lombardi there was no room for sentiment in running a football team. As soon as he got the job in Green Bay, Lombardi began looking at film from the previous season, and players who couldn't cut it physically were traded or released. "Fellas," he told the team, "there are planes, trains, and buses leaving here all the time. And if you don't produce for me, you're going to find yourself on one of them."[15]

Those who remained may have envied Ferguson, who finished his career with the Los Angeles Chargers of the American Football League. Lombardi was also looking at something beyond just physical skill; he wanted players who were mentally tough, and he began instilling that toughness from day one.

Players ran wind sprints at the end of practice and the last man to finish had to run laps. After one practice, Lombardi barked at Alex Hawkins, a rookie running back, to start running.

"But, coach," Hawkins protested, "I wasn't last."

"Take two laps," Lombardi yelled back. "I said you were."[16]

Because of such incidents, Lombardi developed the reputation as a martinet who pushed his players relentlessly with little or no regard for their feelings. "He shouted, bullied, drove us, underpaid us and refused to spoil us," said Packer lineman Jerry Kramer.[17] Kramer's teammate Henry Jordan said famously of Lombardi, "He treats us all the same—like dogs."[18]

But Lombardi's genius was that he *did* treat his players differently. He was a master psychologist who knew which players needed prodding, which needed coddling, and which needed a kick in the pants.

Kramer was in one of his first practices under Lombardi when the coach started riding him especially hard. Lombardi called Kramer an "old cow" and said he was the worst guard he had ever seen. After practice, when Kramer was ready to quit football for good, Lombardi walked up to him, tousled his hair, and said, "Son, one of these days you are going to be the greatest guard in the league." Said Kramer, "I was ready to go back and practice for another four hours."[19]

Lombardi's handling of Bart Starr was especially masterful. Starr had shown little evidence that he could play quarterback in the NFL, let alone become a championship leader like Lombardi demanded. That first season in Green Bay there were four quarterbacks on the roster, including Starr, Joe Francis, Babe Parilli and Lamar McHan. By far, McHan was the most physically gifted and Lombardi named him the starter. "McHan was big and strong and athletic, and could throw a football through a brick wall," said receiver Gary Knafelc.[20]

But McHan was also hotheaded, outspoken, and in many ways not the kind of player Lombardi could count on. After one difficult game in which Lombardi benched him, McHan later confronted his coach. "He was back in less than five minutes," said Knafelc. "He never started another game and was traded soon after. No one told coach Lombardi what to do."[21]

That still left the problem of Starr. "He could be good," Lombardi mused, "but he's too damn nice."[22] Anyone who ever met Starr called him one of the kindest, gentlest persons they had ever met. Lombardi saw it too and wondered if his quarterback, who didn't have the great physical gifts of other athletes, had the personality to succeed in the NFL.

The coach set out to build that coveted mental toughness, refusing to let Starr come out games when ill or slightly injured. Lombardi would sometimes plant phony stories with reporters about benching Starr or finding a new quarterback. He was testing to see how Starr would react, whether he would sulk or accept the challenge.

It was difficult at first for the shy quarterback. When Lombardi chewed him out in front of the team, Starr believed it made him impossible to lead. He grew despondent and admitted his fears to his wife. Cherry Starr told him "to march into the coach's office the next morning and ask him never to do that again."[23]

Starr listened, confronted Lombardi, and slowly gained the confidence that transformed him into an NFL Hall of Famer. As he grew into the position, Starr showed the mental toughness Lombardi so valued. He challenged his own teammates who he didn't feel were playing their best, and became one of the few players to stand up to Lombardi. "Bart would stand up in front of the team," said teammate Bill Curry, "and say, 'Wait a minute, coach. Don't be criticizing us about that because that's not true. Let's get it right.' And Lombardi would actually concede to him."[24]

As Starr grew into the job, and into a championship quarterback, Lombardi backed off in his criticism. He still pushed his quarterback, but mostly in private as Starr requested. Lombardi had eventually learned to handle Starr differently than he did Kramer, Jordan and other Packers. And he learned to handle Paul Hornung differently as well.

Hornung was a special case. He and receiver Max McGee were the "bad boys" of the Packers; guys who stayed out all night drinking and chasing women, yet were able to perform at a high level the next day. In some ways, Lombardi looked at Hornung as a son, and it hurt him deeply when the NFL suspended Hornung for a year in 1963 for gambling, and it hurt him again when Hornung's skills declined in 1967. "I had to put Paul on that list," he said to Jerry Kramer about his decision to make Hornung available to the expansion New Orleans Saints. "This is a helluva business sometimes, isn't it?"[25]

And yet, said Kramer, "[Lombardi] constantly chewed out Hornung. He knew that Paul expected to be yelled at and thrived on it, and he knew that other players would accept his lashings if Paul had to take it. Yet Lombardi almost never said anything unkind to Max McGee. He knew that Max couldn't stand being embarrassed in front of his teammates and that if his confidence faltered he might lost his remarkable ability to rise to occasions."[26]

While Lombardi's motivational ability has long been documented, his skill as a technician and football strategist sometimes goes undervalued. He developed the concept of zone blocking while an assistant at West Point, which led to his famous "run to daylight" philosophy. His book, *Vince Lombardi on Football*, published after his death, was incredibly detailed, especially in diagramming the offense.

It is true that Lombardi valued simplicity and had only a handful of plays compared to other teams. "It wasn't complex, it was simple," noted *Sports Illustrated*. "It was football at its more basic: survival of the strongest and the toughest."[27] But Lombardi insisted those plays be run with precision and coordination, which called for endless repetition. "If we call the sweep twenty times," he said, "I'll expect it to work twenty times—not eighteen, not nineteen. We do it often enough in practice so that no excuse can exist for screwing it up."[28]

The sweep was Lombardi's signature play because it symbolized everything he believed about football. "You think there's anything special about this sweep?" Lombardi once asked a writer. "Well, there isn't.

Five. *The Power of Myth* 85

It's as basic a play as there can be in football. It's my number one play because it requires all eleven men to play as one to make it succeed, and that's what 'team' means."[29] "I think when he first got there, we broke it down for a week," said tackle Bob Skoronski. "I never saw anyone, anywhere go through something more thoroughly than he did that one play."[30]

Another coaching legend can attest to that. As a young assistant coach, John Madden once signed up to attend a Lombardi coaching clinic in Reno, Nevada. Lombardi would often travel around the country giving such clinics and coaches from all over the country would come to hear him speak. While it seems hard to believe, Madden insists that Lombardi spent eight hours going over one single play—the Green Bay sweep. "He stood up there at the blackboard with a piece of chalk and dissected the Green Bay sweep player-by-player," said an incredulous Madden. "Each player's assignment against every possible defense, against every possible stunt, against every possible blitz, against every possible coverage."[31] Bill Yeoman, a bit of a legend in his own right for developing the veer option formation at the University of Houston, also visited a Lombardi coaching clinic. "Vince would get so excited talking about the sweep," Yeoman recalled, "I thought we was going to have an orgasm right there at the chalkboard."[32]

It was called "Red Right 49," and tight end Ron Kramer's job was to block a linebacker, an assignment he handled through seven seasons and three championships. Years later and long retired, Kramer was at home watching news coverage of Operation Desert Storm. General Norman Schwarzkopf was detailing an assault by U.S. forces, when Kramer suddenly realized he had seen the maneuver before. "I wrote a letter to General Schwarzkopf," Kramer said. "I sent '49' to him and told him he had plagiarized Vince."[33] Schwarzkopf had indeed played football at Army under offensive assistant Vince Lombardi.

That Lombardi's power sweep ended up 50 years later on a Kuwaiti battlefield demonstrated his ability to translate Xs and Os into a bigger picture for his players. "All plays succeed on the blackboard," Lombardi often said, "but men make them work."[34] Lombardi's ultimate success came not on the blackboard, but in the locker room and on the practice field. He was not a student of football as a theoretical concept, but as a training laboratory for life. "We're better people for having been exposed to him," said Starr. "The preparation that is necessary in order to succeed; the total commitment to practice and teamwork. Without these things you cannot be successful, and with them you cannot fail."[35]

"The lessons Lombardi taught were only incidentally about football," said Jerry Kramer. "They were about life. Any time I think of taking a shortcut, of just going through the motions, I hear Lombardi's raspy voice, I see his shiny eyes, and I just can't do it."[36]

He was a larger than life legend that in many ways was not unlike another giant of the times, General Douglas MacArthur. Major William Ganoe served under MacArthur at West Point and his description of the general also perfectly describes Lombardi—"[He possessed] a gifted leadership, a leadership that kept you at a respectful distance, yet at the same time took you in as an esteemed member of his team, and very quickly had you working harder than you had ever worked in your life, just because of the loyalty, admiration and respect in which you held him."[37]

That is part of the mythology that Vince Lombardi brought to the NFL, and for all his other football gifts, it may be the most important contribution he made to the league. Other coaches had more wins (Lombardi barely even cracked the top 50; his 96 far behind Don Shula's 328), higher winning percentages (John Madden's .759 beats out Lombardi's .738), and more championships (Paul Brown won a combined seven titles in the NFL and AAFC).

But none of them gave the NFL a soul as did Lombardi.

"Myth helps you to put your mind in touch with this experience of being alive," wrote Joseph Campbell, who studied, taught and wrote about comparative mythology. "We're so engaged in doing things to achieve purposes of outer value that we forget that the inner value, the rapture that is associated with being alive, is what's it's all about."[38]

The NFL has always had that outer value—the games won and lost, the touchdowns scored and the records set. Lombardi gave voice to that inner value, that rapture, that helped it transcend from a game into the obsession of a nation.

The Lombardi mythology was based on the fundamental values of pride, character, and desire. It was a combination of Horatio Alger, Frank Merriwell and Teddy Roosevelt, who famously observed, "There is no effort without error and shortcoming. [One] who knows in the end the triumph of high achievement, and who at worst, if he fails, at least fails while daring greatly."[39] This was much more in line with Lombardi's philosophy than the most famous quote attributed to him—"winning isn't everything, it's the only thing." While Lombardi certainly wanted to win, "there was a crucial distinction between paying the price to win and winning at any price. He showed no interest in winning the wrong way, without heart, brains and sportsmanship."[40]

Every year at the beginning of training camp, Lombardi would address his players. In this opening meeting, Lombardi did not talk about winning, strategy, or schedules. "One thing about the Packers, it's a team with a great tradition," he began. "That glory that is the Packers has been developed from one thing only, and that's pride. Everybody has ability, but pride in performance is what makes the difference. How do you develop pride? Pride is developed from a winning tradition."[41] "He molded us from losers into winners," said Jerry Kramer, "and into men as well. [Because of] the principles he urged on us, the dreams he stirred in us."[42]

Part of the appeal of Lombardi's mythology was a desire to return to "simpler" times. As American culture became increasingly commercialized, corporatized, and regimented in the 1950s, there was a sense that the country was losing an essential part of its spirit. There is a story about President Eisenhower in a room full of America's best and newest supercomputers. The president asked one of the machines, "Is there a God?" After several moments of blinking lights and turning wheels, a voice replied, "Now there is."[43]

The story demonstrated the fears many Americans had during that time period, and still have today to an even greater extent. "What we have today is a demythologized world," said Campbell. That's why mythology is so important, because it reminds us "that technology is not going to save us. Our computers, our tools, our machines are not enough. We have to rely on our intuition, our true being."[44]

In 1959, there was already a sense that the NFL was becoming demythologized, thanks to the success of men like Paul Brown and "Automatic" Otto Graham in Cleveland. Along came Lombardi to remind everyone that the game was about something much more.

Even Lombardi's flaws added to his mythology. Perfection, wrote Campbell, is inhuman because "humanity, the thing that makes you human and not supernatural—that's what's lovable."[45] Lombardi was hotheaded, impatient, and often difficult to be around. He had strained relationships with his children, and especially his daughter Susan, who as a teenager rebelled with drinking and partying. "I did a lot behind his back, but he found out," she said years later. "He was a very hard man."[46] A devout Catholic, Lombardi attended mass every day at St. Willebrord in Green Bay. According to Bart Starr, "If you heard him every afternoon in practice, you'd understand why he had to go to Mass everyday."[47]

There is an element of tragedy in all mythology—Icarus flying too close to the sun—and while the Lombardi children have made peace with their famous father, "he knew what it was like [for them] to live in a town of 60,000 where your father was god."[48] Wife Marie also suffered "as a tragic figure in the Lombardi mythology. Alcohol helped her cope with a volcanic and abusive husband, even as she publicly served as the good-wife."[49] Her problems continued after Lombardi's death. "My first reaction after he died was that I was very angry at football," she said. "I felt football had taken too much out of Vince."[50]

It was that tragic death from colon cancer in 1970 at the relatively young age of 57 that elevated the Lombardi mystique to mythological proportions. Books, documentaries, stage plays have all been written about him. Every year, thousands of people who had no connection to the coach or the Packers, make a pilgrimage to his old house in Green Bay—677 Sunset Circle—as if it were some holy shrine. They come unannounced, knocking on the door or peering in the windows, hoping to be invited inside by the present occupants. Many want to go downstairs to the basement "rec room," where Lombardi would unwind by hosting cocktail parties for friends and invited guests. "I don't pretend to understand it," Vince Lombardi, Jr., says. "It was a long time ago. I don't understand it."[51]

Campbell believed that the rebirth narrative—the cycle of death, burial, and resurrection—is a common thread that runs through mythology. The idea that from death comes life, and "from sacrifice, bliss."[52] Had Lombardi lived out the course of a more normal lifespan and retired with several more championships, he might not have the same hold over the football consciousness. His accomplishments were heroic while he lived; in death they came legendary.

That legend was grown and cultivated, often times willingly but sometimes unwillingly, by the sports media. The Green Bay and Milwaukee media people, mostly newspapermen but later also television reporters, soon learned that Lombardi wanted as much control over them as he did his team. He instituted a rule that reporters covering training camp had to stay at the camp as well. Lombardi restricted interview access and when he did answer questions, usually barked at reporters and cut off their questions. "He just put the fear into everybody," said Bud Lea, who covered the Packers for 50 years for the *Milwaukee Sentinel*. "We were afraid of asking a stupid question. He'd just glare at you or tell you, 'That's a stupid question.' The guys I felt sorry for were at the *Green Bay Press-Gazette*. They had to deal with him every day."[53]

As the team began winning, Lombardi loosened up a bit more with reporters, especially at his famous "5 O'Clock Club" meetings. Every afternoon at training camp, and then at the hotel when the team was playing a road game, reporters were invited to meet with Lombardi and his coaches in a more relaxed atmosphere that often times included his wife Marie. Lombardi would drink a Scotch and water, read through some newspapers, watch some television, and speak off the record. As scared as they were, the reporters respected Lombardi and he gradually came around to respect them.

The Lombardi image also began to soften with the production of a television documentary in 1964 that gave viewers an inside tour of training camp. For the first time, people could see the human side of Lombardi, such as his interaction with players, coaches, and even the nuns who lived at the St. Norbert facility. Even though Lombardi sometimes seemed stiff and self-conscious, the show, which ran on ABC television, held "a special place in the Lombardi mythology."[54]

But no medium, no reporter, no single individual contributed more to the development of the Lombardi mythology, and the mythology of the NFL as a whole, than did NFL Films.

In 1962, the same year Lombardi and the Packers were winning their second consecutive title, an overcoat salesman in Philadelphia with aspirations of a film career approached NFL commissioner Pete Rozelle about film rights to the championship game. Ed Sabol's film experience consisted of home movies of his son Steve playing football, but he doubled the bid from the previous year and somehow convinced Rozelle he could do the job. Sabol named his company Blair Productions after his daughter.

At the time, NFL highlight films consisted of stringing together some scoring plays with marching band music as accompaniment. The action was shot from up high in the press box, giving the game a distant feeling. Most teams produced their own highlight films at the end of the season and used them as promotional tools. Some local business would sponsor the film, which would then be shown to various organizations around town to help increase ticket sales. In part because the films were usually uninspiring and of poor technical quality, teams continued to put more promotional emphasis on live television broadcasts and local newspaper coverage.

Ed Sabol immediately sought to do things differently. He wanted "to portray football the way Hollywood depicts fiction—with dramatic flair; with eyes bulging, the snot spraying, the sweat flying, and passion and the sound."[55] He hired his son Steve, a college player himself at Colorado College, to help out and their first big project was the 1962 championship game between Lombardi's Packers and the New York Giants. The film, called *Pro Football's Longest Day*, included footage of players and locales away from the football field. It was the first time viewers had seen such a personal approach and they responded positively. "We wanted to show emotion," said Steve. "Football is a visceral sport; that's the way I wanted to portray it. Like it had never been seen before."[56]

As Blair Productions evolved into NFL Films, the experimentation continued. In 1966, composer Sam Spence was hired to score music, and he replaced the marching bands with compositions so dramatic and compelling that they often overshadowed the film itself. Perhaps the most important addition was Philadelphia newscaster John Facenda, who agreed to leave his television job to join the Sabols. He had a rich, baritone voice—one that Steve Sabol called the "voice of God; one that could make a laundry list sound dramatic"[57]—that immediately gave NFL Films credibility and resonance. "For those of us who grew up in the 1970s and 80s," writes Rich Cohen, "it remains the voice in our heads, lending drama to even the most mundane decisions."[58]

NFL Films firmly established itself in the American sports consciousness in 1967 with *They Call It Pro Football.* Dramatic close-ups and slow-motion shots, Facenda's powerful narration, and Spence's dramatic music all combined to present the game in a new and personal way. Steve Sabol called it the "Citizen Kane" of football movies, and Rozelle remarked, "That's not a highlight film, it's a real movie."[59]

They Call It Pro Football showcased the emerging style of NFL Films—"lean and weighty narration, symphonic music punctuated by grunts, collisions, and shouts caught by wireless microphones, slow motion and tight close-ups, [and] romantic, melodramatic, mythic story."[60] That style made NFL Films, and by extension the NFL itself, increasingly rich and successful. To date, the company has produced some 10,000 features, won more than 100 Emmy Awards, and become a programming staple on multiple television networks. "As much as George Halas and Sid Luckman, or Tom Landry and Roger Staubach, it was Ed and Steve who created the modern game, a contest more in tune with the speed and violence of modern America than any other sport."[61]

Lombardi was an obvious and natural choice for NFL Films, and Steve Sabol would later admit that "no one in the NFL was documented on film more thoroughly than Lombardi."[62] In Sabol's office he kept boxes of note cards on not just football, but poetry, history, and other topics. Vince Lombardi was the only figure who had a box all to himself. "The story is not Lombardi in his time," wrote Sabol on one card, "but how he lives in ours. His spirit still summons up the best we have to offer."[63]

Because of a friendship between Ed Sabol and Lombardi, the coach granted NFL Films almost unprecedented access to practices, meetings, and even into his home. On several occasions, Lombardi permitted himself to be wired up with a microphone during games. The result was a fascinating and unparalleled look at not just a coach, but a man, husband, and father.

Perhaps no game or moment more symbolized the relationship between Lombardi and NFL Films than the Ice Bowl. When the Packers and Dallas Cowboys met for the NFL championship on December

Five. *The Power of Myth* 91

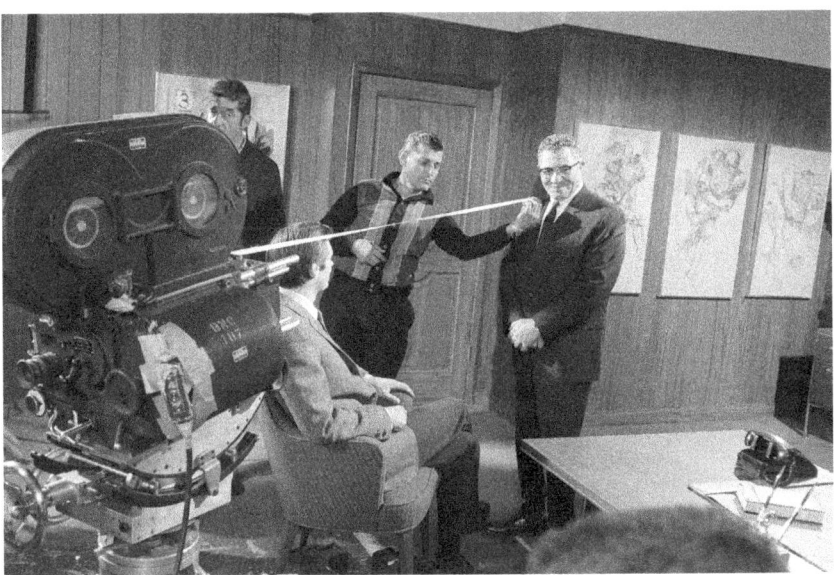

The relationship between Packers coach Vince Lombardi and NFL Films helped create the mythology of the NFL. Lombardi's teams won five titles in nine years, and NFL Films transformed them from champions into legends. *Getty Images/Bettmann Collection.*

31, 1967, the temperature in Green Bay was 15 below zero. Days before the game Lombardi had bragged to reporters how his electrified system of wires running under the field would keep the playing surface warm. But now the system failed, and Lambeau Field turned into a sheet of ice.

The dramatic visuals from the game were powerful enough—groundskeepers sweeping ice from the field, players huddled in makeshift tents on the sidelines wearing any assortment of protective clothing, and everywhere the continual puffs of smoke as fans breathed out the frozen air. But the game added even more drama.

When Dallas scored a touchdown at the start of the fourth quarter, the Cowboys took a 17–14 lead and seemed to have secured their first NFL title. Since scoring two early touchdowns, the Green Bay offense had done nothing and had spent much of the second half going backwards. When the Packers got the ball back with 4:50 to play and 68 yards from the end zone, everyone in the stadium sensed that this was going to be their last chance. "We went out for the huddle," said Starr, "and decided that if we were going to do it, it had to be now."[64]

The final drive, as captured by NFL Films, was everything Lombardi stood for—desire, toughness, and heart. The Packer offense huffed and puffed, and chugged its way downfield a few yards at a time. It finally arrived at the one yard line with 20 seconds to play and no times out left. Dallas had stopped Donny Anderson twice and if it did so again, Green Bay would not have time to run another play.

Figuring Anderson couldn't get decent traction, Starr decided to call his own number. After conferring with Lombardi, who told him to "run the play and let's get the hell out of here," Starr quarterback sneaked in for the winning score with just 16 seconds left. The NFL Films shot of Jerry Kramer blocking Jethro Pugh just enough to let Starr sneak in, became an iconic moment in NFL history. The 21–17 win gave Lombardi and the Packers an unprecedented third straight NFL title. "This game," said Packer tackle Bob Skoronski, "was our mark of distinction."[65]

The Ice Bowl moved Lombardi from legend into myth. Eight months after the game, CBS pre-empted the *Ed Sullivan Show* to televise an NFL Films production simply called *Lombardi.* Suited more for a mass television audience, the film did not have many of the signature NFL Films elements, but it did capture some essential Lombardi. "What the hell is going on out here?" Lombardi screams during a game with the Los Angeles Rams. "I tell you, Lee Roy," he says to linebacker Lee Roy Caffey, "if you don't shape up, you're not going to have a job."[66]

By the time the show aired, Lombardi had retired as coach, remaining as the Packers general manager. He returned to coaching the following year in Washington and led the Redskins to their first winning season in 14 years. He seemed poised to recreate the success of the Packers when he died suddenly from a virulent form of colon cancer in September 1970.

Current and former players made a pilgrimage to his bedside to say goodbye, many of them too choked up to do anything more than hold Lombardi's hand. "He wanted us to be better human beings," said Jerry Kramer. "He cared for us as human beings. He believed in us."[67]

NFL Films was at the funeral and ever since that time has continued to churn out programming in his name. "Lombardi," began one such program from the 1980s, "a certain magic still lingers in the very name. It speaks of duels in the snow and the cold November mud."[68]

If magic still lingers in the Lombardi name, it is in great part because of NFL Films. Lombardi brought an important sense of mythology to the league, but he could not have done so without the influential power of the visual media, and most especially NFL Films. Together, they created a mythology of pro football that has survived work stoppages, concussion and health dangers, drug issues, and increasingly bad player behavior.

"He coached and become popular in an era with flower children and the Vietnam War," said Steve Sabol. "He kept alive old-fashioned values like hard work and discipline, yet he took the idea of love and put it on the football field."⁶⁹

"In an era of debunking," author Michael Oriard wrote of NFL Films, "it has not just sustained but increased football's cultural power. NFL Films has sustained a sense of mythic grandeur in our decidedly antimythic times."⁷⁰

Lombardi made his mark in the 1960s, but it all started in 1959 with his first season in Green Bay when the Packers became winners after years of losing. "Players and fans alike sensed a new era dawning," wrote John Eisenberg. "Though a season had just ended, the Packers seemed at a beginning."⁷¹

Thanks to Lombardi, so did the NFL.

Six

Alphabet Soup

Like millions of others around the country, a 26-year-old Texan named Lamar Hunt watched with fascination as the 1958 championship game between the Colts and Giants unfolded. Hunt had a special interest in the game as his former college teammate at Southern Methodist University, Raymond Berry, was now a star receiver for the Colts. Berry had a sensational game, catching twelve passes for 178 yards and a touchdown in Baltimore's dramatic overtime win.

Also like millions of others watching the game, Hunt was a frustrated athlete. He had a great enthusiasm for many sports, especially football, but not the requisite talent to become an outstanding player. Hunt, nicknamed "Poor Boy" by his SMU teammates, languished on the bench his three varsity seasons, never rising above third string end. Even so, he called it a great experience and was proud of the fact that he made the team as a non-scholarship player. "Since he played behind three ends who later made pro teams," noted *Sports Illustrated*, "the fact that he hung on as an overshadowed substitute is a tribute to his tenacity rather than a reflection on his ability."[1]

Unlike millions of others, Lamar Hunt had the financial wherewithal to scratch his football itch. He was the son of H.L. Hunt, a multimillionaire Texas oilman who used his gambling winnings to secure oil properties, including the rights to the East Texas Oil Field, at the time the largest known deposit of oil in the world. Even as his fortune grew to a reputed two billion dollars, H.L. never liked to brag about his money. When asked how rich he was he would simply reply, "I'm plenty rich."[2] Whatever his holdings at the time, H.L. Hunt was one of the four or five richest men in the country.

After earning a degree in geology at SMU, Lamar joined his father in the family business, which meant he too was worth millions. And as Hunt watched the dramatic ending of the Colts overtime win from a hotel room in Houston, he began thinking about football and how to use some of that money. "You can't overemphasize the dramatic impact

Six. Alphabet Soup

of that 1958 NFL championship game between the Colts and Giants," he recalled. "Pro football was just starting to grow. It suddenly had its first overtime in a championship game with the nation watching on television."[3] In February 1959, on a flight from Miami to Dallas, Hunt had what he described as a moment when "the light bulb came on"[4] and he decided to get into the pro football business.

Hunt would soon show the same tenacity in dealing in his new enterprise as he did on the SMU football team.

He started first by trying to buy an existing NFL franchise, and the most likely candidate was the shaky Chicago Cardinals, then owned by Violet Wolfner, who inherited the team when her husband Charles Bidwell died. The Cardinals were currently in a losing battle with George Halas and the Bears for the city of Chicago (see Chapter Seven) and would within a year move the franchise to St. Louis, the hometown of her new husband, Walter Wolfner.

Hunt approached the Wolfners with the idea of buying a 20 percent stake in the team and moving it to Dallas. He was apparently unconcerned about the abject failure of the first NFL team in Dallas, the 1952 Texans (see Chapter One). Sitting on the SMU bench that year he saw crowds of 50,000 and 60,000 come out to see the Mustangs and Raymond Berry, and he believed people would also come out to see professional football.

Another Texan millionaire oilman thought the same thing. Like Lamar Hunt, K.S. "Bud" Adams played college ball, but mostly watched from the bench at the University of Kansas. Adams, about ten years older than Hunt, also had a rich oil father—the chairman of Phillips Petroleum—and he too wanted in professional football. While Hunt was described by almost everyone who met him as a shy, bookish man who "totally dislikes anything that makes him stand out,"[5] Adams looked and played every bit the part of the brash, swaggering Texas oil man, complete with a cavernous office that included a barbecue pit and pool with lily pad. After the Wolfners turned down Hunt's offer, Adams stepped in and believed he had a deal made to move the Cardinals to Houston. He valued the franchise at $1.5 million and offered to buy 50 percent. Again the Wolfners balked, not wanting to give up control of the team.

Hunt then went to NFL owners about the possibility of an expansion franchise and was told "unequivocally that there would be no franchise in Dallas."[6] George Halas softened the blow a bit, inviting Hunt and Adams to his office in Chicago for a clandestine meeting. "Why don't you wait until we expand," he told them, "do it in an orderly fashion, and we'll get you in."[7] Hunt and Adams left Chicago discouraged;

their attempts to buy the Cardinals had failed and they were highly skeptical of Halas's promises.

It was natural that the two oilmen would turn to each other. They had dinner together in Houston, and before Hunt left for home in Dallas, Adams blurted out, "Maybe we ought to start our own league." When the two met again a few months later Hunt had lined up four other prospective owners and asked Adams if he wanted in. "Hell, yes!" was his immediate answer.[8] When the group of six grew to eight, with each team putting up only $25,000 as an entry fee, the American Football League was born. AFL owners held their first meeting on August 14, 1959, and announced plans to begin play in 1960.

Adams and Hunt were not the only ones in the group with deep pockets. Hotel magnates Barron and Conrad Hilton owned the Los Angeles franchise, and actor and broadcaster Harry Wismer backed the New York team. Hunt said everyone he approached about joining the new league accepted, including Bob Howsam in Denver and Max Winter in Minneapolis, two others who also failed to pry the Cardinals out of Chicago.

All that money would be necessary if the AFL hoped to take on an established league that had grown in power and popularity in recent years. In 1959, fresh off the excitement of the Colts–Giants game, the NFL drew 3.3 million fans to its games and set an attendance record for the eighth straight year. Led by a young and forward-thinking commissioner in Pete Rozelle, the league was on the threshold of unprecedented success in the 1960s. No wonder that at one of the first AFL owner meetings Wayne Valley of Oakland said, "this is a really foolish group. We ought to call ourselves the Foolish Club."[9]

Hunt did not want a fight with the NFL and believed the two leagues could co-exist. "I told myself I didn't want to go into this if it meant some kind of battle," he said. "Of course, this was one of the more naïve thoughts in the history of pro sports."[10] Almost as soon as the AFL was announced, Pete Rozelle and the NFL set out to squash it like bug on a west Texas windshield. "The National Football League decided, 'We need to bust this Lamar Hunt,'" said Dallas attorney Ed Kemble, a good friend of Hunt's. "So there were a lot of bad feelings about that."[11]

One of the first things the NFL did was to undercut Hunt's new team in Texas. Just months after the league told Hunt he could not have a franchise in Dallas, NFL owners reversed course and announced an expansion franchise to begin play in 1960. The new team, finally named the Cowboys, was owned by Clint Murchison, Jr., whose family had made almost as much money in oil as had the Hunts. Now, two Texas oil barons would battle it out in a city that had failed miserably in pro football and a year before had no teams at all.

Six. Alphabet Soup

Hunt immediately cried sabotage and suggested some sort of lawsuit or congressional action. "It's obvious what they're trying to do," he said. "I think some congressman and senators from states where we will have teams are not going to stand for it."[12] The lawsuit would come shortly, but in the meantime Hunt suddenly had competition in his hometown and could do very little about it.

Having dropped a bomb on Hunt in his own backyard, the NFL now set its sights on the rest of the league. Minneapolis businessman Max Winter had agreed to back an AFL franchise, but changed his mind when approached with an offer for an expansion team in the NFL to begin play in 1961. Winter felt more comfortable going with the prestige and security of the NFL, even though the entrance fee—$600,000 compared to $25,000—was much higher than for the AFL. "And you could pay for it in monthly payments,"[13] Winter gloated, adding that he did not have an oil fortune to fall back on.

Winter announced his defection as AFL owners met for dinner in Minneapolis. Harry Wismer of the New York franchise looked across the table at Winter and hissed, "Nice going, Judas." After Winter left, Wismer told the remaining owners, "Boys, this is the last supper."[14] It did appear that divine intervention would be needed to save the fledgling league. The NFL had landed two massive broadsides, but determined to keep going the AFL hastily replaced Minnesota with a team in Oakland and pressed on.

The AFL then countered with two strategies—money and legal action. Men like Hunt, Adams and Hilton could absorb

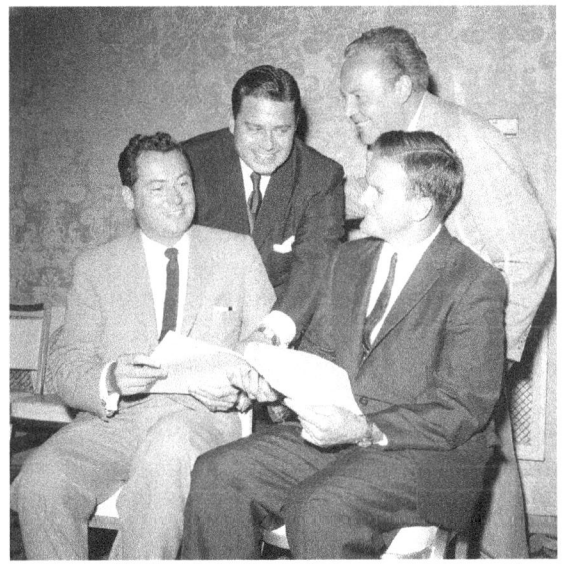

Four original founders of the American Football League in 1959 met to discuss plans. Barron Hilton (far left), Bud Adams (second from left), and Harry Wismer (standing right) all played an important role in the AFL, but it was Dallas oilman Lamar Hunt (seated right) who was the driving force that kept the league going, especially in its early years. *AP Photo/DAD.*

the financial losses that were certain to come until the league could get on its feet. As the Dallas Texans struggled in the early going, a reporter went to Lamar Hunt's father and warned him that the team was losing around a million dollars a year. "At that rate," H.L. Hunt replied, "he'll be broke in a hundred years."[15]

Hunt and his fellow AFL owners got out their checkbooks and started spending serious money for college talent, stealing it away from an angry NFL. Even before the league played its first game it had signed such college stars as Ron Mix (USC with the Los Angeles Chargers), Johnny Robinson (LSU with the Dallas Texans), and most notably Heisman Trophy winner Billy Cannon of LSU with Bud Adams's Houston Oilers.

Lamar Hunt may not have wanted a war with the NFL, but one was now on and it was going to prove very costly for both sides.

The Cannon signing was controversial in that before he signed his Oilers contract he had also signed one with the Los Angeles Rams. The Rams, still led at the time by general manager Pete Rozelle, had made Cannon the very first pick in the NFL draft and wanted him badly. Cannon signed a three-year deal with the Rams with the contract dated after the Sugar Bowl so he would not lose his eligibility. When Adams found out he offered to double the Rams offer, and then had Cannon sign the contract on the field after the Sugar Bowl in front of a live television audience.

The frustrated Rams, in possession of a contract with Cannon's signature, sued him and the Oilers in federal court. In something of a surprise move, considering Cannon had first signed with Los Angeles, the U.S. District Court in Southern California ruled in favor of the Oilers, saying that the undated contract in reality "constituted no more than an offer" and did not entitle the Rams to relief.[16]

In all, nine players signed contracts with both the NFL and AFL and three ended up in U.S District Court. The most interesting case was that of Ralph Neely, a talented offensive lineman who signed with both the Cowboys and Oilers. The suit dragged on until finally an appeals court reversed a previous ruling and gave Neely to Houston. By that time Neely had already played two years in Dallas and would become an All-Pro player. To settle the case, Dallas gave the Oilers four draft picks and also agreed to a series of exhibition games between the teams. The courts favored the AFL in all three cases, but chastised athletes who "agree to play football for a stated amount for one group, only to repudiate that agreement the following day or whenever a better offer comes along."[17]

Arguments over player contracts would not be the only reason the leagues would face off in court. Almost immediately after the AFL kicked off its first season in 1960, the league filed an antitrust lawsuit claiming the NFL monopolized professional football and used as part of its argument the dirty dealings in Dallas and Minnesota. In 1962, a U.S. District Court in Maryland found in favor of the NFL and dismissed the charges. Lamar Hunt was doubly disappointed when the court added, "Interest in and attendance at both NFL and AFL games in Dallas has been disappointing, and may indicate that the city is not as good a location for a professional football team as was generally believed."[18] Hunt would eventually realize that Dallas could not support both teams, and in 1963 moved his team to Kansas City and renamed it the Chiefs.

The court decision was a tough setback for a league that stumbled out of the gate its first few years and earned the reputation, deserved or not, as a second-class outfit. Aside from Cannon and a few other headliners, most of the players were NFL castoffs or worse. The NFL thought of their competitors as "Mickey Mouse" or flag football and ridiculed the AFL's wide-open style of play, which featured lots of passing and scoring. "The feeling," said NFL player turned broadcaster Pat Summerall, "was that it was the Major Leagues against the Triple A's."[19]

AFL facilities were also considered substandard. Hunt and his Texans played in the relatively modern Cotton Bowl and reported good crowds, including 42,000 for the first-ever home game against the Chargers and 37,500 the following week for the New York Titans. The Cowboys could only draw half that many and complained that the Texans were padding their count with freebies and giveaways.

But the Oilers used a high school field and the Oakland Raiders played in a decrepit park named after a local undertaker. The New York Titans could not draw flies, and much of the problem was the crumbling Polo Grounds. By 1962 the *total* attendance for the Titans seven home games was just 36,161. "We had more people watching practices at Bear Mountain [training camp] than came to the Polo Grounds,"[20] said Titans linebacker Larry Grantham, a continuing issue that eventually forced Wismer to declare bankruptcy and sell the team.

The Denver Broncos had a good facility in Bears Stadium, but they also had problems drawing fans. From a high of 19,141 in October 1960, the Broncos fell to 5,861 for the home finale against New York as the team went winless the last two months of the season. Denver was further embarrassed by its mustard-and-brown uniforms which featured vertically-striped socks bought used from a college team. "The most ridiculous thing I ever saw in my life,"[21] Broncos tackle Bud McFadin said of the socks, which were publicly burned before a preseason game in 1962.

Even Lamar Hunt's own father didn't believe the league would last. H.L. Hunt wrote a letter to the Dallas newspapers saying the Texans would likely fail and drag down college football with them. Still a gambler, H.L. liked to bet on college games and had a special phone installed in his office to contact his bookie, but chances are he would have given very long odds on the survival of the American Football League. The Raiders lost a half million dollars in their first season and needed a $400,000 loan from Buffalo owner Ralph Wilson to keep going. The league took over the New York franchise in 1962 when Wismer could no longer meet payroll.

The AFL might have gone under completely if not for a series of bold moves. The first of these was the signing of a five-year national television contract with the ABC network in 1960. The contract brought in $2.1 million split evenly among the eight teams as part of a revenue sharing deal. When that deal expired the AFL signed an even more lucrative contract with NBC worth $36 million over five years. The television contracts gave the AFL visibility, credibility, but even more importantly, financial stability. Without a doubt, television kept alive Lamar Hunt's dream. "The NBC contract with the American Football League put them in the ball game," said NFL sportswriter and author Paul Zimmerman. "The size of the contract showed that the AFL would be able to survive."[22]

That second television contract was made possible by new ownership of the New York franchise. David "Sonny" Werblin was a big shot talent manager at the Music Corporation of America who acquired the rights to the Titans and changed their name to the Jets. "I believe in the star system," he said after taking over the team. "It's what you put on the stage or playing field that draws people."[23] In 1965, Werblin had a chance to put a really big star on the AFL stage—University of Alabama quarterback Joe Namath.

Namath had the star power and charisma to put the AFL in the headlines. Both the Jets of the AFL and the Cardinals of the NFL had drafted him, and when the Cardinals dragged their feet in contract negotiations, Werblin moved in. He signed Namath to a record contract worth an eye-popping $427,000 in an age when veteran players made about $12,000 per season. "It's utterly ridiculous," wrote Arthur Daley in the *New York Times*. "No untried collegian is worth even half that much."[24]

But Werblin understood Namath's appeal, not just as a quality quarterback, but also as a gate attraction. Putting it in theatrical terms, Werblin said, "A million-dollar set is worthless if you put a $2,000 actor in the main role."[25] Now Werblin had his leading man, soon to become known as "Broadway Joe," and as Namath prepared for his first training camp, *Sports Illustrated* ran a cover photo of him in full uniform standing in front of a backdrop of New York City nightlife. The headline read, "Pro Football Goes Showbiz."[26]

Namath was the brightest star of the new league, but by no means the only one. AFL teams were extremely successful at luring top college talent and soon the new league featured such stars as receiver Lance Alworth of the San Diego, quarterback Daryle Lamonica of Oakland, and linebacker Bobby Bell of Kansas City. They joined former NFL players like George Blanda in Houston, Len Dawson in Dallas/Kansas City, and Don Maynard in New York, who made the most of the second chance they received.

The battle for talent between the AFL and NFL, especially for the best college seniors, turned into all-out war. The NFL created "Operation Hand-holding" in which some 125 babysitters would fan out across the country weeks before the draft and attach themselves to prospects, trying to keep them from the other league. In some cases, this led to escapades worthy of a James Bond novel, none any more cloak-and-dagger than the case of Otis Taylor.

In 1965, Taylor was a prized receiver from Prairie View A&M, drafted by both the Chiefs and Eagles. NFL hand holders stashed Taylor in a series of motel rooms in Dallas, changing not just rooms but motels as well. Kansas City scout Lloyd Wells used Taylor's girlfriend to find his location and then registered at the same hotel using an assumed name. Posing as a newspaper reporter, complete with camera hanging around his neck, Wells got past NFL babysitters and arranged to sneak out of the hotel with Taylor around midnight.

When some NFL scouts recognized Wells and called police to report a prowler, Wells left thinking he had blown his opportunity. But Taylor called Wells and asked to be picked up, so Wells returned, snuck Taylor and another player out of the hotel room window, and drove them to the airport for a flight to Kansas City where Taylor signed with the Chiefs. Taylor made two Pro Bowls and two All-Pro teams during his eleven-year career in Kansas City.

Once a player signed with a team in the AFL or NFL, he was considered "property" of that league, part of an unwritten agreement between the leagues not to poach one another's players. But that was shattered in 1966 when the New York Giants signed kicker Pete Gogolak, whose contract with the AFL's Buffalo Bills had expired. Al Davis, managing partner of the Raiders who had temporarily become AFL commissioner, reacted quickly. He signed eight prominent NFL players, including quarterbacks Roman Gabriel and Sonny Jurgensen, to future AFL deals once their current contracts expired. The Oilers offered San Francisco quarterback John Brodie a salary unheard of in those days—$750,000 for ten years. Brodie turned down the deal after a substantial raise from the 49ers, but "when Houston approached him, it convinced the NFL of the potential disaster."[27]

The disaster was that the cost of signing college players had created financial problems for both leagues. In December 1965, *Life* magazine ran a cover story featuring linebacker Tommy Nobis from the University of Texas who had been drafted by both the Oilers and Falcons. Bud Adams of the Oilers vowed to break the bank to get the homegrown star and in addition to salary offered Nobis gas station rights and a hundred head of longhorn cattle. Nobis even felt pressure from miles above the earth. During one of the orbital flights on Gemini 7, astronaut Frank Borman radioed back to mission control, "Tell Nobis to sign with Houston."[28]

In the end, Nobis felt more comfortable with the stability of the NFL and signed with Atlanta. Afterwards, even the flamboyant and combative Adams realized he and pro football had reached a tipping point. "The fighting over college talent is not good," he said. "Within two or three years at the present rate salaries are going up what we'll have is almost every team out of the black and into the red. Either a merger or common draft is coming."[29]

Adams was prescient, as secret merger talks had begun featuring Lamar Hunt and Cowboys general manager Tex Schramm. The two met clandestinely in a parked car at Love Field airport in Dallas, trying to work out an agreement to stop the financial bleeding of both leagues. "We could have done our business for another thirty years," said Browns owner Art Modell, "but we sought [a merger] to prolong the success of pro football before things got out of hand and we couldn't control them."[30]

What finally emerged in the summer of 1966 was an agreement to bring together the two leagues. The NFL and AFL would meet in a yearly championship game beginning in January 1967 and then play a common schedule as one NFL in 1970. Pete Rozelle would remain commissioner of a league that nearly doubled in size overnight. The AFL had suddenly reached parity, even if it had to poach three teams from the NFL (the Browns, Steelers and Colts) to play in the new American Football Conference, and even if the AFL franchises had to pay millions of dollars in indemnity fees to the established NFL clubs. "I don't see why we should pay them for existing,"[31] fumed an AFL spokesman.

That animosity remained burned in AFL veterans for years. In New York, the Giants had treated the cross-town Jets as a poor cousin, even

Six. Alphabet Soup

after Jets won a Super Bowl in 1969. "[The Giants] never spoke of the Jets," said sportswriter Mike Vaccaro. "They never even pondered the Jets ... never once said the name 'Joe Namath' in public. And the Giants lorded over their upstart neighbors at every turn."[32]

When the teams met for the first time ever in a 1969 exhibition game, the players from both sides treated it more like a playoff game. "Giants fans still don't feel we're on a parity with their team and we feel we've got to prove it," said Jets linebacker Larry Grantham. "A lot of people, NFL fans, still regard the Super Bowl as a fluke."[33] Grantham, along with NFL castoffs Bill Mathis and Don Maynard, was a captain for the game, and like most regulars he played almost the entire way. Joe Namath threw three touchdown passes as the Jets humiliated the Giants, 37–14. "You saw what we did out there today," said Jets running back Matt Snell after the game. "You know it wasn't the $250 we earned that made us do it, so it had to be the glory. And, man, was it glorious today."[34]

Lamar Hunt must have felt just as glorious. The man once ridiculed and rejected by NFL owners had taken on and beaten one of the most powerful sports organizations in the world. Perhaps "beaten" is an overstatement, but certainly Hunt had made himself and the AFL an equal. Hunt enjoyed a special measure of satisfaction when his Chiefs beat the Vikings in Super Bowl IV, the last game in AFL history before the merger. In the Chiefs noisy locker room after the game, Hunt called it "a satisfactory conclusion to the ten years of the American Football League." Some AFL hardliners were not so gracious. "Hell," said former AFL Commissioner Joe Foss, "maybe we shouldn't have merged."[35]

Lamar Hunt and the AFL had done what no other challenger had ever accomplished. "Sometimes it was scary," he said of the ten-year battle with the NFL. "My neck was on the line, both financially and personally. We should have been scared."[36] And with good reason, for the NFL had a long history of fighting and beating an alphabet soup of rival leagues—the MFL, AAFC, and three versions of the AFL—and would go on to take down even more in the WFL, USFL, and the XFL. Each of those leagues had many of the same advantages as the AFL, yet none of them could duplicate its ultimate success. "They're running out of space in the Graveyard of Failed Football Leagues," according to Rodger Sherman of *The Ringer*.[37]

The All-America Football Conference, which started play in 1946, came the closest. AAFC owners were rich, even richer than NFL owners at the time, and had money to burn in a new league. The Los Angeles AAFC group included actors Don Ameche, Bob Hope and Bing Crosby. Dan Topping of the New York Yankees baseball team came over to own an AAFC team of the same name. So well-heeled were AAFC owners that league meetings were often described as "the millionaires coffee klatch."[38] Attendance was decent during the four years of play, and in some cases even better than the NFL. In 1946, for example, the Cleveland Browns had the highest attendance in either league (606,022), and the Los Angeles Dons (337,940) did respectably against the cross-town Rams (426,858).

But the league suffered in that it did not have competitive teams in its biggest cities (New York, Chicago, and Los Angeles), and did not have much competition in general. The Cleveland Browns won the AAFC title all four years and did so in such dominating fashion that the league died from boredom. A bigger problem was the lack of television. Television money and exposure saved the AFL and might have done the same for the AAFC if the league had come along a decade later.

By 1949, most AAFC teams were in serious financial trouble, and so on December 9 the two leagues announced a merger, although "it was not so much a merger as the dissolution of the AAFC."[39] The NFL took the popular and financially solid Browns and 49ers franchises, and threw in the Baltimore Colts, while the other teams were dissolved and their players redistributed in an NFL allocation draft. Even the small concession awarded to the AAFC—renaming the NFL as the National American Football League—was quickly dropped before the 1950 season started.

The AAFC originally set out to peacefully co-exist with the NFL and sought to reach agreements to that effect between the two leagues. According to AAFC historians Ken Crippen and Matt Reaser, "The NFL, however, did not see things the same way [and] wanted nothing to do with the AAFC."[40] Just like the AFL, the AAFC had to learn that lesson the hard way. It would be a lesson learned again and again in the years after the success of the AFL.

Peace had barely descended on the pro football landscape with the NFL-AFL merger in 1970 when another upstart league tried its luck. The World Football League announced plans to begin play in 1974 with twelve teams in U.S. cities as well as Toronto. The WFL had a national television contract with syndicated network TVS for its first season, giving the league exposure that was so vital to the survival of the AFL. Attendance at several games surpassed 40,000, better even than the AFL's first season in 1960. Publicly, the league had modest aspirations, and assigned team spending limits so as to avoid an expensive battle with the NFL for players.

Privately, things soon ran off the rails. WFL founder Gary Davidson was a high-rolling attorney who had already started other sports leagues

Six. Alphabet Soup

such as the World Hockey Association and American Basketball Association. Davidson, who served as the WFL's president and commissioner, envisioned a league that would one day have teams in Europe, Japan, Mexico and "encompass the entire world."[41] Davidson pushed owners to challenge the NFL by signing established stars, and soon more than fifty had jumped leagues, including Miami Dolphins stars Larry Csonka, Paul Warfield and Jim Kiick who signed multi-million dollar deals once their NFL contracts expired. The former Dolphins each got three-year deals worth a combined $3.5 million.

The problem was that the WFL didn't have that kind of money. John Bassett, who signed Csonka, Kiick and Warfield, didn't have the oil bankroll of Lamar Hunt or Bud Adams. His Toronto franchise ran into trouble and moved to Memphis, while other teams barely managed to survive. Two teams relocated midway through the first season, including the New York Stars abandoning the biggest market in the country for Charlotte, North Carolina.

Stories began to leak out about the league's shoestring operation. Shortly after moving to Charlotte, the team had its uniforms impounded for failure to pay bills. Several teams went months without receiving paychecks, including the Detroit Wheels whose players paid expenses out of their own pockets before the team declared bankruptcy. After the WFL World Bowl championship game, the winning Birmingham Americans had jerseys and other property confiscated to pay off debts. The Internal Revenue Service took a percentage of the gate receipts as partial payment for a $237,000 tax bill. "At this point," said Bassett, "the league has no credibility."[42]

Any credibility the WFL had vanished when it was discovered that many teams had lied about attendance figures and papered games with free tickets. When news of "Paper-Gate" got around, many of the NFL stars who had signed future contracts got nervous and sued to break their deals. Hawaii team owner Chris Hemmeter took over for Davidson as commissioner and promised reorganization, but midway through its second season the WFL collapsed for good having lost $30 million in eighteen months of operation. "There wasn't a single overriding factor in the decision," said Hemmeter. "As responsible people we realized that the risk had become too great."[43] Some newspaper headlines called the decision a "mercy killing."

Perhaps the problem was trying to compete directly against the NFL by playing games in the fall. The league's twenty-game regular season started in July when NFL teams were in training camp and ended in November. So when the next challenger to the NFL stepped forward it decided to take a different approach.

The United States Football League began play in the spring of 1983 with its championship game designed for late summer so as to avoid the NFL. USFL Founder and New Orleans businessman David Dixon believed a league could successfully fill this void on the pro football calendar and he followed a plan very similar to the AFL and WFL: secure NFL-caliber stadiums, put teams in big markets, get a national television contract and control spending. Each team started with a salary cap of $1.8 million.

The USFL followed that approach its first season and did fairly well. The league had a national television contract with ABC. Only two of the league's twelve teams drew less than 14,000 fans per game, and the league as a whole averaged about 25,000. More than 50,000 fans came to Denver's Mile High Stadium to watch the Michigan Panthers beat the Baltimore Stars for the first USFL championship. When the league added Heisman Trophy winners Doug Flutie and Mike Rozier, joining such stars as Herschel Walker and Reggie White, the USFL looked to be on solid ground for years to come.

Not satisfied with its modest success, the USFL wanted much more. And like the AFL did more than a decade before, the league started a bidding war with the NFL for players. "We're fighting for players," USFL Commissioner Chet Simmons said at the time. "If we didn't have them, we would be off Broadway. And we want to be on Broadway."[44] When the NFL's Houston Oilers offered Rozier $2.8 million for three years, the Pittsburgh Maulers offered him eight million—guaranteed. The Los Angeles Express lured quarterback Steve Young with a contract for $40 million spread over 43 years.[45]

A turning point may have come in 1984 when New York business mogul Donald Trump bought the struggling New Jersey Generals. "He was the air pump into the tire," said Charley Steiner, who broadcast games for the Generals. "He gave the league the air it needed, elevated it to another level, pumped it up real good, and kept pumping till it exploded."[46] Trump immediately pumped up the league with an infusion of much-needed cash and exposure. Reasoning that you had to do things big in New York, he signed Flutie to a deal—five years for $7 million— that along with the Rozier, Young and Walker contracts blew away Dixon's plan for controlled spending. "Donald does everything big, right?" said Mike Tollin, who worked in the USFL and later produced a documentary about the league's demise.[47] "And he made a big mistake—capital B, capital I, capital G."[48]

Trump's big mistake, often blamed on his hubris and his desire to own an NFL team, was convincing other USFL owners to change from a spring league and move the games to the fall to compete directly with the NFL. Other owners were rightly concerned, including WFL holdover John Bassett who owned the popular Tampa Bay Bandits franchise that led the USFL in attendance. Trump dismissed their complaints and plowed ahead. "He was a bully," Tollin said of Trump. "He was good at finding and exploiting an opponent's weakness."[49]

The USFL announced the change for the 1986 season. "If God wanted football in the spring," Trump reasoned at the time, "he wouldn't have created baseball."[50] Privately, Trump bragged that the move would either force a merger with the NFL or make the USFL just as rich and successful.

It did neither. ABC had little interest in televising the USFL against the established NFL on CBS and NBC. With losses now reaching $200 million, USFL owners pinned their hopes on a $1.69 billion anti-trust lawsuit against the NFL, arguing that the NFL had conspired to keep them off national television. The USFL ended up winning the battle, but losing the war. In July 1986 a U.S. District Court in Manhattan ruled in favor of the USFL, but said the league had caused many of its own problems and awarded only one dollar in damages. With damages trebled for anti-trust cases, the final amount came to $3.76, with interest.

The USFL, which had counted on a huge payout to save the league, suspended operations and never played another game. "It was a hard thing to watch unfold," said Jerry Argovitz, owner of the Houston Gamblers. "Donald didn't love the USFL. To him, it was small potatoes. Which is terrible, because we had a great league and a great idea. But then everyone let Donald Trump take over. It was our death."[51] For his part, Trump denied any culpability. "I've had a lot of false press on the USFL," he insists. "Without me, the USFL would have been dead immediately. It was a league that was failing badly."[52]

Not since the USFL has another football league had the resolve (some say foolhardiness) to take on the NFL. Certainly there have been pretenders, such as Vince McMahon's XFL in 2001. McMahon brought the same over-the-top entertainment production to the league as he did with his World Wrestling Federation, and the result was an almost cartoonish product that lasted just one season. The XFL played its games after the NFL season ended, as did the Alliance of American Football, which also had a short life. The AAF did not make it through its first season and suspended operations in April 2019.

A toned-down version of the XFL returned in 2020 and got off to a promising start. "This version of the XFL took its time in reaching kickoff," noted *USA Today* when the season got underway in February, "and the results have been good football, enthusiastic fans and reasonable results."[53] But insiders had a much more realistic view of things. ESPN's

Steve Levy, who broadcast the games, warned, "This is the last shot at this, you know what I mean? If this one does not work, it's just not going to work."[54]

When the new XFL declared bankruptcy in the spring of 2020, the NFL stood alone as all other challengers had fallen by the wayside. Only the American Football League had the resources, strategy and just plain luck to survive, and even the AFL ceased operations after ten years when its teams were merged into an enlarged NFL.

So why did the AFL succeed when so many others failed?

It would seem that for any league to mount a serious challenge to the NFL (or any new league in any professional sport) would require a combination of rich ownership, television exposure, star power on the field, and good timing (see Figure 2).

The All-America Football Conference certainly had rich ownership and good timing, starting play right after the end of World War II when the public was hungry for more sporting entertainment. But it simply could not attract the television exposure it needed, even in the early days of television when the medium was desperate for programming. There were plans to televise the 1948 championship game between Cleveland and Buffalo, and beam the signals back to viewers in those cities, but the deal fell through at the last minute, as did an effort to get the game on NBC television to its affiliates in the Midwest. "The network couldn't find one single sponsor for the game. Such was the AAFC's lack of prestige with the corporate world."[55]

The AAFC also suffered from a lack of star power. That's not to say the league did not have good players, especially on the four-time champion Cleveland Browns who featured future Hall of Famers Otto Graham, Marion Motley and Lou Groza, among others. But without media exposure, they played mostly in anonymity outside their home areas. Not until the Browns joined the NFL did their good players become widely known stars.

The WFL understood it needed marquee names and moved to raid NFL talent, but the league went out of business before it could showcase its new stars. The XFL and AAF never attempted to sign NFL stars because of the expense involved, and fans quickly lost interest in the product. By contrast, the USFL had several star players, mostly from the college ranks, but the high cost of prying them away from the NFL strained the league's finances. Even so, well-heeled owners like Donald Trump seemed to have enough capital to survive, especially with a strong television contract with ABC.

But the USFL ultimately fell victim to bad timing, most of it created by the move from spring to fall to directly challenge the NFL. Star

Six. Alphabet Soup

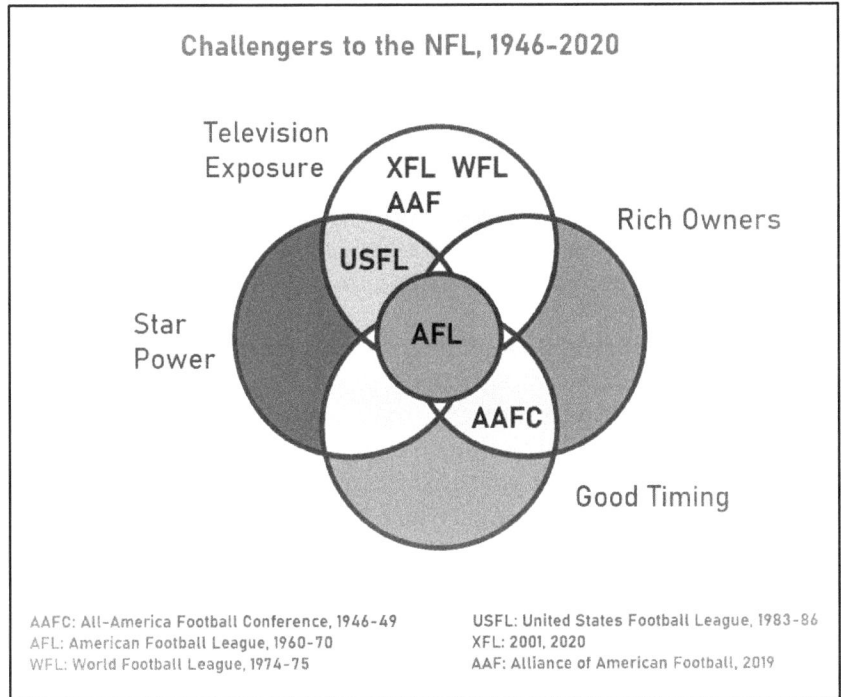

Leagues that tried to challenge the NFL needed a unique combination of good timing, star power, television exposure and rich ownership to succeed. Only the American Football League had all the ingredients to survive and eventually force a merger with the NFL.

power, rich ownership and television exposure all are important commodities for an upstart league, but perhaps good timing may be the most important. The AAFC had it, but couldn't overcome its other disadvantages. The USFL seemed to have it, but threw it away. And the most recent incarnation of the XFL most certainly did not have it. Just when the league was building a solid fan base with modest success on television, the coronavirus pandemic shut down the league in March 2020. The league cancelled its games and eventually declared bankruptcy.

While the American Football League stands out as the success story, it's hard to imagine the AFL surviving a global health crisis in its first year of operation, or succeeding without the help of a burgeoning television industry. Those that came before and those that came after suffered the same eventual fate—victims of poor timing and extenuating circumstances that consigned them to the graveyard of pro football leagues. Only the AFL, or at least part of it, survived to leave a lasting legacy, and its contribution is still being felt today in all levels of football.

"The NFL was there first," said broadcaster Bob Costas, "and it had the most teams, but you can make the case that the genesis of modern pro football was the AFL."[56]

Part of that genesis was the AFL's emphasis on opening up the game to blacks and minorities. The NFL had integrated in 1946, but in 1960 was still primarily a white league with unwritten quotas on how many blacks each team could have. Some owners, like George Preston Marshall in Washington, were avowed segregationists and resisted using black players until pressure from civil rights groups forced them to do so (see Chapter Eight).

Certainly there was an egalitarian reason for the AFL to reach out to black players, but much of it was simple practicality. The new league needed any quality players it could get and could not afford to be choosy. Lamar Hunt's Texans/Chiefs franchise put a special emphasis on finding minority talent, and did so thanks in great part to scout Lloyd Wells. Wells helped the AFL become a haven for black players, many of whom were denied opportunities through the NFL's quota system, in which "no more than five blacks could be on a team," according to Ron Mix, a Hall of Fame lineman with the Chargers. "What a difference in the AFL. The AFL could not afford that luxury."[57] Wells scoured the black colleges and the AFL ended up signing such talents as Taylor, linebacker Willie Lanier, and defensive tackle Buck Buchanan.

The AFL's other lasting contribution to pro football was the wide-open offenses that became a signature of the new league. Whether by accident or design, the AFL realized it had to offer something different than the three yards and a cloud of dust of Vince Lombardi's NFL. In 1961, Bart Starr led the Packers to a convincing NFL title, crushing the Giants in the championship game, 37–0. The Packers led the league in rushing that year and Starr threw but 16 touchdown passes the entire season. In the AFL that same season, the Houston Oilers won the title and led the league in passing. The Oilers threw for 48 touchdowns, including 36 from NFL castoff George Blanda.

The passing revolution came from such brilliant minds as Sid Gillman, whose San Diego Chargers threw the ball all over the field. Oakland's Al Davis coached under Gillman and called him "the father of modern-day passing. It had been thought of as vertical, the length of the field, but Sid also thought of it as horizontal."[58] A young assistant with the Cincinnati Bengals, Bill Walsh, took Gillman's concepts and went even further, refining and developing what eventually became the West Coast offense. "'Nickel and diming' they called it," said Walsh. "The pass just wasn't used that way"[59] (see Chapter Eleven).

The West Coast offense flipped the traditional run-first philosophy of football on its head, using short, controlled passing to set up the run. While such an approach viewed passing like a scalpel, other teams used it like a bludgeon. Al Davis and the Raiders believed in the deep vertical passing game and used it to become consistent championship contenders. Joe Namath believed in it also, and in 1967 he became the first pro passer to ever surpass 4,000 yards passing (4,007). The NFL would not have a 4,000-yard passer until 1979, and fittingly it came from an old AFL team as Dan Fouts of the Chargers passed for 4,082 yards.

The record season Fouts had in 1979, under the tutelage of another passing guru, Don Coryell, presaged a passing revolution in the NFL. In 1980, Fouts and Brian Sipe of Cleveland both eclipsed 4,000 yards. In 1984, three quarterbacks did it, and starting in 1988 at least one quarterback did it every year through 1996. In 2008, Drew Brees of the Saints became the first 5,000-yard passer (5,069), and in 2011 Brees, Tom Brady and Matthew Stafford all surpassed 5,000 yards. That same year saw a record eleven NFL quarterback pass for at least 4,000 yards.

All of this has trickled down to the college and even high school levels. Colleges want to attract the best high school talent, and that talent wants one day to play in the NFL. It's a big advantage for colleges to run the same offenses as the pros because they can sell themselves to recruits as an easy transition to the NFL. It works the same way for high schools that want to develop players that are college ready. Even in the stodgy Southeastern Conference—the land of Herschel Walker, smash-mouth football and Bear Bryant's Wishbone—passing has taken root. Since 2010, three SEC quarterbacks (Cam Newton at Auburn, Johnny Manziel at Texas A&M and Joe Burrow at LSU) have won Heisman Trophies, mainly by putting the ball in the air. That's also translated into championships, including six by Nick Saban at Alabama. "This is where the game has gone," says Gary Danielson, who broadcasts SEC games for CBS, "and it's hard to see that changing back."[60]

The misadventures of the XFL and AAF will give serious pause to anyone thinking of creating a new league to challenge the NFL. "The world doesn't need another football league," wrote *The Ringer's* Rodger Sherman. "It seems pretty convincing that there isn't enough interest in a second-tier football organization to provide the cash for the many expenses of football. The only thing that will lead to another football league's success is the NFL deciding that its own football product could be improved by the presence of another football league."[61] Former television executive Eddie Einhorn, the executive producer on WFL telecasts, came to the same conclusion twenty-five years ago. "I learned once again how hard it is to start up a league, even with maximum exposure," he said. "[The NFL] was dealing with all three networks at the time, and if you can't get one of the big networks to jump with you, well, the USFL had the same problem. I don't think you'll see any new leagues in the major sports ever again."[62]

But chances are, even now, someone somewhere is thinking about taking on the NFL. That person, or persons, believes he has enough money, a foolproof business plan and access to television exposure. While the chances of success are obviously remote, in 1959 those were also the thoughts of a former third-string end on the SMU football team who wanted nothing more than to bring pro football to his hometown of Dallas. Lamar Hunt never got off the bench to make a dent on the football field, but he made a giant impression as founder of the American Football League. And what he started in 1959 continues to evolve and shape the future of the NFL.

Seven

Oh, Canada!—And Beyond

On December 24, 1950, the Cleveland Browns won their first-ever NFL championship, beating the Los Angeles Rams, 30–28, on a late field goal by Lou Groza. It was a cold, raw day at Cleveland's Municipal Stadium, and the attendance of just 29,751 suggested that either the weather or perhaps last-minute shopping gave fans a reason to spend their Christmas Eve elsewhere.

Just a month before, on November 25, Canadian football held its annual Grey Cup championship game at Varsity Stadium in Toronto. The crowd—27,101—was about the same, even though the game was played in a steady rain which turned the field into mud. In a game that came to be known as the "Mud Bowl," the Toronto Argonauts won their ninth Canadian title, 13–0.

As the NFL struggled to gain its footing in the 1930s and 40s, Canadian football had long been established. The first Grey Cup game was held in 1909 and the Argonauts franchise dates back to 1873, making it one of the oldest sports teams in North America. Canadian football evolved out of rugby and like its brethren in the National Hockey League was established mostly on an amateur basis. Amateur teams could challenge to play for the Cup, just as they could with the Stanley Cup in the early days of the NHL.

The game evolved through the years, becoming fully professional with the formation of the Canadian Football League in 1958. Yet it held on to the traditions that made it distinctly Canadian, including its distinctive rules. Compared to American football, the Canadian field is bigger (110 yards vs. 100 yards), the game more wide-open (only three downs to move the ball instead of four encourages more passing), and the scoring more unique (a single point, called a "rouge," is scored when a team kicks the ball into the end zone and the other team does not run it out). The season starts in the heat of summer and ends with the annual Grey Cup championship game at the end of November before the harsh winter arrives. Hockey is and always will be Canada's lifeblood and national sport, but even today 63 percent of all Canadians "believe that the CFL is integral to Canada's sporting identity."[1]

Canadians bristle at the notion that their sport is inferior to the NFL, and take pride that many NFL innovations, including replay and end zone celebrations, were first tried in the CFL.

"As a Canadian, the CFL is something that is yours," says sportswriter Donnovan Bennett. "It's part of your history. It's played by, run by, and increasingly coached and managed by Canadians. Plain and simple, the CFL has an impact on people. It's important to people."[2]

Perhaps that's why Canadian footballers were eager to test themselves in exhibition games against American teams. In August and September 1941, even as the world was plunging itself into war, the Columbus Bulls (or Bullies) of the American Football League[3] decided to spend part of their summer training camp in Winnipeg, Canada. Their trip included three exhibition games against the Winnipeg Blue Bombers, still a collection of amateur players.

The Bulls were the defending AFL champs and would win the league title again in 1941. That prompted one Winnipeg newspaper to designate the games the "amateur-pro championship of North America."[4] That was a bit of wishful thinking considering the AFL was vastly inferior to the established NFL, and in the previous year's NFL title game the Chicago Bears set an all-time scoring record, destroying the Washington Redskins, 73–0.

The locals had a chance to crow a bit after the Blue Bombers beat Columbus in the first game, 19–12, but Columbus then won the follow-up games, 6–0 and 31–1. The shellacking in the final game was enough to convince Winnipeg sportswriter Herb Manning that the Canadian game was not up to the standards of the Americans, even as played in the AFL. "[The Bulls] left an indelible impression of a football team which knew and could execute all of the game's finer points," he wrote. "A team which could paste the home-town boys and still retain the favor of the fans. They also left behind them a sadly disillusioned group of footballers wearing the Blue and Gold, though the Bombers are sadder, surely too, they are wiser."[5]

As the AFL faded into the sunset, so too did the idea of games between Canadian and American teams, at least for the better part of a decade. The NFL and Canadian leagues decided to hold a pair of exhibition games in Ottawa during the 1950 and 1951 seasons, which was still a time the NFL was trying to get itself firmly established. The attitude of the league and Commissioner Bert Bell was one of selling the game to new fans, anywhere, any place, and any time, especially during the preseason. NFL teams played exhibition games in such places as

Hershey, Pennsylvania; Abilene, Texas, and Akron, Ohio. "Aside from giving teams high revenue and low expenses," wrote NFL author Mark Ford, "the summer games also gave the NFL a chance to sell pro football. The NFL could take it show on the road, introducing its brand of football to cities and towns that weren't likely to get a pro team but might watch on TV."[6]

If the Canadians thought the AFL Bulls were impressive in 1941, they got a look at the real deal when the New York Giants came to Ottawa to play the Rough Riders on August 12, 1950—the first ever NFL game played outside the United States. The game was played with Canadian rules in the first half, which prohibited blocking five yards beyond the line of scrimmage, and the Giants led, 13–6. Using NFL rules in the second half, New York went on to win the game, 27–6, before 11,025 fans. "Actually, it wasn't a true test for the American style of football," Jack Koffman wrote in the *Ottawa Citizen*. "Against another American squad, against a team fully versed and equipped for the U.S. code, it might have been a spectacular show. As it was, there was something missing for the big crowd in the second half."[7] The Giants returned the next year and were even more impressive, beating Ottawa, 41–18.

Just as the NFL was evolving in the 1950s, so too was Canadian football. By 1955, amateurism had given way to professional players, and in 1958 the Canadian Football League was formally founded as a merger of the Western Interprovincial Football Union and the Interprovincial Rugby Football Union. With professionalism now firmly entrenched, the NFL took a different view of their Canadian neighbors, who suddenly became competitors for football talent rather than just friendly rivals.

One of the first American players to jump to Canada was Bud Grant, who left the Philadelphia Eagles in a contract dispute after the 1952 season for more money in Winnipeg. "The Eagles offered me $8,000 and I went to Winnipeg for $11,000," Grant said. "That's not tough arithmetic."[8] While he is best remembered for losing four Super Bowls as coach of the Minnesota Vikings, in Winnipeg Grant became a Western Conference All-Star three times, and after his retirement in 1956 coached the Blue Bombers to six appearances in the Grey Cup and four championships.

As it would do with the American Football League in 1959, the NFL looked down on Canada as inferior. When Grant was coaching the Blue Bombers, he and Vince Lombardi tangled over a player named Mike Wright. Green Bay had drafted Wright, but Grant had signed him to a contract. When Lombardi found out, he called Grant and chewed him out. "Why would he want to play in a Mickey Mouse league like the CFL?" Lombardi growled. Grant replied evenly, "Well, I'm sorry, but I'm not sorry. I think it's in his best interest." Lombardi yelled back, "Well you no good son of a ... blah blah blah."[9]

Like many NFL coaches, Lombardi looked at the CFL like a farm team, often trying to grab players when someone got hurt or he needed a roster spot filled. Most of the American players in the CFL felt the same way, and viewed Canada as a proving ground or stepping stone to the NFL. However, others saw the CFL as a legitimate opportunity that was denied them by the NFL. This was especially true for black players.

In 1951, Johnny Bright of Drake University was assaulted during play in a game against Oklahoma A&M (now Oklahoma State) in Stillwater, Oklahoma. The Oklahoma players seemed to target Bright because of his skin color, and he was knocked out three times and left the game with a broken jaw. After graduation, Bright turned down an offer with the NFL Eagles to play with the Calgary Stampeders. "I would have been their [the Eagles] first Negro player," Bright said. "There was a tremendous influx of Southern players into the NFL at the time and I didn't know what kind of treatment I could expect."[10] Bright led the Canadian league in rushing three times and eventually made the CFL Hall of Fame.

No position benefited black players more than quarterback. It was unthinkable that the NFL would allow a black to play quarterback in the 1950s, and it was still extremely rare in the 1960s and '70s. Marlin Briscoe broke the color line for quarterbacks in 1968 with the Denver Broncos of the AFL, but the following year he was traded to Buffalo and switched positions to wide receiver where he stayed the rest of his career. The thinking was that blacks could succeed as receivers and running backs, but lacked the intelligence required to handle the quarterback position. "A black has never been given a real chance at quarterback in the NFL," wrote Dink Carroll in the *Montreal Gazette*. "They are signed by NFL clubs ... but are quickly converted to defensive halfbacks and flankers when they turn professional."[11]

The same year Johnny Bright turned down the Eagles to play in Calgary, the Cleveland Browns drafted Bernie Custis of Syracuse University with plans to move him from quarterback to defensive back. Custis instead went to Hamilton and in 1951 became the first black starter in the league. Twenty years later, Chuck Ealey came to Hamilton from the University of Toledo after telling NFL teams he would only play quarterback. In 1972, Ealey won CFL Rookie of the Year, led the Tiger-Cats to the Grey Cup title, and won player of the game honors in the championship. It was a similar story for Condredge Holloway of the University of Tennessee, who in 1975 was drafted by the New England Patriots in the twelfth round with the idea of converting him to defensive back.

Holloway quarterbacked the Toronto Argonauts to a Grey Cup championship in 1983 and was later inducted into the CFL Hall of Fame.

The all-time success story is Warren Moon, who after leading the University of Washington to a Rose Bowl win in 1978, went to Canada after no NFL team selected him in the draft. In six CFL seasons in Edmonton, Moon won five Grey Cup titles, and when he finally came to the NFL in 1984, Doug Williams and James Harris had already showed that black quarterbacks could succeed in the league. Moon played in the NFL 17 years, joining Bud Grant as the only players inducted into both the NFL and CFL Halls of Fame. "One of the more refreshing things about being up there was I never felt that racial tension," he said of his CFL experience. "In the NFL, you felt it all the way around. You heard the things that were yelled at you."[12]

Not only was the CFL siphoning away talented minorities, it was also attracting players not considered big enough, strong enough, or fast enough for the NFL. Undersized quarterbacks Joe Theismann of Notre Dame and Doug Flutie of Boston College both enjoyed great success in Canada before coming to the NFL. Flutie was named the CFL's Most Outstanding Player a record six times, helped his teams win three Grey Cups, and is generally considered the greatest CFL player of all time. "I felt Doug was perfectly suited to the CFL," said teammate Dave Dickenson. "Very creative. A trendsetter. He didn't want to be put in a cookie-cutter. He wasn't worried to make a mistake."[13] Flutie still holds CFL record for most passing yards in a season (6,619 in 1991), most touchdown passes in a season (48 in 1994), and most passing yards per game for a career (306.3).

But any pretensions the CFL had that it could compete with the NFL on the field were shattered during a series of games that started in 1958.

On September 14, 1958, the CFL played a regular season game in Philadelphia between Hamilton and Ottawa, the first Canadian game ever played outside the country. It was the brainchild of a Philadelphia promoter named Bud Dudley, who wanted to use the proceeds to help a local children's hospital. The CFL agreed, in part because it viewed the game as chance to gain some footing on American soil.

Despite good weather, the game turned into a disaster for the CFL. The game attracted only 15,110 fans, many of whom bused in from Canada, and the cavernous 102,000 seat Municipal Stadium "resembled a dozen or so people sitting in Ottawa's Landsowne Park."[14] Needing 17,000 ticket sales just to break even, the game instead lost $26,000.

With the NFL preseason underway and baseball pennant races entering the final stretch, American media ignored the event. Hamilton beat Ottawa, 24–18, but the game featured 31 punts and enough rule differences to confuse fans. "The evidence was irrefutable," Jack Kinsella wrote in the *Ottawa Citizen,* "that Hamilton and Ottawa had combined successfully to kill any illusions that the game of Canadian football is the superior product on the market. Canadian football was made to look awfully foolish, if not actually second-rate. [Bert] Bell and his NFL cohorts must have enjoyed a few satisfactory chuckles before the afternoon was over."[15]

Whether or not Bell and the NFL laughed, the league decided to return to Canada for a series of exhibition games starting in 1959. With the CFL embarrassment in Philadelphia, and the excitement generated from the 1958 overtime championship game between the Colts and Giants, the NFL was now viewed as the far superior league. Playing in Canada, on unfamiliar fields with different rules, seemingly could do nothing to help this reputation. If the NFL teams won, it was expected; if they lost, it would be a monumental upset and blow to league pride.

However, by playing and beating CFL teams, the NFL would send a clear message to aspiring college players that if they were serious about football as a career, the NFL was going to be their best option. This was especially important in terms of the battle for talent between the NFL and AFL. And much like the CFL tried in Philadelphia, the NFL wanted to see if there was a market for the game beyond its own borders. Whether it even realized it at the time or not, the NFL's return to Canada signaled the first tiny steps toward turning the league international.

By the time the Chicago Cardinals met the Toronto Argonauts on August 5, 1959, in Toronto, the CFL has revamped its schedule. The Canadian season now began in early summer and finished around Thanksgiving, which means while the August game was simply a tune-up for the Cardinals, it came right in the middle of the CFL regular season. The once-proud Argos, ten times winners of the Grey Cup, had fallen on hard times and were in the middle of a 4–10 season.

The Chicago Cardinals weren't much better, and in fact were considered one of the weaker teams in the NFL. One of pro football's original franchises, the Cardinals enjoyed success in the 1920s, winning a disputed title in 1925 over the Pottsville Maroons. The team fought bitterly with the cross-town rival Bears, building its fan base on Chicago's Southside while the Bears stayed on the Northside. Games between the teams were like the mob wars of the era, with each team trying to protect its turf and unafraid to use violence to do so. In a 6–0 Cardinals win over the Bears on Thanksgiving in 1922, the *Chicago Herald-Examiner* noted, "The struggle between the post-grad teams of north and south side ended with a score of 6–0 in favor of the south siders, after a battle which included a half-riot, two fist-fights, and finished peacefully enough with the clanging of patrol wagons bringing the reserves."[16]

In the ensuing years, the richer and more successful Bears began to wear down their rivals in a battle of attrition. The Cardinals staggered through the Depression and into the war with ten straight losing seasons, including two winless campaigns. A brief glimpse of glory brought an NFL championship in 1947 and a loss in the title game the following year, but by the 1950s the franchise descended back into mediocrity. "Imagine a football team that played as poorly as the 1962 New York Mets, not just for a season or two but for an entire decade," lamented the *Chicago Tribune*. "These were the Chicago Cardinals of the 1950s. Rosters changed not just year to year, but week to week."[17]

The roster changed drastically on February 28, 1959, just months before the trip to Canada. The talent-starved Cardinals traded their one true star, running back Ollie Matson, to the Los Angeles Rams for what seemed like a staggering haul—eight players and a draft pick. "As far as I'm concerned," said Matson, "the Rams got the best deal. They got an established ballplayer, a dedicated ballplayer who loved the game. I did well in every position they put me in."[18]

Although he was never the superstar he was in Chicago, Matson, a former Olympic medal winner as a sprinter, went on to a Hall of Fame career. True to form, none of the players the Cardinals acquired distinguished themselves and the team would finish 2–10 in 1959. Starved for money, and unable to pry Chicago's love away from the Bears, the Cardinals moved to St. Louis in 1960.

But as the Cardinals prepared for their exhibition game in Toronto, they were still looked upon with awe by their hosts. An NFL team, even a bad NFL team, was considered the cream of the pro football crop. "Argos against the Chicago Cardinals," sportswriter Jim Hunt asked in the *Toronto Star*, "the mismatch of the century or a football game?"[19] It turned out to be a mismatch, but not in the beginning.

As in previous exhibitions, the game would feature a mix of Canadian and American rules, although Canadian rules on kicking would be used. It also marked the opening of Toronto's new Exhibition Stadium, and while the 27,770 fans who attended had plenty of room once they got inside, traffic outside was another matter, as 12,000 cars jockeyed for position in 7,000 parking spaces.

The Cardinals had only been in training camp ten days and they quickly fell behind, 13–1, but soon the American advantages began to show. The Cardinals' linemen outweighed their counterparts by about twenty pounds apiece, and as the Canadians were still playing one-platoon football, the Argos began to wear down as the game continued.

Don Caraway, considered the best of the Toronto defensive players, broke a foot midway through the second quarter, and three more starting Argos suffered injuries. Not only did the Cardinals roar back to win, 55–26, but the injuries crippled Toronto for the rest of the season and the team finished in fourth place. "We're Still Minor League," read the headline in the *Toronto Star*, where Hunt admitted that "Canadian football and the mighty National league are still a world apart."[20]

They were still worlds apart when the Pittsburgh Steelers came to Exhibition Stadium the following year to play the Argonauts, and two years later when the Cardinals returned to Toronto. In 1960, the Steelers trounced the Argonauts, 43–16, and the following year the Cardinals, now playing out of St. Louis, administered another beating, 36–7. Both NFL teams won easily despite the fact that they would not have winning records during the regular season, and that they played "Canadian football on a Canadian field before a Canadian crowd under Canadian rules."[21]

Three days after the St. Louis Cardinals' win in Toronto, the Chicago Bears beat the CFL's Alouettes in Montreal, 34–16. The Alouettes gained only nine yards in the first half and had seven played helped off the field with injuries. The game also featured a brawl that saw three players ejected. Ignoring all that, Bears coach George Halas charitably noted afterwards, "You have a good, lively game of football up here. Just what the Canadians have been telling me for years."[22] It was not the Bears first visit to Canada. The previous August the Bears and Giants played an exhibition game in Toronto, the first game between two NFL teams played outside the United States. In a game that featured mostly unknown rookies trying to make the team, Chicago won, 16–7.

The last American-Canadian exhibition took place on August 8, 1961, as the AFL's Buffalo Bills played in Hamilton. The league was only in its second year of operation and the Bills were not even a good AFL team, finishing in fourth place that season with a 6–8 record. NFL executives probably got a good laugh as the Tiger-Cats won, 38–21, before 12,000 fans.

Then, just like that, the goodwill exhibitions ended. Part of it was the dominance of the NFL teams, including the crippling injuries suffered by the Canadians, and part of it was the difficulty of scheduling, as Canada was in its regular season while the NFL was just starting preseason play. "[The] honeymoon with the NFL is over," wrote the *Toronto Star*, "and like all mismatches the breakup was a sad thing to watch."[23]

The NFL made a half-hearted attempt to return to Canada in 1969 when the Lions and Patriots played an exhibition game in Montreal

The Chicago Cardinals of the NFL beat the Toronto Argonauts of the CFL, 55–26, in August 1959. It was the first of three straight years that an NFL team played an exhibition game in Canada, marking the first small steps toward globalization. *Toronto Star/PARS International*.

hosted by the baseball Expos. "Only 8,212 turned out at Jarry Park for an exhibition that was supposed to be a yardstick for interest here," noted the *Montreal Gazette*, "but nobody seemed to really care. The crowd, such as it was, was markedly unresponsive."[24] Just 5,401 turned out to watch the Bears play the Giants in that 1960 exhibition game.

But there were encouraging signs, at least for games involving Canadian teams against the NFL. There were 27,770 fans who came to Toronto for the Cardinals–Argos game in 1959, 23,750 watched Pittsburgh and Toronto in 1960, and when the Cardinals returned in 1961 the crowd was 24,376. Those kinds of attendance figures may seem small compared to NFL games, but they were consistent with good crowds in Canada. The league also found success with another experiment in the Steelers–Argonauts game. That game "went over pay TV to a nearby town of Etobicoke in what was believed to be the first such showing of a pro grid battle."[25]

Pay broadcasting and expansion of the game on international soil—the NFL had taken small steps into its future. But they were only baby steps as the league was not in a position to take advantage of either circumstance quite yet.

The key factor seemed to be timing. In 1959 the NFL was coming off a hugely successful overtime championship game and did not yet have competition from the American Football League. The league pushed boldly into Canada seeking not only to assert its dominance but also test the waters of international interest. But when the AFL proved to be a serious challenger, as did later the World Football League and United States Football League (see Chapter Six), the NFL had to pull back and regroup to fight a series of costly internecine wars. Only when these other leagues were defeated or absorbed could the league again turn its attention outward.

By 1976, the NFL was again in an expansive mood, adding Seattle and Tampa Bay as new franchises. That August, the Chargers and Cardinals flew 13 hours to play in Tokyo for the first-ever NFL game outside of North America. Unlike Canadians who had a basic understanding of football, the Japanese knew next to nothing about the game and spent the afternoon yelling "Banzai," often at inappropriate times. Still, 40,000 came out to watch in the rain as St. Louis won, 20–10. "I remember leaving Tokyo and us saying, 'Well, we must have started something,'" said Pat Curran of the Chargers. "I bet you this will be carried on from here, because it was so well-received."[26] Two years later, the Eagles and Saints played the first-ever NFL game in Mexico. Even on what Eagles quarterback Ron Jaworski called "the worst field I've ever played on,"[27] the game attracted a decent crowd and demonstrated Mexico's growing interest in American football.

Starting in 1986 the NFL played a series of yearly exhibition games in foreign countries. The games started in London, transitioned to Japan, and then moved on to Montreal, Mexico City, and Berlin. The game was called the American Bowl and the first version, held August 3, 1986, in London, drew a sellout crowd of 82,699 to Wembley Stadium. That should have been no surprise considering the previous year's Super Bowl "was watched by 3.6 million [in England], an astonishing figure considering only about six million watch rugby union internationals. For a period men like Joe Montana and William 'The Refrigerator' Perry were almost as famous"[28] as England's top soccer stars.

Even though it was just a preseason game, the event had the star power of the defending Super Bowl champion Bears against the popular Dallas Cowboys. Chicago won, 17–6, with Perry delighting the crowd by scoring a touchdown. The Fridge was a constant topic for the London tabloids, as were the Dallas Cowboy cheerleaders who made the trip. Soccer-mad England seemed to take the game to heart, even with intermittent rain throughout the game. "By most accounts the tour had been a fabulous success," said *Sports Illustrated*. "The NFL will do no more than break even financially, but that ... is more than enough. The beachhead has been established."[29]

The same week the Bears and Cowboys thrilled the crowds in London, a federal court in Manhattan announced the damages awarded to the USFL in its monopoly case against the NFL—one dollar, automatically trebled to three dollars under the law. The USFL had sought $1.69 billion and the decision effectively gave the league its death sentence. Suddenly, the NFL had no more challengers to fight and could move forward with its ambitious plans to colonize the world.

Given the success of the London exhibition games, the NFL was eager to plant its flag in Europe and in 1989 league owners unanimously voted to create a spring developmental league. The World League of American Football had teams in Europe (Barcelona, Frankfurt, and London), Canada (Montreal), and the U.S. (Birmingham, Sacramento, San Antonio, New York, Orlando, and Raleigh-Durham, North Carolina). Play began in the spring of 1991, and while interest lagged in the U.S. and eventually doomed the effort, attendance was surprisingly strong in Europe where London led the league.

After failing in its U.S. cities and folding in 1993, the WLAF returned in 1995 with only European teams. Rupert Murdoch of Fox television, fresh off landing rights to televise NFL games, pumped new money into the league and became a part owner. Observers and sports fans in Europe called it "the biggest push yet towards the idea of globalised American football,"[30] but interest started to wane as attendance averaged less than 15,000. The name changed in 1998, this time to NFL Europe. By then, the bedrock London franchise was shut down after average attendance dropped to less than 6,000 per game.

Despite yet another name change to NFL Europa in 2006, the league could not survive and disbanded in 2007. "By NFL standards, NFL Europe was a financial turkey," wrote the *Manchester Guardian*. "The league never sniffed a profit as a European-only enterprise. Like any start-up, it was continually tweaked, re-tweaked, re-painted and rebranded."[31] Finally, the NFL had had enough and pulled the plug.

Given the failure of the WLAF and its successors, why would the NFL continue to have an interest in spreading outside the U.S.? As the NFL considers the answer to that question it should carefully consider the experience of the Canadian Football League and its attempts at international expansion.

The NFL incursion into Europe emboldened the Canadian Football League and in 1993 the CFL added expansion teams in Sacramento and San Antonio, although the latter franchise dropped out before ever playing a game. The following year the CFL reached further into the U.S. with teams in Baltimore, Las Vegas, and Shreveport, Louisiana. The Baltimore team was originally called the Colts, but dropped the name after a dispute with the NFL. It went nameless for a time, and then became the "Baltimore FC" before settling on Stallions. "You try calling a game for a team without a name," said television announcer Bruce Cunningham, who broadcast Baltimore games in 1994. "Sometimes it was 'the Baltimores.' We made it up. It wasn't easy."[32]

Whatever the team was called it was immediately successful both on and off the field. Baltimore led the CFL in attendance its first season and made it all the way to the 1994 Grey Cup game before losing to British Columbia, 26–23. Baltimore came back the next season and became the only U.S. team to win a CFL title, beating Calgary in the championship.

With now ten U.S. teams it appeared Canadian football had finally made a foothold in America, but closer examination showed that most of the franchises were on shaky financial ground. Outside of Baltimore, the other teams did not have good attendance and the league suffered from lack of television exposure. When the Cleveland Browns announced plans in 1995 to move to Baltimore, the Stallions knew their time in the spotlight was over. The franchise moved to Montreal, the other U.S. teams folded, and the CFL experiment in the U.S. ended.

Many north of the border greeted the retreat back to Canada with a great sigh of relief. Even though the product on the field had improved, there was a sense that the Canadian game was losing its identity. Baltimore did not have a single Canadian player on its roster that won the Grey Cup and many CFL fans were rooting against them in both championship appearances. Baltimore's success "was a wakeup call to Canadian fans," wrote Erik Malinowski in *Rolling Stone*. "CFL rosters are ... consciously Canadian, stocked with players who were born in Canada and played their college ball there."[33]

Unlike Canadian teams that win the Grey Cup, Baltimore got no rousing victory parade after its championship. The Browns were already making plans to relocate and certainly no one in Canada wanted to celebrate. Twenty years after the championship, the remaining players and executives got together to remember the only CFL team ever to win eighteen games in a single season. "This team never truly got the sendoff that it should [have]," said team over Jim Speros. "It's the greatest team that ever played."[34]

The problems of the NFL and CFL in expanding their product can both be traced to identity and timing. Canada embraces the CFL brand of football as *its* game, as much a part of its national identity and heritage as the Mounties, poutine or maple syrup. While CFL fans would gladly welcome American stars such as Doug Flutie and Warren Moon, they could not tolerate the idea of their sport becoming dominated by U.S. teams. "How do you feel as a Canadian with the Grey Cup sitting in Baltimore," wondered Mike Cosentino, then in the front office of the Toronto Argonauts. "I think I hate it. I'm sure for some people it was enraging."[35]

The NFL tried again in Canada beginning in 2008 when the Buffalo Bills hosted an annual series of home games in Toronto's Rogers Centre. While the league pushed it as a means of introducing the game to new fans, the unspoken reason for the games was to test Toronto as a possible landing site for the Bills if the franchise decided to move. The first game in 2008 attracted a decent crowd of 52,134, but that was 20,000 less than the Bills were averaging in Buffalo. Attendance in Buffalo soon dropped, and attendance for the games in Toronto declined every year to the point that only 38,969 fans watched the game 2013. "It's an idea that, at its very core, makes absolutely no sense," said *USA Today* of the series. "It spits in the face of communities and laughs at the familial-like bonds the professional sports teams create within their markets."[36]

That kind of cultural resistance is what the NFL is fighting against, especially in places like Europe. It's tempting to think of a "European culture," but the reality is dozens of different cultures spread across the continent. *Sports Illustrated* observed that American football meant something diffcrent in each country—"disciplined and efficient in Germany, fiery and emotional in Italy and a game of the people in Sweden."[37] All of them defied the NFL's "one size fits all approach." "There is no outcome at the end of day with the NFL for development of football in our country," said Robert Huber, president of the American Football Association of Germany, "because we are too different. We are just too different."[38]

So again, why does the NFL keep trying and exactly what is it trying to accomplish?

Part of the answer, at least in terms of the why, is that for the NFL there are really no more domestic worlds to conquer. The league's most recent expansion came in 2002 with the addition of Houston, which brought the NFL to a bulging 32 teams. Almost every square inch of the country has been covered with the NFL footprint and adding more teams would make scheduling and the playoffs unwieldy. That means most of the changes today are relocations, such as the Rams returning to Los Angeles or the Raiders leaving for Las Vegas. Any growth is going to have to take place outside the U.S.

To that end, the NFL is finding some fertile international ground for its game, especially in Mexico. Mexico has the largest NFL fan base outside the U.S., and with 20 million followers it is now the second most popular sport in the country behind soccer. Youth football programs have become popular, including more than three million boys and girls playing in some 15,000 leagues across the country. In 2005, the NFL staged its first-ever international regular season game when the Cardinals and 49ers played in Mexico City before a then-record crowd of 103,467. The biggest crowd ever to watch an NFL game—112,376—was for a 1994 preseason game between the Cowboys and Oilers in Mexico City. The NFL now schedules a regular season game in Mexico City every year and the tickets usually sell out quickly.[39]

The league also has multiple regular season games in London on a yearly basis, which reflects something of a change in philosophy. Some believe the WLAF and its brethren failed because they focused too much on the athletic aspect of the sport. As a developmental league, the WLAF was filled with bottom-tier players whose appeal quickly wore off over the course of a season. "To be quite honest, the World League should've been in the States," says Jason Hall, who played with the Cologne Centurions. "I understand the desire to 'globalize' the game [but] it wasn't the right strategy."[40]

The NFL strategy now appears to have shifted from sport to spectacle. A summer-long season of football might not excite Europeans, but the occasional visit with an emphasis on entertainment rather than competition is something different. "Football is the new kid in town in Europe," writes Pat Evans, "and provides the viewers with more 'glitz and glamour'" than the hatred often association with British soccer.[41]

The NFL featured four regular season games in London in 2019, two at Wembley Stadium and two at Tottenham Stadium. The bigger Wembley Stadium drew 84,771 to see the Jaguars and Texans, and another 83,720 for the Rams and Bengals. Both games were staged as "experiences" for London fans, with accompanying cultural activities

Seven. Oh, Canada!—And Beyond

and sideshows. The idea is to export American football as "entertainment as much as sport, intended to appeal as much to the party animal as the family audience."[42]

Given that kind of success, the NFL is once again debating whether to put a permanent franchise overseas, and London is the logical choice given that the UK now has more than 15 million fans. But there are a mountain of problems to overcome—permission from the NFL Players Association, time zone differences, scheduling, simple logistics of getting teams and players back and forth—that make an overseas franchise unlikely in the near future. A team in London would likely not be an expansion franchise but rather a relocation, and no current NFL owners have suggested an interest in moving. Supporters on both sides of the Atlantic, including the Tottenham Hotspur soccer team, which spent millions to upgrade its stadium to NFL specifications, remain undeterred. "Clearly we wouldn't be putting all this into the stadium," said Tottenham chairman Daniel Levy, "if there wasn't the prospect of one day a team eventually coming to London. I think we're all putting the effort in the hopes that they will do it."[43]

More likely, the NFL will continue its "less is more" approach by staging occasional games on a permanent basis. This could even possibly include a Super Bowl, and Estadio Azteca in Mexico City, which can seat 130,000, would seem to be an attractive choice. "There's been much speculation," said Arturo Olive, the managing director of NFL Mexico. "One game a year at this point is good to get people engaged and keep growing. But who knows what the future may bring?"[44]

One thing that complicates the international picture for the NFL is the continuing growth of media technologies. Much like it does with its "Sunday Ticket" package inside the U.S., the league is marketing its game in Europe through "Game Pass," which offers more than 300 games on demand per season. Subscriber numbers have grown 75 percent in England and the UK, and 69 percent in Germany. It should also help local interest in Germany that games are available on free over-the-air television as they are in the U.S.

The future is exciting but uncharted as the NFL seeks to expand its tentacles overseas. Canada seems closed, but Mexico and Europe remain enticing frontiers. "It's a little bit like an iceberg," says former WLAF coach Jim Tomsula. "We're looking at the tip here in the States, but there's a whole bunch under water over there."[45]

In a very real sense, it all started with a series of Canadian exhibition games in 1959. There was no thought of Europe or Mexico at that point; no inkling of how to use television or other technologies to reach international audiences. The NFL went to Canada in 1959 almost on a lark, trying to send a message to its upstart neighbors (and the American Football League) that it had the superior brand of professional football.

That it most certainly did, but in the process the league discovered that there might be an audience for its game outside the United States. The NFL was in no position to take advantage of the situation, but the opportunity was there and required only better timing. The seed was planted in 1959, even if it took several decades to take root.

Eight

Man with a Vision

If one were going to create a Mt. Rushmore of the early NFL, say before 1959, there would be little debate as to the central figure carved in stone. No one man better defined the league than one of its original founders, George "Papa Bear" Halas. It was Halas who put up $100 in 1920 to get the Decatur Staleys into the American Professional Football Association, and it was Halas who eventually got the name changed to the National Football League. When asked about the new name, Halas said simply, "The other name stunk."[1]

The name of the Staleys eventually changed as well, to the Chicago Bears, who under Halas came to be known as the "Monsters of the Midway." They were a tough, violent, pugnacious group of players, perfectly fitting the personality of Halas, their owner and coach. Under Halas, the Bears dominated the 1930s and 40s, winning five NFL titles and playing in nine championship games. One of Papa Bear's greatest contributions to the game was the development of the T-formation, which replaced the old single wing and opened up the game. The Bears used the T to crush Washington 73–0 in the 1940 title game, still the biggest rout in NFL history.

Halas won his first championship in 1921 and his last in 1963—seven all told—and stayed with the team in some capacity for more than 60 years. No team would be more closely associated with one man than George Halas and the Chicago Bears, who were "conceived, built, and nurtured with loving adoration with every fiber of his being as long as he lived."[2]

Another figure on that Mt. Rushmore would be Jim Thorpe, the legendary Olympic gold medalist and sometimes-professional baseball player. Thorpe played with the Canton Bulldogs in 1920, the very first year of the league in what is now considered the birthplace of pro football. He later played for the Cleveland Indians, Rock Island Independents, New York Giants, Chicago Cardinals, and befitting his heritage, the Oorang Indians. Thorpe was already 33 when he began play, and his statistics—at least the numbers that exist—weren't that impressive. But his mere participation in the league, including serving as its first president while he was still playing, helped it survive its bumpy beginnings. "When a team was organized in Canton in 1915, his name insured gate receipts," according to the league office. "When pro football organized in 1920, his name gave the president's office instant prestige."[3]

Just as Thorpe was leaving the NFL, Red Grange was entering, forgoing his senior season at the University of Illinois to join the Chicago Bears (see Chapter Two). Grange was the most recognizable name in football, college or pro, and his joining the league most likely saved it from financial disaster. Where once crowds numbered in the hundreds, they now packed in by the thousands just to get a glimpse of the "Galloping Ghost" as he and the Bears barnstormed the country. Since Grange got a cut of the gate, as well as a salary and promotion deals, the tour made him wealthy. More importantly, it made the NFL viable. "When I played for the old Providence Steamrollers," said longtime player and coach Jimmy Conzelman, "just about everybody in the human race had a higher standing than a professional football player. The colleges frowned on us. On top of that, we were playing before 'poverty' crowds. Then Red Grange came into the act."[4]

George Halas, Jim Thorpe, Red Grange. Who else for the fourth and final spot?

The most likely candidate is De Benneville "Bert" Bell, who just as much as Halas, gave his heart, life, and soul to the NFL. He was neither as powerful as the Papa Bear, nor as popular as the glad-handing Art Rooney, owner of the Steelers. But it was Bell who made the monumental decisions that shaped the emerging league.

Born in Philadelphia, Bell played at the University of Pennsylvania and in 1933 founded the Philadelphia Eagles. In an era when team revenue depended almost completely on ticket sales, the Eagles were constantly in trouble because of their poor performance on the field. The team suffered through ten consecutive losing years, including three seasons in which it won only one game. Bell, who also served as coach for parts of five seasons, won only ten of 58 games for a winning percentage of .179. It's the worst percentage in NFL history for anyone who coached at least 50 games.

Only the necessities of World War II, which forced some teams to merge in order to cut costs and share dwindling manpower, pulled the Eagles out of the bottom division. By that time, in a complicated deal with Rooney, Bell acquired a stake in the Steelers and the teams merged for the 1941 season. Both franchises were already in financial trouble, even without the war pressures, and Bell had to borrow heavily

Eight. Man with a Vision

throughout the Depression. In the 1933 home opener, only 1,750 fans showed up to watch as the Eagles lost to Portsmouth, 25–0.

As Bell sank deeper into debt, he pondered the difficulty of his problem—he couldn't bring fans to the stadium without a winning team, but he couldn't build a winning team without the money provided by paying customers. The rich teams like Chicago and New York could outbid the Eagles for the best players. "I made up my mind that this league would never survive unless we had some system whereby each team had an even chance to bid for talent against the other," Bell decided.[5]

At the annual league meeting in 1935, Bell addressed his fellow owners, telling them "pro football is like a chain. The league is no stronger than its weakest link. Every year the rich get richer and the poor get poorer. Four teams control the championships [and] because they are successful, they keep attracting the best college players in the open market—which makes them more successful."[6] With that, Bell introduced his proposal for the college draft, where teams would have exclusive rights to college players they selected. Those teams at the bottom of the standings would pick before those at the top, ideally evening out the talent disparity.

The successful teams, including the Bears and Giants, initially balked, but eventually they came around to see the wisdom of Bell's proposal. It was an idea that did nothing less than save the NFL, and it was eventually copied by the other major American sports leagues. Years after he tried to block it in that league meeting, Halas admitted, "The National Football League college draft has been the backbone of the sport and the primary reason it has developed to the game it is today."[7]

True to Bell's luck, when the Eagles had the first overall pick in the very first draft in 1936, their selection—Heisman Trophy winner Jay Berwanger from the University of Chicago—turned down the offer to play pro football and instead went in to private business. The draft would eventually turn the Eagles into champions, but Bell would not be around to see it. After more than a decade of running losing teams on a shoestring budget, Bell jumped at the chance to become NFL Commissioner in 1946.

The commissioner at the time was Elmer Layden, who had drawn the ire of NFL owners for his mishandling of many league issues, including the emergence of a competitive league, the All-America Football Conference. Led by Halas, the owners refused to extend Layden's contract and unanimously voted in Bell. The man who had once saved the league with the player draft would now step up to save it again. "His hiring came at a critical moment," said NFL author Michael MacCambridge. "In the indefatigable presence of Bert Bell, they found their beacon of hope, a man whose unquenchable love for football was so close to blind adoration as to make no difference."[8]

Bell's first order of business was to deal with the threat of the AAFC. When talks of a rival league surfaced in 1945, the NFL and Commissioner Layden were dismissive. "There is nothing for the National Football League to talk about as far as new leagues are concerned," he said stiffly, "until someone gets a football and plays a game."[9] But when the league did get a ball and start playing in 1946, it startled NFL owners—51,000 showed up in Chicago to watch the home team play Cleveland, more than 70,000 came to Cleveland to see the Browns and 49ers, and announced attendance for the league after that first season was 1.25 million. Soon, AAFC owners were making overtures to established NFL players and a bidding war for talent ensued. The NFL responded with a five-year ban for any of its players that jumped leagues.

Almost from the outset, AAFC owners pushed for some kind of merger with the NFL in the long term, and a possible championship game between champions of the two leagues in the short term. With Layden gone, Bell would now have to navigate through the negotiations, not only with the rival AAFC but also with hardline factions in his own league that resisted any conciliation. Representatives from both leagues met in Philadelphia in 1948 to discuss a possible deal, but only on Bell's terms, and "those terms had been made clear to the AAFC—the Browns and 49ers would join the NFL, and the rest of the AAFC would disintegrate and blow away."[10]

Even as both leagues continued to lose money, the AAFC finally gave in. The merger announced in December 1949 was in reality a capitulation. Bell and the NFL got everything they wanted, most especially the Browns and 49ers franchises with the Baltimore Colts thrown in for good measure. Bell would also continue on as commissioner of the league, his contract extended from five years to ten.

Bell put his mark on the expanded NFL of the 1950s, helping it grow "from the point where every dime was counted to a business which rose to challenge even baseball in popularity with America's sports loving public."[11] It was Bell who first recognized the importance of television to the NFL, and it was he who charted its course through some bumpy times. In 1950, each time had the right to cut its own television deal, and in Los Angeles the Rams decided to televise all their games, home and away. "The result was a qualified disaster [as home] attendance dropped by nearly half to 110,000."[12] When the Rams televised only road games the following season, attendance jumped back to 234,000.

Bell convinced owners to give him the power to decide television policy for the entire league, and in 1952 he instituted the NFL's first blackout policy, which allowed the league to prevent showing games within a 75-mile radius of the home stadium. Bell also worked a deal with the Dumont network for the televising of a national game every Sunday, and annually televising the NFL championship game. "Bell had placed the league on a prosperous platform from which it was about to embark on an extended period of expansion, thanks in large part to an enlightened television policy."[13]

Bell had also moved quickly to address the growing problem of gambling in the game. He dealt harshly with Frank Filchock and Merle Hapes, two players offered bribes before the 1946 championship game (see Chapter One). He made annual trips to training camps to address the issue, warning players "don't fool around with strangers. You've got to be careful. Do no betting and give no advice. You're smart enough to know these things."[14]

As the NFL players moved toward unionization and collective bargaining, it was Bell who played an instrumental and decisive role (see Chapter One). After a series of defeats in court, the NFL came to realize that a player's association was inevitable. Bell had to convince reluctant owners to accept the union and eventually the idea of collective bargaining. Whether Bell's support for the players was genuine or simply a matter of convenience remains unknown.

Bell's death on October 11, 1959, has become part of NFL legend. He was attending a game between the Eagles and Steelers—two teams he previously owned—at Philadelphia's Franklin Field, where he once starred as a player for the University of Pennsylvania. Though born into a prominent Main Line family, Bell chose not to sit in the press box, but in the stands. "He hated being from high society," said his biographer Richard Lyons. "He was a football guy. He walked with a swagger and talked out of the side of his mouth."[15]

Almost as if scripted from above, the exact moment the Eagles scored a touchdown to win the game, 28–24, Bell dropped dead from a massive heart attack. "The 65-year old Bell succumbed while doing the thing he loved best," read newspaper reports, "watching a pro game."[16] The implication was that Bell had given everything to pro football, even his own life, to make the NFL successful. "It was a fantastic ending," admitted his son Upton, who was at the game when his father died. "He went probably the way he would have wanted to go. Some people think it's a fantastic ending to a great life."[17]

If Bell was indeed martyred for the cause, it was in some ways a necessary death for the growth of the NFL. The events of fall 1959, most especially Bell's death, signaled a dramatic turn in the fortunes of professional football.

For all the success he brought to the league, there was a sense that Bell was still very much a provincial 19th-century man. He kept the league offices in Philadelphia even as the country's media attention was concentrating on the coasts. There was also a feeling that he didn't take the threat of the American Football League seriously when the AFL announced plans to begin play in 1960. Bell turned down an offer to become AFL commissioner, and even as he talked positively about the new league in public, behind the scenes he was solidly against it. "I really liked Bert Bell," said AFL founder Lamar Hunt. "I really thought we could get along," an idea Hunt later called "one of the more naïve thoughts in the history of American sports."[18]

On January 26, 1960, Lamar Hunt was named president of the American Football League. That same day, after a tortuous meeting of NFL owners, a new commissioner was finally named to replace Bell. Although he was a compromise candidate and chosen almost by accident, the league had stumbled upon the man with a vision who would carry it into the future.

League treasurer Austin Gunsel had served as NFL interim commissioner since Bell's death and was considered the front-runner to earn the job, especially among the older owners who resisted change such as George Preston Marshall in Washington. Meanwhile, a group of younger owners, most of them on the west coast and pushing for reform, backed 49ers legal counsel Marshall Leahy. Thus, it was a divided group of owners that met for their annual meeting in Miami Beach to select Bert Bell's replacement. What promised to be a relatively simple procedure soon became "a nine-day emotional tug-of-war that was part filibuster, part stubborn anger, part tunnel vision, and total confusion."[19]

After the first round of balloting, with eight votes (two-thirds of the twelve owners) needed for election, Leahy had seven votes, Gunsel four, while George Halas and the Bears abstained. As the balloting continued, Halas steadfastly abstained while Colts executive Don Kellett suddenly entered the picture, replacing Gunsel as Leahy's main rival. When the weary owners prepared for a 23rd ballot with no winner in sight, a compromise candidate emerged. There are various stories as to who made the suggestion to the owners—Paul Brown of Cleveland, Art Rooney of Pittsburgh, and Wellington Mara of New York have all been mentioned—but all agree it was a surprising, if not shocking choice. Alvin "Pete" Rozelle was an unknown, very young (33) Rams executive whose primary (and possibly only) selling point was that he wasn't old enough to have made enemies of anyone.

Apprised of the situation, Rozelle bolted to the restroom to avoid reporters, washing his hands some twenty times in a half hour. That's where Colts owner Carroll Rosenbloom found him to announce results of the latest voting. Rozelle had pulled the needed eight votes, with one voting against (San Francisco voted for Leahy) and three abstentions. The NFL had its new commissioner. "I can honestly say I come to you with clean hands," Rozelle told Rosenbloom upon hearing the news.[20]

Neither the vote nor the reaction to it was unanimous. Critics called Rozelle the "Child Czar" or the "Boy Wonder." In its story on the meeting, the *Miami Herald* called him "Pete Roselle." "They finally picked Pete as a compromise because both sides thought they could control him," said Tex Schramm. "But they were wrong. Pete was a lot stronger than any of them realized."[21]

That included Marshall, who wondered what destructive changes the new leader might have in mind. Rozelle had only three years of NFL experience working for the Rams, and before that worked at a public relations firm in San Francisco. Even Rozelle wondered what he had gotten himself into. "Don't worry," Paul Brown told him, "you'll grow into the job."[22] "Almost by sheer luck," wrote sportswriter Jerry Izenberg, "[NFL owners] elected a leader who ... set the pace for every innovation that followed anywhere in America's professional sports."[23]

Rozelle's most immediate challenge was the American Football League, which would begin play that fall. The same owners meeting that elected Rozelle dragged on so long in part because of dissension over expansion. Led by Halas, some owners believed the league had to expand to counter the AFL. Others, including Marshall in Washington and Walter Wolfner with the Chicago Cardinals, believed that adding more teams would devalue their own, especially in terms of television appeal and revenue. "Expansion is a must for the National Football League,"[24] Rozelle declared right after his election, and that seemed to settle the issue. Owners voted to admit Dallas to begin play immediately in 1960, followed by the Minnesota Vikings in 1961.

The issue reflected the deep divisions between the owners, particularly Halas and Wolfner, both fighting over the city of Chicago. The Bears had long dominated the city in terms of money, success, and popularity, but Halas would seemingly not be satisfied until he had run the poor-cousin Cardinals out of town. At one time or another, each owner had offered the other hundreds of thousands of dollars to leave, but both men stubbornly refused. Rozelle realized something would have to be done, and he maneuvered the Cardinals toward St. Louis, which not only solved the Halas–Wolfner feud, but also shut off that territory for the AFL. When Wolfner balked at the $500,000 cost to move, Rozelle found an anonymous owner who was willing to pay the cost for the good of the league.

Young, inexperienced Pete Rozelle (center) is congratulated as the new NFL commissioner in January 1960. Rozelle was not the first choice of NFL leadership, including Bears owner George Halas (far left), Eagles president Frank McNamee (second from left), Redskins owner George Preston Marshall (second from right) and Eagles executive Joe Donahue (far right), but he soon led the league to unprecedented power and popularity. *AP Photos/ Harold Valentine.*

That owner, of course, turned out to be George Halas. "With little publicity and great skill, Rozelle pulled off a major triumph. The commissioner had brilliantly put a ribbon around the entire package with that master stroke."[25] Halas got Chicago to himself, Wolfner got a nice market he didn't have to share, plus moving expenses, and the league was able to blunt the encroachment of the AFL. "[Rozelle] was able to accomplish things because he was able to bring diverse groups of egotistical, strong-minded owners and managers together," said Tex Schramm, "and do things that were necessary to be done for the betterment of the league."[26]

There was no more egotistical or strong-minded owner in the

league than George Preston Marshall of the Redskins. Marshall had many visionary qualities that contributed to the success of the league, but he was also an unapologetic racist. At the time, Washington was the southernmost team in the NFL and the only one without a black player. "We'll start signing negroes," he once famously said, "when the Harlem Globetrotters start signing whites."[27] Longtime Washington sportswriter Shirley Povich responded by taunting Marshall in print. Povich often referred to the team colors as "burgundy, gold and Caucasian," and after Cleveland running back Jim Brown had a big day against Washington, he wrote, "Jim Brown integrated the Redskins' end zone three times yesterday."[28]

Despite Povich's entreaties, and picketing by civil rights groups like the NAACP and CORE, Marshall remained adamant. If anyone realized the importance of image it was the former public relations man Rozelle, and he worked quickly. Rozelle intervened to prevent segregated seating at a preseason game in Roanoke, Virginia, right in Marshall's backyard. He then met with Marshall in August 1961, urging him to draft black players, which Marshall promised to do for the following season.

Pressured by Rozelle, and the federal government, which owned the land for the Redskins' new stadium, Marshall finally backed down. The team had three black players on its roster in 1962, including Bobby Mitchell, who led the league in catches and receiving yards. "Rozelle's powers of persuasion would be hard to overstate," wrote the *Washington Post*. "In one of his keenest accomplishments, Rozelle got Marshall to line up with the rest of the league."[29]

Marshall's attitude had been driven largely by his own personal racism, but there was also reasoning behind it. He had promoted the Redskins as the "Team of the South," building a radio and television network of nearly 100 stations that carried games down into the Carolinas and Georgia, and west into Tennessee, Arkansas, and Kentucky. "We take most of our players out of Southern colleges and are trying to appeal to Southern people," Marshall said. "Those colleges don't have any Negro players."[30] At the time, each NFL team cut its own broadcast deals, and Marshall certainly wanted to protect his monopoly on NFL football in the south.

Rozelle knew that such regional thinking was not going to work in his vision of the new NFL. In June 1960, the AFL had signed a deal with ABC television that pooled the television revenue and distributed it evenly to all the teams. Rozelle wanted something similar for the NFL and in 1961 he signed a two-year deal with CBS that would pay the league $9.3 million and split the revenue among league teams. But those individual television stations that had already signed a deal with

NFL teams cried foul and filed a lawsuit charging the league with violating the Sherman Anti-Trust Act. (The AFL did not face antitrust scrutiny because as a new league there were no television contracts already in place that could be legally challenged.)

Rozelle's solution showcased perhaps his greatest skill: glad-handing, arm-twisting, and working behind the scenes to eventually get what he felt was best for the league. With the help of the NFL's well-connected owners, it took Rozelle only three months of lobbying to get a bill passed. The Sports Broadcasting Act of 1961 exempted the NFL (and other major sports) from anti-trust legislation and allowed teams to engage in revenue sharing. Before the SBA, the New York Giants were making $350,000 from their television deal while the Packers could only get $35,000 in the smaller Green Bay market. After the SBA, Rozelle went back to CBS and cut a deal worth $14.1 million that the teams would share equally. "What Pete Rozelle did with the television receipts," said Vince Lombardi, "probably saved football in Green Bay."[31]

Revenue sharing aside, Rozelle had a genius for understanding the entertainment value of television. Yes, the SBA ended the in-fighting among teams and owners, but more importantly it put the NFL on a national stage. Rozelle understood that if football was ever going to supplant baseball as the most popular sport in America, it would have to succeed as entertainment. And in the 1960s, the proving ground for entertainment was television.

No one understood that better than Pete Rozelle, whether it was supporting the birth and success of *Monday Night Football* or using television to reach new audiences. "He wanted us to find more ways to engage existing NFL fans and attract new ones," said longtime assistant Joe Browne. "Our games were on all three networks at the time and he convinced the TV execs to promote those games during weekday programming that had mostly female viewership. It helped us grow our fan base among women."[32]

Rozelle's legislative skills were also put to the test in 1966 when the NFL and AFL began merger talks. U.S. Congressman Emanuel Celler of New York was dead set against the merger and had it stalled in committee. Rozelle performed an end run by going through Louisiana congressman Hale Boggs, who got the pending merger moved to a senate committee chaired by another Louisiana politician, Senator Russell Long. As the bill came up for vote, Rozelle told Boggs, "Hale, I don't know how to thank you enough for what you are doing." Boggs replied, "What do you mean, you don't know how to thank me? New Orleans gets an immediate franchise in the NFL. Isn't that our deal?"[33] Eleven days after the approval of the NFL–AFL merger, Rozelle came to New Orleans to announce the city had received an NFL franchise.

By 1963, Rozelle had indeed "grown into the job" as Paul Brown had suggested. Two crises would threaten his leadership that year, but in the end he navigated the challenges and firmly established himself as the most powerful and dynamic leader in professional sports.

The first crisis came with the shocking revelation of an extraordinary gambling problem in the NFL. Two players were found to have made bets on their own teams, but these were not just any two players. Paul Hornung of the Packers and Alex Karras of the Lions were two of the league's best and most recognizable faces. Hornung, the "Golden Boy," had just led Green Bay to back-to-back NFL titles as a runner, pass catcher, and kicker, and two years before had been named the league's player of the year.

Here was a supreme test of wills for Rozelle. The league had suspended Frank Filchock and Merle Hapes before the 1946 NFL title game for considering bribes, but neither of those players had the star power of Hornung. To suspend Hornung meant removing one of the most popular players in the league and ran the risk of a fan backlash. To not suspend him would damage the NFL's credibility and make it seem weak.

Rozelle conducted an investigation, which included 52 players on eight on the league's 14 teams. On April 17, 1963, he announced his decision—an indefinite suspension for Hornung and Karras, fines for assorted players on the Lions who had bet on games, and another fine for the Lions organization for withholding a police report of alleged wrongdoing. All the players involved, except for Karras, admitted to the charges the investigation uncovered. "These investigations have disclosed no evidence of criminal wrongdoing," said Rozelle, "but [the league] believes them to be in the best interests of the game, the players and the fans."[34]

While the Packers and Hornung were contrite—the player expressing regret about how the news would affect his mother—Karras was defiant. "I haven't done anything that I am ashamed of and I am not guilty of anything," he told reporters upon hearing of the suspension, adding dramatically, "I don't know what I'll do if my family is out of food."[35] Karras threatened legal action and spent his year of suspension as a pro wrestler. He never did admit guilt or forgive Rozelle, which some blame for his exclusion from the Hall of Fame.

Rozelle now faced pressure from Karras and increasingly from NFL fans who felt the punishment did not fit the crime. "Indefinite suspension" suggested maybe a year or maybe forever. "Cab drivers and sportswriters and fellow athletes and ladies in elevators hailed [Hornung] and told him how Pete Rozelle ought to be strung up by his strait laces," wrote John Underwood in *Sports Illustrated*. "At a banquet in Worcester, Mass. he was given a hero's ovation. 'Everywhere I went the people were behind me,'" said Hornung.[36]

Rozelle did not back down. "The decision to suspend Hornung and Karras was mine alone," he said almost defiantly, "and it had to be done."[37] Rozelle found it harder to break news of the suspension to Lombardi than he did Hornung, sitting down with the Packer coach for four hours sipping scotch in a local bar. But it was the support of Lombardi, and other players, coaches, and sportswriters, that solidified Rozelle's position. "I am shocked and hurt," said Lombardi, "however, there was a definite violation of the player contract and constitution and bylaws of this league in regard to gambling. The commissioner had no other alternative."[38]

That seemed to be the consensus—Rozelle had stuck out his neck and made a tough decision, but he did so courageously in order to prevent a bad problem from becoming much worse. "The greatest benefit is the assurance that the integrity of the sport must and will be maintained," wrote Lloyd Larson in the *Milwaukee Sentinel*. "Rozelle and responsible owners obviously are willing to let the chips fall where they may. The crackdown is stern [and a] fair warning to players, coaches and club officials."[39]

Sports Illustrated went even further, naming Rozelle its Sportsman of the Year for 1963. "The men of the NFL have one plan of their own," the magazine observed, "which can be stated in two words: 'Keep Pete.' No man was more valuable to sport in 1963. No sport is in more competent hands for the years to come."[40] "Pete Rozelle's handling of the investigations," said Tex Schramm, "was the thing that made everybody accept him as commissioner and no longer a boy playing the part. He gained once and for all everybody's complete respect."[41]

Rozelle called the Hornung-Karras suspension the most difficult decision of his career, but the one that caused the most controversy came just a few months later. The emotional aftershocks of President Kennedy's assassination on November 22, 1963, virtually paralyzed the country. Partly from shock, and partly in tribute to the fallen president, all across America stores, movie theaters and concerts shut down. The American Football League announced its games that Sunday would not be played, and the Army–Navy game scheduled for Saturday was postponed. No one seemed to be in the mood for any type of public performance.

Except for the National Football League.

Once Rozelle got word of the assassination on Friday afternoon, he wanted to confer with an old college friend, Pierre Salinger, the White House press secretary. It was no easy task, as Salinger was on a diplomatic flight over the Pacific, now rerouted back to Washington. When the two finally did talk, Salinger encouraged Rozelle to play the games. "Jack would have wanted you to play," he told Rozelle. That weighed heavily on Rozelle, and when he announced the league would play its full schedule, his statement read in part, "It has been traditional in sports for athletes to perform in times of great personal tragedy. Football was Mr. Kennedy's game. He thrived on competition."[42] Rozelle said he did not believe playing the games would be disrespectful and added that perhaps the games would provide needed emotional diversion.

Almost the entire nation disagreed with him, including most of the NFL players and coaches who had no choice but to play. In Philadelphia, Eagles owner Frank McNamee announced he would miss his first home game in 15 years, even as Mayor James Tate tried unsuccessfully to get a court order to stop the game. Dallas players, who were finishing a practice just a few miles from the scene at the time of the assassination, would require extra security for their game in Cleveland. Even as coach Tom Landry was diagramming on a blackboard before the game, the team learned that Jack Ruby had gunned down the accused assassin, Lee Harvey Oswald, on live television.

For its part, CBS television decided not to show any of the games, opting instead to continue its coverage of the assassination and its aftermath. By Sunday, two days after the shooting, national indignation against Rozelle had not diminished. In the *New York Times*, Red Smith said of the decision to hold the games, "For that exercise in tasteless stupidity there is neither excuse nor defense, as nothing could illustrate more clearly than the banal, empty phrases with which Rozelle sought to justify the decision."[43]

There is some evidence to suggest that Rozelle knew what he was doing. The game between the Cardinals and Giants in New York, with Rozelle in the stands brooding over his decision, attracted 66,992 fans. "Some came, they said, reluctantly," Dick Young wrote in the *New York Daily News*, "[and] some came with a feeling of complete justification."[44] But they did come. Sellouts were reported in Philadelphia for the Redskins and Eagles, and in Milwaukee for the Packers and 49ers. Attendance across the league that Sunday would turn out to be higher than the NFL average for the season.

Even so, Rozelle forever regretted his decision and called it the biggest mistake he ever made as commissioner. But the passage of time has cast Rozelle in a more favorable light. Looking back, it is possible to appreciate the difficulty of the decision, even if one does not agree with the decision itself. "I felt badly over all the criticism Pete took because I believe he did the absolute right thing," said the Giants' Frank Gifford. "I played that Sunday in New York, and I believe, at least in this city, it got us moving again."[45]

In 1963, Rozelle was still too popular and too powerful to let the Kennedy decision diminish his star. By the end of the decade, in addition to all his other accomplishments, he moved league offices from Philadelphia to New York, steered the NFL through its battle with the AFL and was instrumental in building up the league pension fund. Rozelle also spent several years convincing NFL owners to think beyond Sunday afternoon football, which culminated in 1970 with the success of *Monday Night Football*. "I firmly believe that when the final history of the National Football League is written, the all-time hero of the NFL, the man who contributed the most to changing America's Sunday afternoon watching habits, is Pete Rozelle," said Edwin Pope in the *Miami Herald*.[46]

Rozelle spent much of the 1970s as the unquestioned leader of the most powerful sports organization in America and the prototype of the emerging CEO-model of the modern sports commissioner. But as the sports landscape continued to evolve, Rozelle found his power waning, and shifting into the hands of the players and owners he had successfully controlled for so long. Writing about commercialism and professionalism in ancient sport, E. Norman Gardiner said, "The very popularity of athletics was their undoing."[47] The popularity of the NFL, and the money that came with it, would be Rozelle's undoing as well.

As more and more money poured in to the league from television contracts, the players began to demand more of it. Salaries escalated, but so too did player militancy. Players temporarily refused to report to training camps in 1970 and 1974, but by far the most damaging work stoppage was the 1982 strike that lasted 57 days, forced cancellation of seven weeks of the season, and cost the league $200 million. Rozelle was highly criticized for not being able to broker a quick deal, and as the strike dragged and he looked on somewhat helplessly, Rozelle came to be viewed by many as a football emperor with no clothes on. "I quit smoking and then I started again," he lamented. "That, of course, is the stress from the problems we have. It's something that won't go away."[48]

Another problem that would not go away was Raiders boss Al Davis. Rozelle began his tenure as commissioner with the ability to control NFL owners through counsel, compromise, and sometimes coercion. But Davis was altogether a different matter. His distrust of Rozelle, and a hatred for the established order that bordered on paranoia, went back to his combative days as commissioner of the AFL. It was Davis who proposed all-out war with the NFL by signing the league's stars to future AFL contracts, and it was Davis who opposed the merger in 1966, preferring to fight it out to the death. "Al's exit strategy was not a merger," said his coach of the Raiders, John Madden. "Al's exit strategy was to take them on, become their equals, and then become better than them."[49]

That attitude prevailed even after the merger, and Davis would become an increasingly irritating burr under Rozelle's saddle. He fought constantly with the commissioner's office, and while he always insisted everything he did was in the best interest of the league, there was also a sense of personal vendetta. "[He had a] resentment of the NFL," said football author Michael MacCambridge, "and his increasing sense of paranoia over the league being 'out to get' the Raiders, dated at least as far back as 1970."[50]

For his part, Rozelle liked to say he considered Davis "like a charming rogue,"[51] but that opinion changed as Davis began to move his disputes from NFL offices to the court system. It began in 1976 when Rozelle had to appear in court as part of a dispute between the Raiders and Steelers over dirty play. A decade later, after Davis ignored a unanimous vote by league owners and announced his intention to move the Raiders from Oakland to Los Angeles, Rozelle said, "In this instance, he's become outlaw."[52]

The ensuing trial in U.S. District Court in Los Angeles, called by some "possibly the most devastating court action in the league's history,"[53] took three years just to get to court and seemed to drain the life from Rozelle. He appeared to age drastically during the ordeal, and the ultimate verdict in the Raiders' favor, after suits and countersuits, only further diminished his stature. "I have said before that when I came to a point where this ceased being fun," Rozelle had said during the players' strike in 1982, "I might consider resigning."[54] Now, with the fun of the job seemingly all drained away, that moment seemed close at hand.

He lasted until 1989, when he announced his retirement after 29 years as commissioner, and almost immediately the plaudits rained down. Rozelle was seen as "forward-thinking," "revolutionary," and "ground-breaking." Cooper Rollow wrote in the *Chicago Tribune* that Rozelle had "stamped himself with immortality [and] became the most competent and admired sports commissioner since Kenesaw Mountain Landis of baseball legend."[55]

When Bert Bell died in October 1959 the National Football League was a fairly solid, if unspectacular, organization that still lagged behind baseball in the hearts of the American sports public. When Rozelle retired forty years later, the NFL was unarguably the most successful, powerful, and compelling sports empire in the country, if not the world. Of all the tributes and eulogies for Pete Rozelle, former quarterback and Congressman Jack Kemp may have had the best. "He was a man of vision; boy, did he have vision," Kemp said. "Could he see things the rest of us could not see."[56]

Nine

By the Numbers

Considering how disastrously the NFL's first venture went with the Dallas Texans (see Chapter One), it raised more than a few eyebrows when the league decided to return to the city with an expansion team in 1960. But when the American Football League began play that same year, and had a team in Dallas (also named the Texans), the NFL felt it had no choice. "This is an act of war," AFL Commissioner Joe Foss said when the NFL announced its plans. "An out-and-out attempt to put the AFL team in Dallas out of business. We will go to court or Congress to prevent them from killing off the Dallas team."[1]

No such thing happened, of course, in part because the AFL had similarly invaded NFL territory by placing teams in New York, Los Angeles, and the San Francisco Bay area. Texas oil millionaire Clint Murchison, Jr., owned the Dallas NFL franchise, which would compete directly with the AFL Texans and their multimillionaire oil owner, Lamar Hunt.

While Hunt was more directly involved in running his franchise, Murchison stayed behind the scenes and delegated operations to Tex Schramm, a former television executive with CBS who also had experience in the Rams front office. Schramm became the general manager and his first order of duty was to find a name for the team. The first choice was Steers, but Schramm didn't like the idea of naming the team after a castrated bull. Then came the Rangers, in honor of the state's famous law enforcement group, but a local minor league baseball team also had that name. To avoid confusion, Schramm finally settled on Cowboys.

As the Texans and Cowboys searched for a coach, they both zeroed in on the same man. The candidate had all the right credentials—a Texas native, a star halfback for the University of Texas, a pilot in World War II who had flown 30 missions over Europe, a man of solid Christian faith, and an NFL veteran who had survived for seven years as a defensive back with the Giants despite underwhelming physical talents.

But what made Thomas Wade Landry especially attractive was his growing reputation as a coaching genius, especially on defense.

It started during Landry's playing days, when he used film study to compensate for lack of size and speed. "The Rams used to have a sprinter named Bobby Boyd," said Dick Nolan, who played in the defensive backfield with Landry and later coached with him in Dallas. "The guy could fly and would just take off and run past the defensive back. Not Tom. Tom would study the guy thoroughly and give him fits."[2]

Eventually, Landry became a player-coach and finally just an assistant coach in charge of the defense. At the time, most teams were playing the 6-1 defense—six defensive linemen with one linebacker. Giants coach Steve Owen refined that into the "umbrella," where the two outside lineman would sometimes fan out to cover backs and passes. Landry took that even further and created the modern 4-3 that is still used today. In 1950, when the Browns ran roughshod over the league in winning the NFL title, they averaged 29 points a game against every team but the Giants. Against New York and Landry's defense, the Browns scored zero, eight, and 13 points in three games, and won a special playoff game by a score of 8-3.

Perhaps the greatest testament to Landry's defense came in the near championship year of 1958. Again the Giants played the Browns three times, and again the New York defense under Landry dominated. The Giants won all three games, including a special playoff game to determine the Eastern Conference championship in which New York shut out Cleveland, 10-0. In that game, the Giants held Browns star Jim Brown, who had led the league in rushing with 1,527 yards, to eight yards on seven carries and limited Cleveland to 86 yards of total offense. "Only one man could have done that to us," said Browns lineman and kicker Lou Groza. "Tom Landry."[3] After the game when Giants lineman Andy Robustelli handed him the game ball, Landry called it one of his proudest moments in sports.

When the Colts and Giants met again in 1959 for the NFL championship, Landry's defense held Johnny Unitas and Baltimore to a single touchdown through the first three quarters before tiring in a 31-16 loss. Landry could not have known that during the game, and others that season, he had been scouted by Tex Schramm. "[I] went to their games and was surprised by what I saw," said Schramm. "Here was an assistant coach—a defensive coach—who was looked upon by his players as almost a god. They were the best defensive club in the league for several years, and Tom Landry was the reason."[4]

Landry was thinking of leaving football and would only stay if he could get a head coaching job in Texas. To keep him away from Lamar

Hunt and the Texans, and from Bud Adams and the Houston Oilers who also expressed interest, Schramm had to give Landry much of the same control that Lombardi had in Green Bay. The new coach would be in charge of drafting, training, coaching, and evaluating the players—everything except their contracts, which Schramm would handle. Landry signed a five-year deal that averaged $34,500 a year, and at 35 became the youngest coach in the league. A few months earlier, Schramm signed a former baby photographer, Gil Brandt, to be his director of scouting.

In the fall of 1959, as Schramm was putting together the pieces of the Steers/Rangers/Cowboys, a young immigrant from Uttar Pradesh in northern India arrived in Cleveland to begin a teaching fellowship at the Case Institute of Technology (now Case Western Reserve University). A. Salam Qureishi was an expert in mathematics, statistics, and data analysis, and was soon hired by International Business Machines (IBM) to work with their computers. Qureishi knew a great deal about soccer and cricket, a little bit about baseball, and absolutely nothing about American football. "I thought football was about people piling on people," he said.[5]

He also struggled with the English language, and in an era of hard-drinking, harder-partying football players, the small, bookish Qureishi did not smoke, drink, or swear. It was the unlikeliest of marriages—the Cowboys and the Indian—but together with Landry, Brandt, and Schramm, Qureishi would help create a dynasty and launch the NFL into the future.

As Landry began assembling this first Cowboys team, his immediate problem was talent acquisition. Dallas was not even allowed to take part in the 1960 NFL draft and had to build its roster with leftovers from other teams in the league. Those teams could protect their best players, with the Cowboys selecting the unprotected players at the bottom of their rosters. Although that process brought to Dallas solid players in linebacker Jerry Tubbs and receiver Frank Clarke, the rest of the lot was eminently forgettable and a main reason the Cowboys went 0–11–1 in their first season.

Landry, Brandt, and Schramm decided to build their team through the draft, but even that was an inexact science. Scouting a player was difficult and imprecise, and teams often made their picks based on newspaper and magazine articles, or on performances in a bowl game. As a classic example, the Lions made USC quarterback Doyle Nave their number one pick in 1940 after the fourth-stringer came off the bench to help the Trojans beat Duke in the Rose Bowl. Nave was the sixth overall pick of the draft, but never played a down in the NFL. By contrast, the

Colts took a flyer on Raymond Berry in the 20th round of the 1954 draft, and he went on to the Hall of Fame. "I decided that I would have to find an objective method of deciding on the worth of a football player," said Schramm. "We had to find a way to judge players without emotion."[6]

Enter A. Salam Qureishi.

Schramm went to IBM with his problem and that eventually led to Qureishi. They were the oddest of odd couples—the blustery Texan who spent his life in football and the shy Indian with the thick accent who knew nothing about the game. "With my heavy Indian accent and his Texas accent, we understood each other poorly at first," admitted Qureishi. "Somehow, we hit it off after a few initial missteps."[7]

The first thing Schramm and Qureishi had to do was define and quantify what it meant to be a good football player. It wasn't enough to measure weight, height, and speed; all of those were physically measurable. Qureishi and Schramm came up with five intangibles—character, quickness and body control, competitiveness, mental alertness, and strength and explosiveness. Scouts and coaches also had to learn how to measure those characteristics so that the numbers entered in the computer would be the same no matter who did the evaluation.

The new emphasis led the Cowboys to find players where no one else was even looking. This included small colleges, like Ft. Valley State, which contributed Hall of Fame lineman Rayfield Wright, and Florida A&M, which had Olympic gold medal sprinter Bob Hayes. "Other clubs thought the Cowboys were crazy to pick Hayes," said NFL author Joe Patoski. "Even though he was a high profile track-and-field Olympic athlete, he had never really played football before and went to a small, obscure black college better known for its marching band."[8] All Hayes did as a receiver was revolutionize the league with his speed, force the invention of the zone defense, and make the Hall of Fame.

The Cowboys computer also found some players who did not even play college football. Receiver Pete Gent and defensive back Cornell Green played basketball instead. "One of the things I did was go after great athletes," said Schramm. "Gil Brandt knew as many basketball coaches as football coaches, and he would ask them, 'Who do you see who won't make it in the NBA but who's a hell of an athlete?'"[9] Schramm admits it was a hit-or-miss system. The Cowboys hit with Green and Gent, but drafted Lou Hudson, Pat Riley, and John Havlicek, all of whom went on to star in the NBA.

Qureishi and the Cowboys tinkered with the system and gave it a trial run with a mock NFL draft in 1964. The computer spit out the names of Joe Namath, Dick Butkus, Gale Sayers, and Fred Biletnikoff, all of whom made the Hall of Fame. When the actual draft came along,

Tucker Frederickson was taken number one overall by the Giants, followed by Ken Willard with San Francisco. While Sayers, Butkus, and Namath were all first-round selections, Biletnikoff was not drafted until the third round.

Once they got it up and running, Qureishi and Schramm's computer model built the Cowboys into one of the most successful sports dynasties in history. Hayes, Mel Renfro, Jethro Pugh, and Walt Garrison were some of the early fruits, and in 1964 alone the Cowboys picked three future Hall of Famers—Bob Hayes, Mel Renfro, and Roger Staubach. Dallas delayed the draft six hours waiting to get medical reports on Renfro (there was no "on the clock" back then), prompting Packer coach Vince Lombardi to wander over to the draft table of the Cowboys. "What happened," he asked Schramm and Brandt. "Did your computer break down?"[10]

But when those Dallas stars began to age, it was the computer that led Dallas to another crop of great players—Harvey Martin, Randy White, and Ed "Too Tall" Jones. The result was 20 consecutive winning seasons and 18 playoff appearances in 19 seasons—an NFL record. "We missed on quite a few picks," said Brandt, "but so did a lot of teams in those days. But when we hit, we hit big."[11]

Even with the contributions of Schramm, Qureishi, and Brandt, the one who turned the numbers into results was Tom Landry. If ever one coach was perfectly suited for the introduction of computer analysis into the NFL, it was the man whom sportswriters often called "Old Computer Face."[12] Actually, that may be one of the kindest descriptions his critics had of Landry. Running back Duane Thomas famously called his own coach a "plastic man."[13]

If Qureishi and Brandt introduced computerization into scouting, then it can be safely said that Tom Landry introduced it into the coaching profession.

Up through the 1950s, most coaches were of the Knute Rockne mold, emphasizing inspiration and motivation. The pregame and halftime pep talks were staples of this approach, and were used with success by men like Vince Lombardi. Lombardi certainly understood strategy, and demanded execution, but essentially his approach was an emotional one designed to inspire hate, fear, love and ideally, some combination of them all. "Some people try to find things in this game or put things into it which don't exist," Lombardi said in a not-so-veiled swipe at Landry. "Football is two things. It's blocking and tackling. I don't care anything about formations or new offenses or tricks on defenses."[14]

Lombardi made those comments after the Packers destroyed the Giants, 37–0, to win the NFL championship in 1961. When Green Bay went on to win four more titles under Lombardi, including the first two Super Bowls, the other teams in the league took notice. The road to success, they nodded in agreement, was a fundamental one. It was a brutal, basic straight line from point A to the end zone.

Tom Landry did not agree.

"The Green Bay system of offense," he said, "we call it the basic system, was that you were going to run the power sweep regardless of what the other team put up against you. So Lombardi had to develop the players to an emotional pitch; the Packers had to stay very emotionally high to win. Once Lombardi's players slipped down, they had problems."[15]

The problem, as Landry saw it, was that it was difficult if not impossible to maintain that emotional peak play after play, game after game, and year after year. If one could remove the emotion from execution, it would eliminate the inconsistency that so often led to defeat. As Landry refined this approach in the following years, it came to be known as "the system."

First and foremost, Landry's system was based on his near encyclopedic knowledge of schemes and formations. It was Landry who refined the basic 4–3 defense, and then attacked it on offense by creating multiple formations and shifts. He then counter attacked his own offense by creating the "flex" defense, with defenders staggered off the line of scrimmage instead of head up over the offensive lineman. "[The flex] developed Doomsday I, it developed Doomsday II, two of the greatest defenses in NFL history," said Cowboys receiver Drew Pearson. "The NFL is such a me-too league, a copycat league, but nobody copied the flex despite its success, because of one simple reason: nobody could teach it."[16] "The term genius gets overused in football," noted NFL Films, "but Tom Landry was a gridiron savant, a brilliant innovator who unlike any coach in the modern era, changed the way football is played on offense and defense."[17]

Landry emphasized reading keys, recognition, and staying in assigned gaps, which often challenged a player's basic instinct to follow the ball and chase down the ball carrier. Defensive back Dick Nolan once questioned something Landry had written on the blackboard. "Tom," he said, "what if I commit myself that completely and the wingback isn't there?" Landry looked at Nolan and without changing his expression said, "He will be."[18]

Don Meredith, who quarterbacked the Cowboys during the difficult early years, said, "I've learned one thing: Tom is right. You get tired of a guy being so right so often, but that's the way it is. The hardest thing to do with Tom's system is believe it."[19]

Perhaps no one player chafed under Landry's system more than

Meredith, a fun loving, free wheeling Texas kid who often came into the huddle singing country and western songs. Landry needed a quarterback who studied and took his position seriously; Meredith needed a coach who would give him the attention and adulation his insecurity so desperately needed. Neither got what they wanted. "Meredith finally came to believe that Landry was a football genius," wrote Steve Perkins, who covered the team for the *Dallas Times Herald*. "That is, he believed it intellectually. He never believed it viscerally, and this essential gap probably cost the Cowboys a couple of championships."[20]

The fact that the Cowboys eventually became winners under Meredith was as much a testimony to the quarterback's courage and leadership as it was to Landry's system. "We would have done anything for him," offensive guard Jim Boeke said of Meredith. "Anything!"[21] Meredith endured countless beatings—from the press as well as opposing players—and often played when he should be have been in a hospital. Newspaper reporters, both in Dallas and around the league, labeled him a loser for what they perceived as Meredith's failures in big games. It left deep emotional scars that contributed to Meredith's early retirement in 1969 at the age of just 31.

When he went to Landry to announce his retirement, Meredith wanted his coach to talk him out of it; to tell him how badly the team needed him. "I went into Tom's office with tears in my eyes," said Meredith, "halfway hoping he would talk me out of quitting."[22] Instead, Landry said Meredith was making the right decision. Landry had analyzed the situation, crunched the numbers, and with a younger, healthier Craig Morton waiting in the wings, decided Meredith's retirement made sense. It was simply not in his emotional makeup to do otherwise.

That cool, analytical efficiency came to symbolize the Cowboys in general and Landry in particular. He was labeled as sanctimonious (because of his willingness to share his Christian faith), stuffy (perhaps because of his habit of coaching in coat, tie and fedora), and unfeeling. That perception filtered down to the team, which was often viewed as cold and mechanical. When the team reached championship caliber in the mid–1960s, it set the stage for a showdown with Vince Lombardi's Packers—one team built with love and character, and the other seemingly connected by circuits and computer wires.

Green Bay beat Dallas in two dramatic NFL championship games in 1966 and 1967, but it was how the games ended that defined the teams. Dallas had a chance to tie the 1966 game, but failed to score from the two-yard line in the waning moments. A year later, on a frozen field that came to be known as the Ice Bowl, Green Bay was in the same situation and won on a Bart Starr quarterback sneak with just seconds to play.

Those heroic wins reinforced the notion that Lombardi's way of doing things was somehow better. The Packers were the John Henry of the NFL, steel driving their way to victory with flesh and blood over the power of machines and computers. "For the Packers, the Ice Bowl was the validation of everything they had learned from Lombardi," wrote the *Milwaukee Journal Sentinel*, "everything the great coach espoused and represented, a victory as hard-fought and as sweet as any they'd ever known or would know."[23]

The failure of Landry and the Cowboys, not just to Green Bay but also to inferior Cleveland teams in successive playoff embarrassments, suggested the organization did not have the heart to become a champion. "People began to wonder as the Cowboys were always one heartbeat away from the ultimate triumph," wrote sportswriter Jim Murray. "It was the best team in the league, but it kept getting beat by the Cleveland Browns. The Packers kept beating it, too, on things like 'second effort' and 'love' and all the things you couldn't find in the Cowboys' playbook."[24]

Landry usually shrugged off such comments, but in private admitted he thought them unfair. "Listen," he once said with a rare edge in his voice, "none of the Cowboys' troubles have been because I was unemotional. In 1966 we were like the Mets [in 1969]. We might have pulled it off, beaten Green Bay, but we probably wouldn't have done it the next year. We weren't mature and experienced enough yet to win year after year."[25]

In actuality, it may have been an emotional moment that turned around the entire Cowboys organization. In 1965, Landry had yet to have a winning season and there were calls for his firing. After a mid-season loss to Pittsburgh that dropped Dallas to 2–5, the supposedly detached coach broke down in the locker room while addressing the team. "We were touched," said defensive tackle Bob Lilly. "Very deeply. I think it humbled all of us. From that point on we were much more attentive and much more diligent. We saw a real man up there."[26] Dallas then won five straight and qualified for the runner-up "Playoff Bowl," before starting a string of eight straight playoff seasons.

Only rarely did Landry let the emotions show through as they did in Pittsburgh. In one training camp, the Cowboys had a linebacker named Ken Hutcherson. He was by almost all accounts, Landry's idea of the perfect player—a big hitter, dedicated, and a Christian. But he just didn't have all the physical tools to play in the NFL. "This is the toughest part of the business," he told the team when he released Hutcherson. "I had to cut a fine young man, a good friend, a Christian."[27] And once more, "Old Computer Face" began to cry.

But the bottom line is that Landry *did* cut Ken Hutcherson.[28] He cut him because Landry's ultimate faith was rooted in the system and not necessarily in the men who made it work. "It wasn't as if real people were performing it," Cowboys linebacker Thomas "Hollywood" Henderson once said of Landry's flex defense. "As much as we were recognized personally we could have been just big, strong marionettes. [Landry] seemed so emotionless, so untouchable, so far from the rest of us."[29]

Like Meredith, like Henderson, the players needed affirmation and validation. But Landry's approach—that belief that the system was so foolproof that it didn't matter who plugged into what position—possibly cost the Cowboys at least a few more championships. Coming off four straight playoff disappointments in 1970, and now with the label of the team that "Can't Win the Big One," Dallas desperately needed some Lombardi-style motivation. Instead, Landry responded with more computer analysis and more performance evaluations; those players that didn't measure up to expectations, like All Pro receiver Bob Hayes, were benched.

Predictably, the 1970 season teetered on disaster. After a humiliating 38–0 loss to the Cardinals on *Monday Night Football*, the Cowboys stood at 5–4 and seemingly out of the division race. "Tom felt he had to put the season on the shelf," said defensive back Mel Renfro. "He felt we just couldn't come back from that. Tom was a statistics and numbers guy, and the statistics and numbers said, 'Hey, you guys, it's over.'"[30]

Dallas then won seven straight games and made the Super Bowl for the first time. To listen to the Cowboys front office, at least according to their highlight film produced that year by NFL Films, the turnaround came because Landry made some technical adjustments to simplify the Dallas offense. It's much closer to the truth to say that the players essentially ignored Landry and the other coaches, and saved the season on their own. Linebacker Lee Roy Jordan told his teammates, "The coaches aren't pulling for us. They've already given up. We are going to do it for us, not for somebody else, not for the coaches or the fans or Tex or anyone else. We're going to do it for *us*."[31] Of course, the Cowboys had to lose another championship game in crushing fashion, as the Colts made a last-second kick to win Super Bowl V, 16–13.

If any one season or moment reflected Tom Landry's commitment to the system, it was the quarterback battle between Craig Morton and Roger Staubach in 1971. Both were highly skilled players who deserved to start, but Landry couldn't decide which one to play. Early in the season he alternated them, starting Morton one game and then Staubach the next. Finally, Landry came up with perhaps the biggest blunder of his coaching career—he decided to alternative them every play in a game against the Bears. "I think he was saying to himself, 'These are just two people,'" said Staubach. "They can pass and hand off. The system is fine.' And if you had two robots, yes, it *would* work."[32]

The move backfired: Chicago upset Dallas, 23–19, and the team was further split as to which quarterback should play. "As far as the offensive linemen are concerned, we need a clear-cut quarterback," said offensive tackle Ralph Neely. "We need to know who's back there, so we'll know his tendencies. When you have a 260-pounder trying to run you over, you need to know the guy you're protecting, not wonder who's back there."[33] When sportswriters pressed Neely as to his preference, he said bluntly, "Either damn one. At this point, I don't care."[34]

In the face of mounting criticism from fans, the press and his own players, Landry had to make a decision. But even in defeat, he *still* believed his alternating system would work. "There's nothing wrong with the two-quarterback system," he said after the Chicago game. "It would have worked today if we hadn't made so many mistakes."[35] Staubach was the ultimate choice, and all he did was lead the Cowboys to two Super Bowl wins on his way to the Hall of Fame.

There is some evidence that Landry's decision was borne of desperation, not genius. For the next three seasons, mainly because of injuries, Landry switched back and forth between his quarterbacks until finally trading away Morton. Landry critics maintain that the Cowboys won most of their games because of Staubach's improvisation rather than the coach's system, and it was Staubach who ad-libbed two of the biggest plays in franchise history: the "Hail Mary" touchdown to Drew Pearson to beat Minnesota in the 1975 playoffs, and the scoring pass to Butch Johnson in Super Bowl XII.

Yet, when Staubach retired in 1980 he gave effusive praise to the "man in the funny hat," whom he called "the nuts and bolts of the Cowboys." Choking back emotion at his retirement press conference, Staubach composed himself and added, "I was successful because the system we had was successful. It was successful before I got here, and it will be successful long after I'm gone."[36]

In that sense, Staubach was absolutely right. Tom Landry set an NFL record by coaching the Cowboys for 29 years. He retired with two Super Bowl wins and 270 victories, which at the time was the third-most in league history. His Dallas teams also set records by making the playoffs nine straight years and 17 of 18 seasons. Most fans today remember him for the unceremonious way he was fired when Jerry Jones took over the Cowboys in 1989.

But Tom Landry, along with Tex Schramm, Gil Brandt, and A. Salam Qureishi, deserve credit for perhaps an even more important contribution.

Nine. By the Numbers

They were the revolutionaries who pushed the NFL into the modern world of computers, statistics, and analytics.

Dallas became an incubator in this process because even as Landry was introducing his brand of complexity into the NFL, Hank Stram was doing the same as coach of the Dallas Texans in the American Football League. Stram didn't copy Landry, but many of the ideas were the same, especially on offense—shifting formations, men in motion, disguised attack. The Texans franchise, which later moved to Kansas City to become the Chiefs, won three AFL titles, and dominated the Minnesota Vikings in Super Bowl IV, 23–7. Stram called the game "the offense of the future against the offense of the past."[37]

When Kansas City won that Super Bowl, and Dallas followed two years later by dominating Miami, 24–3 in Super Bowl VI, it seemed to end the Lombardi era and its emphasis on emotion and simplicity. A young assistant with the Cincinnati Bengals, Bill Walsh, began working on what would become the West Coast offense, spreading receivers all over the field. Another assistant, Buddy Ryan in Chicago, figured if you're sending everyone out as a receiver that left fewer people to block for the quarterback. His "46" defense emphasized pressure, and in leading the Bears to a win in Super Bowl XX, it may have been the single greatest defensive team in NFL history.

As formations got more complex, so too did the terminology. When the Steelers beat the Raiders with the "Immaculate Reception" in the 1972 playoffs, the play was originally called as simply "66 Circle Option." In today's NFL, the plays seem to be as long as entries in the Encyclopædia Britannica. In coach Jon Gruden's system, one of the plays is called "U Zap to West Right Tight F Left Fake 99 Toss Crunch Naked Right."[38]

Consider a play from the Patriots offense in 2016, "G (Gun) Brown Right, 74 Hoss X-Follow." "Gun," refers to the formation, in this case the shotgun, "Brown" indicates an empty set with no running backs and five receivers, "74" refers to the pass protection, and "Hoss" is the combination of pass routes. "On this particular play," noted *USA Today*, "[Patriots quarterback Tom] Brady has to be aware of five receivers running seven different routes while diagnosing the defensive play call. And he has only three seconds to process all of this information before a 300-pound man drives him into the dirt."[39]

Every aspect of the NFL is now more detailed and complex, including team administration. When Dallas entered the NFL in 1960, they had a few dozen employees, and Clint Murchison, Jr., paid $550,000 as an entry fee. In 2020, the Cowboys had more than a thousand employees and were the most profitable sports franchise in the world, with an estimated value of $5.5 billion.[40] While those thousand employees worked in a variety of disparate jobs—maintenance, merchandising, public relations, and so on—much of the sprawling complexity of the organization was focused on the same problem Tom Landry had in 1960: talent evaluation and acquisition.

Perhaps no area of the NFL has seen a greater increase in complexity, computerization, and quantification than the draft. Thanks to A. Salam Qureishi, the Cowboys got a leg up on the rest of the league in analyzing college talent and it paid off handsomely on the field. But imitation is the sincerest form of flattery, and as Drew Pearson noted, the NFL is nothing if not a copycat league. Soon, other teams began developing their own computer methods, trying to duplicate what the Cowboys had done. Even as early as 1973, when the Cowboys were still laden with championship talent, Tex Schramm took note of what happened in that year's draft. "They have caught up with us," he said, referring to the other clubs. "Our scouts have seen it coming. They say it's a jungle out there. Every place they go to look at a player they run over half a dozen scouts from other teams."[41]

Unable to keep talent hidden from other teams, the Cowboys soon began taking gambles on unheralded players that other teams considered risky. There was no bigger gamble than in 1982 when the team selected defensive back Rod Hill from Kentucky State with its number-one pick. Few other teams even had Hill on their radar, and those that did had him listed no higher than a third-round pick. It was widely viewed at the time as a desperation move, and even Landry admitted he was "not a player I felt comfortable taking. There's no surprise when you miss on a Rod Hill because you've taken a real calculated risk."[42]

"America's Team has taken some curiously odd courses in past drafts," sportswriter Jim Lassiter noted at the time, "but this time you feel certain they made their selections after feeding Gil Brandt, the draft 'genius,' into his Apple home computer."[43] Rod Hill played only two seasons in Dallas before moving on to three other NFL teams and eventually playing in Canada. He came to symbolize the draft failures in the 1980s that led to the team's decline.

The same year Dallas drafted Hill, Tex Schramm went to the NFL's Competition Committee with an idea. Back then, if a team wanted to scout a player it had to send coaches and personnel to the individual college campuses, which was expensive, time consuming, and—such as with small schools with few resources like Kentucky State—difficult. Schramm proposed bringing together all the prospects in one place for evaluation under the direction of the NFL. At first, it was called the National Invitation Camp and held in such places as Tampa and New

Orleans. It eventually became the NFL Draft Combine, held now every year in Indianapolis.

If you need any evidence of the obsession the NFL has with numbers and analytics, look no further than the combine.

Every year, hundreds of prospective players head to Indianapolis to be poked, prodded, and pushed by league talent evaluators. The goal is to quantify every conceivable aspect of a player, from the obvious—speed, height, weight, strength—to the esoteric. Players are measured for arm and leg strength, jumping ability, fluidity, and even intelligence with a standardized test called the "Wonderlic." It was Landry and the Cowboys, of course, who pioneered the use of the Wonderlic in evaluating the mental makeup of prospective players, and "Landry was known to put a lot of weight into the results of the test and kept it in consideration when it came to putting together his rosters."[44]

Of course, many players who did not fare so well on the Wonderlic—Terry Bradshaw, Dan Marino, and Jim Kelly to name just three—went on to have outstanding NFL careers, while some who scored high on the test washed out of the league. "The Wonderlic has limited return on investment with its use in the NFL," said professor Brian Lyons of Fresno State University, who published a research paper questioning the validity of the test. "In this context, because it's so physically based, the results point to [the test results] really don't matter."[45]

NFL teams also conduct personal interviews, looking not only for signs of leadership and ability to perform under pressure, but also for red flags such as immaturity or egoism. In many ways, they are trying to quantify the unquantifiable. One player said at an interview that he was asked by a team, "If you were going to kill someone would you use a gun or a knife?" When he went through the combine, former Georgia defensive tackle Jeff Owens said, "One guy did ask me, which one would I take: a pillow or a blanket?"[46]

As flawed as the process can be, the results of all these tests are taken very seriously, and in some cases can elevate the draft status of a player who had an average college career. Such players are called "workout warriors" or "workout wonders," because their great testing numbers overshadow their actual performance, and more than one NFL team has been seduced by a blinding 40-yard dash time or staggering repetitions on the bench press. As just one example, defensive end Vernon Gholston of Ohio State vaulted up the draft lists with his performance at the 2008 combine, which included a 4.65 time in the 40 and 37 reps on the bench press. The Jets took Gholston with the seventh overall pick, but he never lived up to the hype. Gholston failed to record a single sack with the Jets and was gone from the league after three seasons.

Perhaps the greatest cautionary tale of all time is of former quarterback Ryan Leaf. The debate in 1998 was which quarterback, Leaf or Peyton Manning of Tennessee, would go first overall in the draft. Leaf had an outstanding career at Washington State, and teams fell in love with his "measureables"—6'5", 235 pounds, and a rocket arm. By contrast, scouts weren't entirely sold on Manning. "Hell, yes, Manning's good," said one, "but his ball waffles all the time. I didn't like his ball velocity, either."[47] Manning eventually won the debate, taken number-one overall by the Indianapolis Colts, while the San Diego Chargers took Leaf second. Manning played 17 seasons in the league, won two Super Bowl titles, and shattered several career passing records. Leaf was out of the league by age 25, finished with more interceptions than touchdowns, and ended up in prison on drug charges.

Around the time that Leaf and Manning were drafted, major league baseball was also rethinking the role of statistics and numbers in its game. The driving force was the success of the Oakland Athletics, a team that did not spend exorbitantly in free agency, yet had solid success on the field. This success was traced to general manager Billy Beane and the organization's use of non-traditional statistics and analytics. Beane and the A's evaluated players beyond the traditional numbers of batting average, home runs, and runs batted in. When a book and movie—*Moneyball*—came out chronicling this success, Oakland's unorthodox approach became all the rage and was copied throughout baseball.

The NFL also took notice and teams have begun to incorporate some of these "next generation statistics" in their thinking. Players are still measured in terms of height, weight, speed, and strength, but these new statistics measure the velocity of passes, distance traveled on runs, and player acceleration. This is accomplished by tagging equipment with radio frequency chips, with an estimated 250 such devices used in any single game. The league provides the raw data to all the teams, "giving each team the flexibility to develop custom analytics and proprietary statistics."[48] Some of the next gen stats also include such things as a player's "performance above expectation," "play success probability," and "defensive pressure percentage."

Of course, teams want a competitive edge and seek to find it through their own statistics. To that end, every team in the league now has an analytics department, and they often use outside help by employing such firms as Pro Football Focus, Stats LLC, and Pro Scout Inc. to help them make the most of the numbers they are collecting. As might be expected, the Cowboys have fully embraced this new approach. "I don't think it's changed how we've scouted, but it's become a bigger part of the puzzle that we put together each spring," said Chris Hall, the college scouting coordinator for the Cowboys. "We've got a full analytics staff now that's grown over the last few years. They interpret a whole bunch of different things that they bring to the table. Whether it's stats, tendencies, the type of player that fits in different things, there's so many different things to evaluate now. We don't just go with what analytics say, we don't just go with what scouts say, we don't just go with what coaches say."[49]

The Cowboys entered a new era of analytics with the hiring of coach Mike McCarthy in 2020. During his thirteen years coaching in Green Bay, McCarthy was a consistent winner who led the Packers to a win in Super Bowl XLV. But when his last two seasons ended with losing records, McCarthy was fired and his critics complained that his philosophies had become stale. McCarthy kept it somewhat simple in Green Bay, once admitting, "Statistics are for losers."[50]

But during his one-year hiatus from coaching, McCarthy reexamined his approach and promised to embrace technology and analysis. Even before he took the job in Dallas, McCarthy proposed a "football tech" plan:

> There's a flow chart for his proposed 14-person Football Technology Department, including a six-person video unit and an eight-person analytics team. The Chief of Football Technology tops the department, which will run both video and analytics. The top analytics lieutenants will be a Coordinator of Database Management, Coordinator of Football Analytics and Coordinator of Mathematical Innovation. Below them: Football Technology Engineer and two Football Technology Analysts. And finally, a Football Technology Intern.[51]

All of that may sound a bit confusing and more than a little dystopian. Historian and scholar Arnold Toynbee once wrote, "Sport is a conscious attempt to counterbalance the soul-destroying specialization which the division of labor under industrialization entails."[52] Now, that soul—the blood and heart of the game as evidenced in such men as Lombardi and Butkus—seems in real danger and there has been some pushback. "There are a lot of skeptics," said Tony Khan, who runs the analytics department for the Jacksonville Jaguars. "And that's honestly probably on the analysts and the statisticians. You have to be able to explain it to football people on their teams [and] communicate with coaches and scouts on a meaningful level."[53]

In 2005, the Philadelphia Eagles used their analytics to determine that Trent Cole, an unheralded defensive end from the University of Cincinnati, would translate into an effective pass rusher. Ten years later, Cole was second on the team's all-time sack list behind only the legendary Reggie White. But for every hit with analytics, there is also a miss. In 2013, the Browns looked at their numbers and took a chance on undersized pass rusher Barkevious Mingo, drafting him sixth overall. Mingo never lived up to expectation and in 2019 played for his fifth team in seven seasons.

But it is clear that the analytic genie is out of the bottle and is not going back in. Advanced metrics, analytics, and next gen stats are a way of life in the NFL now and are only going to become more important. And for the most part, it can all be traced back to one organization—Tom Landry, Tex Schramm, Gil Brandt and the Dallas Cowboys. "This team established the blueprint for the modern NFL," said NFL author Joe Patoski. "What we know as the NFL today could not have happened without the Dallas Cowboys, who made it up out of thin air."[54]

And don't forget A. Salam Qureishi, the shy man who knew nothing of football when he came to America in the late 1950s. It was Qureishi who took the vision of the Cowboys organization and made it reality. In 2019, Qureishi was long retired from computer science and analytics. In his 80s, he spoke haltingly, and still with a trace of his strong Indian accent.

"It is impossible to describe the impact that football has had in my life," he said.[55] It is not as difficult to describe the impact Qureishi had on football.

Ten

The Door Opens Wider

In July 2020, the Washington Redskins finally did what many inside and outside the NFL had called on them to do for decades—they officially retired the name Redskins and the Indian head logo that had become symbolic of their franchise almost from the very beginnings of the team in Boston in 1932. "This is a good decision for the country, not just Native peoples," said Ray Halbritter, a representative of the Oneida Nation and the leader of the Change the Mascot campaign. "It closes a painful chapter of denigration and disrespect toward Native Americans and other people of color."[1]

It would be nice to think that the Redskins organization made the move willingly and for charitable reasons, but the facts are just the opposite. Team owner Daniel Snyder had vowed for years that he would "never change the name. It's that simple. NEVER—you can use caps."[2] Snyder made the change only at the point of a symbolic gun—the cultural backlash from the death of George Floyd at the hands of police officers. Floyd's death in May 2020 ignited a firestorm of protest that turned once accepted visual symbols into portrayals of racial aggression. Statues and monuments were removed across the country, in some cases forcibly so. Still, Snyder might have held out if his corporate sponsors—notably FedEx, PepsiCo and Bank of America—had not threatened to withhold millions of dollars unless the name was changed.

The whole ugly incident reminded everyone of how resistant the NFL is to change, and especially cultural change. In many respects, the league changes only when forced to do so, which was exactly what happened when the AFL began play in 1960.

On September 11 that year, the Oakland Raiders played the first game in their history against the Houston Oilers. The game wasn't even in Oakland, but instead was played at San Francisco's Kezar Stadium, where only 12,700 came out to watch. Although the American Football League had signed a broadcasting deal with ABC, this particular game was not on television. Fans in the Bay Area could hear the game from Bud Foster and Mel Ventner on local radio, but few bothered to listen.

Thus, it's not exactly known how many people were paying attention when in the second quarter Oakland quarterback Tom Flores threw a 13-yard touchdown pass to Tony Teresa. Later in the game, Flores threw a 46-yard scoring pass to Jack Larscheid, and for good measure added a two-point conversion pass. Flores finished with modest numbers on the day—13 completions in 32 attempts and the two touchdowns—as the Raiders lost to the eventual AFL champion Houston Oilers, 37–22.

Even so, the mere presence of Flores on the field made history as he became the first Hispanic quarterback in pro football history. Flores was born in Fresno, California, but his family came from Durango, Mexico where they mined materials to make explosives and had to contend with bandits. "They didn't fight them off, but they had to avoid them," Flores said of the marauders. "My dad and his brothers had to lay on the floor as bullets came flying through the windows."[3]

Flores made the most of his opportunity, playing all ten years in the AFL and eventually winning four Super Bowl rings—one as a player, one as an assistant coach and two as head coach of the Raiders, who in the 1980s featured Jim Plunkett, perhaps the most successful Hispanic quarterback in league history. It was Flores who paved the way for Plunkett and other Hispanic players that followed, including Ron Rivera, who won a Super Bowl with the Chicago Bears as a player and coached in another Super Bowl with the Carolina Panthers. "He's a pioneer," Rivera said of Flores. "When you talk about me and my Hispanic heritage, it was Tom Flores and Jim Plunkett, guys like that. Those were guys I could look up to and really aspire to be like them."[4]

They were guys who most likely never would have gotten the chance to play in the NFL of the 1950s. It was a league that at the time had an unwritten quota of no more than five minorities per team and had an unrepentant racist in George Preston Marshall running the Washington Redskins (see Chapter Eight). The first Hispanic to play in the NFL was a Cuban, Ignacio Saturnino "Lou" Molinet with the 1927 Frankford Yellow Jackets. But most people looked at his last name and assumed he was of French ancestry. Other Hispanic players that followed, including Hall of Famers Steve Van Buren (Honduras) and Tom Fears (Mexico), were born in Hispanic countries but moved to the U.S. as young children and played college football in America. Fans simply assumed Van Buren was from Louisiana and Fears from California.

The NFL liked to brag that it integrated in 1946, a year before Jackie Robinson broke baseball's color line, but the Los Angeles Rams were practically forced to sign local standouts Kenny Washington and Woody Strode. The Rams had just moved from Cleveland and wanted to sign a lease to play at the Los Angeles Coliseum, a publicly funded park. When the Los Angeles Coliseum Commission met to discuss the lease, representatives of the local black press came to the meeting and pushed hard for integration. The pressure campaign worked as commissioner Roger Jessup announced, "If our Kenny Washington can't play, there would be no pro football in the Los Angeles Coliseum."[5]

Washington, now injured and past his prime, lasted three seasons and Strode just one, but the line had been crossed. Later in 1946, Bill Willis and Marion Motley joined the Cleveland Browns in the All-America Football Conference. In the words of the *Los Angeles Times*, "The door cracked open."[6]

That crack didn't move much until a combination of events jarred it open even further in the late 1950s. The emergence of Rosa Parks and Dr. Martin Luther King pushed the growing civil rights movement into the forefront of American culture, as did a series of legal cases, including *Brown vs. Board of Education*,[7] which outlawed school segregation. John F. Kennedy took over the presidency in 1961 promising to support civil rights, and while his enthusiasm waned in the face of political reality, he did stand behind efforts to integrate previously all-white southern universities. Even as Alabama governor George Wallace famously stood in the doorway to prevent black students from entering the University of Alabama, Kennedy went on television in a nationwide address. "The heart of the question," he said, "is whether all Americans are to be afforded equal rights and opportunities."[8]

That question was also under discussion in the NFL. "Prejudice was everywhere," said Cowboys guard John Wilbur. "Danny Villanueva, our kicker, used to get hate calls, obscene calls, harassing calls all the time in Dallas from fans who hated Mexicans. He was scared to death. His being on the team unleashed the racial tensions existing in Dallas at the time."[9] Into this combustible atmosphere came the American Football League. As a new league in 1960, the AFL couldn't afford the bigotry and elitism of the NFL and needed any player that would be willing to suit up.

Aside from the practicality of reaching out to minorities, AFL leaders, and in particular Lamar Hunt, believed in desegregation and committed the league to that course. Hunt's Dallas Texans began recruiting and playing minority players at a time when most Texas universities were still segregated. "I can look and see Lamar Hunt, the founder of this league, the founder of this team," said linebacker Willie Lanier. "If they did not take the steps they did to create jobs and opportunity, change would not have occurred."[10]

Lanier grew up in Richmond, Virginia, and played college ball at historically black Morgan State University. He was selected by the Chiefs in the second round of the 1967 draft, but had no expectations of playing middle linebacker. No pro team had ever had a black middle linebacker because it was believed that minorities did not have the intelligence to play what was considered the quarterback position of the defense. In that same 1967 draft, three picks before Lanier, the Chiefs took Jim Lynch, who starred at middle linebacker for Notre Dame and was expected to do the same in Kansas City.

Instead, when the team got to training camp, coach Hank Stram noticed how Lanier was ideally suited to play in the middle, and shifted Lynch to the outside. They paired with Bobby Bell, another black player, to form one of the greatest linebacker units in NFL history. Lynch and Lanier broke another barrier when they became road roommates and their eight years together cemented a lifelong friendship. "If [Hunt] and those other men did not found the American Football League," said Lanier, "the opportunity for me to meet Jim Lynch is almost zero. Because he is who he is and they are who they were, is why I'm standing here."[11]

Lanier, Bell and Buck Buchanan—a Grambling College defensive lineman who in 1963 became the first black player ever drafted as the overall number one pick—set the foundation for a Chiefs franchise that would go on to dominate the American Football League. Fittingly, the Chiefs played the last game in AFL history and beat the Minnesota Vikings, 23–7, in Super Bowl IV. That season, Kansas City had 23 black players on its roster, including eight starters on defense. The Vikings had but eleven. "Imagine if there had been no AFL and no Kansas City Chiefs," said Lanier. "Maybe I have to wait five years for my chance to play middle linebacker. And five years in football is an eternity."[12]

Hunt deserves much of the credit for creating opportunities, but even he admitted it wasn't solely because of racial awareness. "He was very adamant that he was not in any way attempting to be a social progressive," said NFL author Michael MacCambridge. "He was not necessarily trying to break down barriers. He just realized that Lloyd Wells would be an asset to what he was trying to do."[13] Wells became the first full-time black scout in pro football and was credited with finding and signing players like Lanier, Buchanan and receiver Otis Taylor. In all, he signed eight players who went on to All-Pro careers. Very rarely does a scout get much public credit for a team's success, but after the Super Bowl IV win, running back Mike Garrett pulled Wells up to the interview podium to share in the spotlight. "Their win came on pro football's biggest and most visible stage," said author Michael Hurd. "It put the

NFL—and other AFL teams—on notice that there was indeed a wealth of talent that needed to be explored at HBCUs (historically black colleges and universities). You could sense the rustle of unfolding road maps by scouts around the league."[14]

Another player that found his way to the Chiefs/Texans franchise was Abner Haynes, a trailblazer who helped integrate the football program at North Texas State University (now the University of North Texas). Haynes was drafted by both the Texans and Pittsburgh Steelers, and recalled when he first met Pittsburgh coach Buddy Parker and quarterback Bobby Layne. Both men, notorious drinkers and hell-raisers, had showed up drunk on Haynes's front porch at 5:30 one morning to give him a recruiting pitch. "I don't think they knew my dad was a minister," said Haynes. "My dad came out front, this big, black guy; talked with a deep voice, and said, 'You won't be going to Pittsburgh.' I said, 'Yes, sir.'"[15]

At least Haynes was drafted by an NFL team. Several minority players didn't even receive that courtesy and went on to become stars in the AFL. Haynes was a four-time AFL All-Star and a member of the all-time AFL team. Receiver Elbert Dubenion, nicknamed "Golden Wheels" for his speed, came out of tiny Bluffton College in Ohio to lead the Buffalo Bills to two AFL championships. He went undrafted by the NFL as did one of pro football's most colorful figures, Ed "Wahoo" McDaniel.

A Choctaw-Chickasaw Indian from Oklahoma, McDaniel came by the nickname Wahoo honestly. "[He] plays middle linebacker as if it were the last wild charge at the Little Big Horn," *Sports Illustrated* wrote in 1964. "Undoubtedly, the New York Jets own better athletes than Ed McDaniel. But no other Jet has ever managed to fascinate and beguile New York's professional football addicts the way Wahoo does."[16]

McDaniel started his career in Houston and spent three years in Denver before arriving in New York, where he became an almost instant folk hero. Instead of the last name on the back of his jersey, McDaniel simply had "Wahoo." Every time he made a tackle the public address announcer would say, "Tackle by 'guess who?'" and the crowd would respond in unison, "Wahoo!"[17] McDaniel wrestled professionally for many years, making more money in the ring than on the football field, and often appeared at matches in full Indian attire, including headdress. He admitted to drinking motor oil and a jug of jalapeno peppers, both on a dare. While at the University of Oklahoma, he threw a soda machine off a second-floor dormitory. In a bit of understatement, his hometown newspaper called McDaniel "an American original [who] had a reputation for doing some wild things that sometimes got him into trouble."[18]

As a wrestler, McDaniel often crossed paths with Ernie "Big Cat"

Ladd, who for years played a villain in the ring. Like McDaniel, Ladd was more of a football player who moonlighted as a wrester. And also like McDaniel, he was a minority who found a home in the AFL coming out of Grambling College. A defensive tackle, Ladd got his nickname from his quickness and size—6'9" and 300 pounds—and in that era, he had about six inches and fifty pounds on the typical offensive lineman. "In his first season in professional football [he] has become one of the most awesome sights in the game," gushed *Ebony* magazine in 1962. "Bigger than the legendary Big Daddy Lipscomb—or any other player on the gridiron—Ladd is the strongest and probably the meanest man in football."[19]

Ladd never quite lived up to that billing, mainly because injuries hampered his career, but he did make three All-Pro teams and played in the AFL All-Star game four times. It was his appearance in the 1965 AFL All-Star game that again reflected the league's openness to minorities and also emboldened the players to speak more openly about racial injustice.

The AFL scheduled its January 1965 All-Star game in New Orleans at the request of local promoters who wanted to showcase the city and its potential as a pro football town. But racial tensions started bubbling almost as soon as the teams arrived. Heading to the French Quarter for some relaxation, black players watched taxis pick up their white teammates but pass right by them. When told that they would need to call a colored cab, Raiders running back Clem Daniels said, "I was ready to turn around and catch a return flight right then."[20] Even when they made it to the Quarter, the players found themselves denied entrance to the clubs, many of which were for whites only. At one venue, the owner adamantly refused to let the players come in, at which point Ladd threatened to pull the door off its hinges. "The doorman had a gun in his waistband," said Oakland defensive back Dave Grayson. "He pointed it at Ernie and told him if he walked through the door, he was going to kill him."[21]

Ladd did not back down, and although no shots were fired a crowd of 200 or so had gathered outside to create a potentially dangerous scene. Those in the crowd, many of them drunk, pushed and jostled, hurling insults and taunts at the players. Outnumbered, the players decided to head back to the hotel, but again ran into problems finding a taxi. At this point, Ladd, who had become something of a leader for the group, had had it. He decided he was going home. "I told Earl [Faison] I wasn't going to play in New Orleans under those conditions," Ladd said.[22] Faison, a teammate of Ladd's in San Diego, talked to some other black players and soon the idea of a boycott was born.

Ten. The Door Opens Wider 167

The black players held a meeting and found the incidents were not isolated. All 21 players had the same problems with taxis, restaurants, clubs, and even riding the elevator at the recently-integrated Roosevelt Hotel. They voted 18–3 not to play in the game, and surprisingly got a lot of support from their white teammates and the AFL. Another San Diego teammate of Ladd, lineman Ron Mix, sat in on the meeting and originally urged the players to stay, arguing that it would set a bad example. Eventually, Mix supported the decision, leading a group of white players that joined the boycott. "I made a decision then that if the game were to go on despite the absence of black players," Mix said, "I would not play. It was important for at least one white player to join them, to say we're with you."[23] AFL Commissioner Joe Foss released a statement saying, "These players are part of the AFL family [and] we can't have them treated like this."[24]

Local promoters and city officials were panicked and begged the players to stay, but to no avail. Many of them never understood why the boycott took place and called it "a grievous injury that has been inflicted on the city of New Orleans."[25] Despite the embarrassment, two years later New Orleans got its NFL franchise. The AFL quickly moved the All-Star game to Houston where it was played without incident. "Someone had to take a stand and stop players from being treated as second-class citizens," said Ladd. "We didn't do it for publicity. We did it because of what was right and what was wrong."[26]

Ladd was among many black players who found an activist voice during this time, one of the most explosive periods in the civil rights era. Rioting broke out in urban areas of Newark, Detroit and Los Angeles. The assassinations of Medgar Evers in 1963 and Dr. Martin Luther King in 1968 convinced many black leaders and athletes of the need to get involved. Part of this effort was spearheaded by Dr. Harry Edwards, a sociologist and professor who described the emerging black consciousness in his book *The Revolt of the Black Athlete*. "My thing is to get them out of their comfort zone," he said of the white establishment, "because their comfort zone is with women chained to the damn stove and the bed."[27] Edwards went on to create the Olympic Project for Human Rights, which called for a black boycott of the 1968 Olympics. Even though the boycott never fully materialized, several prominent athletes, such as basketball star Lew Alcindor, did sit out the games. Two that did go, sprinters Tommie Smith and John Carlos, got themselves kicked out for a raised-fist protest on the gold medal platform after the 200-meter event.

The lightning rod for 1960s black activism was boxer Muhammad Ali, who in 1967 was stripped of his heavyweight title for refusing induction into the U.S. Army, famously saying, "I ain't got no quarrel with them Vietcong."[28] Not long after the decision, some of the most prominent black athletes in the country came out to support Ali. Their meeting, known as the Cleveland Summit, featured Alcindor, NBA star Bill Russell and perhaps the greatest player in NFL history, Jim Brown.

Brown organized the Cleveland Summit and had become an outspoken social activist after his retirement from the NFL two years earlier. He founded an organization that came to be known as the Black Economic Union as a means of empowering minority businesses, and has spent much of his post-football career working for similar minority causes. "Brown's life has resembled a tough, sprawling drama," wrote one biographer, "and includes the seeds of activism that shaped him."[29]

But it's interesting to note that Brown's activism really didn't take off until after his retirement in 1965. In many ways, he had suffered in silence throughout his career, focusing instead on his athletic achievements. "I was appreciative of the fact that God gave me a body and a mind and that I could overcome things if I worked real hard," he said. "Never to judge my work load by other people, but to establish something that fit my mentality."[30] When he suddenly and shockingly retired at the relatively young age of 29, it was as if he finally felt comfortable released from the suffocating confines of the NFL.

Brown was not alone. Other black NFL players, either by choice or compulsion, felt the need to fall in line and not make waves. Green Bay Packer great Willie Davis, who after his retirement became active in helping black business owners, was not a vocal activist during his playing days. Davis was also at the Cleveland Summit to tell Ali that he thought his actions were "unpatriotic."[31]

It seemed as if Davis and others like him chafed under the authoritarian NFL and its symbolic leader, Packer coach Vince Lombardi. In the days leading up to Super Bowl I, the Chiefs outspoken and flamboyant defensive back Fred "The Hammer" Williamson was not shy in predicting how he was going to dominate the game. When Williamson ran into Davis he asked him if the antics bothered the Packers. "They think you got some class, man," Davis answered. "Some of those cats have been dying to express themselves for years, but they won't dare, not with Lombardi around."[32]

While Lombardi and the NFL succeeded to a degree in keeping control, expression erupted on college campuses. Already hotbeds for protest and racial unrest, many universities saw their football programs dragged into the fight. At the University of Wyoming the protests of black players—called the "Black 14"—over what they perceived as lack of support from the coaching staff nearly destroyed the program. At

Ten. The Door Opens Wider

Indiana University, nine black players quit the team, calling the program "mentally depressing and morally discouraging to blacks."[33] A Hoosier team that had recently gone to the Rose Bowl then lost 22 of its next 25 games. When black players boycotted practice at Syracuse University because the school had no black coaches, the players were suspended. They eventually returned, but faced resentment from the white players. "It's too damn late for everybody," one of the players said. "And it's only going to get worse."[34]

This was not just a racial issue. All of football, including the NFL, was caught in a changing generational landscape that pitted the rigidity of the established order, as expressed by coaches like Vince Lombardi, against a new movement of expression and creativity as embodied by the younger players coming into the league. While the players of the 1950s, many of whom had fought in World War II, had no issues with authoritarianism, the players of the 1960s seemed to question everything. Many coaches, described by one psychiatrist in 1969 as "the remaining stronghold of the archaic family structure,"[35] had trouble dealing with what they perceived as open rebellion. "We've always got to understand *them*," said one coach. "Well, maybe I can't. I can't know what it's like to be a Negro. Or live in a ghetto. But that doesn't mean I don't try, and I sure think trying works two ways: they've got an obligation to understand me."[36]

One player coaches could not understand, at least Cowboys coach Tom Landry could not, was Pete Gent. Gent was one of those unlikely success stories the Cowboys had in their search for talent (see Chapter Nine). A basketball player at Michigan State University, he came to Dallas as a free agent in 1964 and made the team despite not having played football since high school. By 1966, Gent became an accomplished receiver, starting ten games and catching 27 passes.

But Gent had a rebellious streak that made him "constitutionally unable to give himself over to authority,"[37] especially the authority of Tom Landry, whom Gent viewed as inflexible and unchanging. "I was the first football player in the National Football League whose hair came out from beneath his helmet," Gent said. "And the Cowboys called me in and demanded I cut my hair. That pissed me off so much I never cut my hair again. It got to the point where the fans in the Cotton Bowl started calling me a hippie."[38]

Gent kept his mouth shut during his career, which lasted only to 1968 due to injuries. But after he left the league, Gent became a leader among the disaffected NFL expatriates who no longer felt the need to conform. He wrote a best-selling novel *North Dallas Forty* that was a thinly veiled reference to what he perceived as segregation, dehumanization and hypocrisy on the Cowboys. Gent and his close friend quarterback Don Meredith were represented in the book by the characters Phil Elliott and Seth Maxwell. In one scene, Maxwell tells Elliott, "Son, you ain't never gonna get off that bench until you stop fighting them suckers. You got to learn how to fool them. I've been fooling them bastards for years."[39] Gent never felt comfortable fighting back until he had left the league.

For a variety of reasons, the young players of the AFL, and especially the blacks, felt more open in expressing these new attitudes. Ernie Ladd went on to a long career in wrestling and became one of "the first black wrestlers to directly antagonize white babyfaces (wrestling good guys) and fans with brash words and uncompromising tactics."[40] Chiefs scout Lloyd Wells, so instrumental in bringing black athletes into the league, later became an adviser to Muhammad Ali. "He was as close to me as a brother,"[41] Ali said years later. Ali was credited with starting the black movement among athletes, but author Maureen Smith makes the point that Ali's emergence into activism came a full two years after the AFL All-Star game in 1965.

Smith also challenged the NFL's contention that it played an important role in the Civil Rights movement as compared to the AFL:

This is an especially important manipulation of the events in part because the NFL makes no effort to distinguish between the two leagues. By claiming the history of [the AFL] as their own, as opposed to a force that acted upon the established league, the NFL sets up an image of the league as being an institution that actively promoted racial equality rather than maintaining the divide.[42]

The implication is clear: while the NFL dragged its feet in an effort to maintain the status quo, the AFL was the fertile ground in which the seeds of young rebellion and black activism were firmly planted.

In almost all areas, the AFL seemed more welcoming and attractive to minority players. The AFL had the first Hispanic quarterback (Tom Flores), the first black number one draft pick (Buck Buchanan), the first black middle linebacker (Willie Lanier), the first black kicker (Gene Mingo), and starting in 1968 the first black quarterback. Coming out of the University of Nebraska–Omaha, Marlin Briscoe wanted to play quarterback in the pros, but was moved to wide receiver. When the Broncos started the 1968 season by losing three straight games, the team figured it had nothing to lose. Briscoe quarterbacked the fourth game and led Denver to a win over Cincinnati. He played the rest of the year, set a team rookie record with 14 touchdown passes and finished second in the AFL Rookie of the Year voting.

"I understood the significance," Briscoe said. "I knew I was the first and what that meant. If I did well, it would make it easier on other guys.

But you have to understand: I had always been a quarterback. It's what I was meant to do. It wasn't a surprise to me."[43] It was a surprise when the Broncos traded Briscoe to the Bills the following season and Buffalo moved him back to receiver. The Bills already had plenty of quarterbacks, including another minority, James Harris. Harris later won two divisional titles with the Los Angeles Rams and became the first black quarterback to start a season opener, to start and win a playoff game, to play in the Pro Bowl, and to be selected Pro Bowl MVP.

James Harris, Marlin Briscoe, Tom Flores, Ernie Ladd and so many others like them found a home in the American Football League. The league also offered a home to their culture, youth, and expression. The landscape of pro football would have looked much different if the AFL had not come along at just the right time to crack open the door for deserving minorities. Much of the credit goes to AFL founder Lamar Hunt.

"He cultivated in the basket of blatant racism and segregation, in his hometown, a power to change professional football," said Curtis McClinton, a running back who starred on Hunt's early Dallas Texans teams and later with the Chiefs. "Lamar goes beyond the American Football League and sports. Lamar goes to a cultural and economic transition for the South and America."[44]

Hall of Fame lineman Anthony Muñoz is trying to bring that same transition to the Hispanic community. A native of California of Mexican descent, Muñoz at first preferred baseball to football before he outgrew the diamond. He starred as an offensive tackle at USC and then played thirteen seasons with the Cincinnati Bengals, made the Pro Bowl eleven times, and earned praise as perhaps the best offensive lineman in NFL history.

During and after his career, Muñoz wondered why more Hispanics had not followed in the footsteps of Tom Flores, Jim Plunkett and Joe Kapp. In 2020, an ESPN poll revealed that 28.7 million Hispanic-Americans considered themselves NFL fans, and yet of the 1,696 players in the league, only sixteen were Hispanic. "It's societal," Muñoz believes. "If they could get away from stereotyping and putting certain cultures in a box, we'd have more Latino players."[45]

Those stereotypes say that Hispanics are best suited for kicking, such as Rafael Septien, the Zendejas family (which at one time had four members kicking in the NFL), and Bill and Martin Gramatica (who became the first Argentineans to play in the league). "There are stereotypes about Mexicans and Latinos, a stigma," said Chargers defensive back Michael Davis, whose mother is Mexican and speaks fluent Spanish. "Mexicans are supposed to be cleaning or doing hard labor, not playing in the NFL. Sure, you could be kickers. I didn't want to be a kicker. I wanted to play offense or defense, be different."[46]

The stereotypes also seemed to value Hispanic players more for their toughness than for their ability. When quarterback Joe Kapp joined the Minnesota Vikings in 1967 after eight seasons in Canada, he was profiled in *Sports Illustrated* as "The Toughest Chicano" and a "Man of Machismo."[47] Kapp was indeed tough, and got into more than his share of fights and eccentric off-field behavior. "Joe Kapp," his Minnesota teammate Karl Kassulke once said, "is one tough son of a bitch."[48] Kapp led the Vikings to an NFL championship and tied a league record by throwing seven touchdown passes in one game, but the image of the brawling, semi-skilled Chicano remained. When Kapp led the Vikings to the Super Bowl the year after Joe Namath did the same for the Jets, one sportswriter observed, "If watching Namath was like watching an artist at work, watching Kapp was comparable to watching a plumber fix pipes."[49]

Slowly, the perceptions have changed. Jim Plunkett won two Super Bowls quarterbacking the Raiders. Just as Anthony Muñoz is regarded as perhaps the best ever at his position, so too is Tony Gonzalez, who shattered all records for tight ends on his way to the Hall of Fame. "Anthony Muñoz was first," said Alejandro Ibarra, who runs a Kansas City Chiefs fan club in Mexico City. "He was a symbol of Mexico for us. Tony Gonzalez broke the barrier and showed everyone a Latino player could catch passes and score touchdown. That made him more influential."[50]

Today, the NFL is using a variety of programs to reach out to Hispanic fans and communities, as are Gonzalez, Davis and Muñoz. Perhaps it's no coincidence that all three players starred with teams that had roots in the American Football League. Gonzalez played twelve years in Kansas City, and during his Hall of Fame induction speech directly thanked the late Lamar Hunt for taking a chance on him in the first round of the 1997 draft. "Lamar said, 'I don't care who you are or what color you are, it's all about what you can do on the field,'" Gonzalez remembered. "Of all the different things he's doing in his life, that was definitely one of the most eye-opening."[51]

And perhaps the greatest legacy of both Hunt and the American Football League.

Eleven

Heir Coryell

The 1961 NFL season ended on a cold, overcast New Year's Eve at Green Bay's City Stadium (later known as Lambeau Field). Playing in their second straight title game under Vince Lombardi, the Packers destroyed the Eastern Conference champion New York Giants, 37–0. Green Bay led 24–0 at halftime, thanks mainly to its punishing ground game headlined by Paul Hornung and Jim Taylor. Playing on special leave from his Army duties, Hornung set a championship game record by scoring 19 points, which included one touchdown, three field goals and four extra points. The league MVP rushed for 89 yards while Taylor added 69 yards on 14 carries.

The Packers rain the ball 44 times in the game for 181 yards, and passed only 17 times. Bart Starr made the most of his limited throws, completing ten for 164 yards and three touchdowns. The Green Bay defense held New York to 130 total yards, harassed Giants quarterback Y.A. Tittle into four interceptions, and beat the Giants for the third time that season—preseason, regular season and championship. "We didn't do anything special," Lombardi said after the game, "but we were the greatest team in the league today."[1]

The rest of the NFL, at heart a copycat league, took notice, especially when Lombardi led the Packers to four more titles in the next six years.

OK, NFL coaches said to themselves. *That's the way you win championships—power running on offense using the ground game to set up a few passes, and a defense geared to suffocate the run and force teams into passing out of desperation.* The NFL retrenched, replacing its aerial attack with foot soldiers for the rest of the decade and beyond. Joe Namath won MVP honors for his performance in Super Bowl III in 1969, but Matt Snell was the real hero, rushing for 121 yards and the Jets only touchdown. Namath didn't throw a single pass in the fourth quarter.

In 1970, the Dallas Cowboys rode their running game and defense into Super Bowl V, where they lost to the Colts on a last-second kick. During a seven-game winning streak that propelled them into the Super Bowl, the Cowboys won games by scores of 16–3, 6–2 and a 5–0 win over Detroit that is still the lowest scoring playoff game in NFL history.

Two years later, 1972, was called "The Year of the Runner" in the NFL as ten different backs broke the 1,000-yard rushing mark.[2] That included two runners in the same backfield for the Miami Dolphins, as Larry Csonka (1,117 yards) and Mercury Morris (1,000) helped Miami to its undefeated season. In a 14–7 win over Washington in the Super Bowl, quarterback Bob Griese threw all of eleven passes. The following season, in Miami's Super Bowl defeat of Minnesota, he threw only seven. In that 1973 season, sixteen of the 26 teams in the league rushed for more yards than they passed, including the good (Super Bowl champ Miami and playoff teams Los Angeles, Dallas, Pittsburgh and Washington), the bad (Chicago, New Orleans, San Diego, all of which finished last in their respective divisions), and the unbelievable. Led by O.J. Simpson's record 2,003 yards rushing, the Buffalo Bills paced the NFL with 3,088 yards on the ground. Their incredible passing totals *for the entire season* included just 96 completions, 997 yards and four touchdowns.

In 1961, as Vince Lombardi and his Packers towered over the NFL, the rest of the coaches and executives in the league looked up at them in awe and figured, if you can't beat them, join them.

A select few were plotting a revolution.

It began in California, and specifically San Diego, where a seismic shift in thinking would eventually rumble through the league like an earthquake. Sid Gillman had spent five mostly unsuccessful seasons as head coach of the Los Angeles Rams, bottoming out in 1959 with a 2–10 record that cost him his job. Gillman wanted to throw the ball, but that Rams team was built around running back Ollie Matson and didn't have the personnel to make his passing game work. Gone were Hall of Famers Norm Van Brocklin and Bob Waterfield at quarterback, along with receivers Tom Fears and Crazy Legs Hirsch. Their replacements were Billy Wade, Frank Ryan and Del Shofner.

In 1960, Gillman landed as coach of the Los Angeles Chargers in the new American Football League, where he found the climate much more fertile for his passing philosophies. He led the Chargers to the AFL title game that first season, and then again in 1961 when the team moved to San Diego. In 1962, the Chargers acquired quarterback John Hadl and receiver Lance Alworth to complement speedy running backs Paul Lowe and Keith Lincoln. In 1963, their offense tore apart the AFL, leading the league in scoring and piling 51 points on Boston in the AFL title game. In the 51–10 rout, San Diego rolled up 610 yards of total offense.

Gillman would lead the Chargers to the AFL championship game in five of the league's first six seasons.

It was success based on a new way of thinking about passing. Football coaches had traditionally viewed a passing attack as vertical. The idea was to pull defenders close to the line of scrimmage and then throw over the top of them down the field. The football equivalent of the home run, called the "bomb" back in those days, was a deep throw to a wide receiver who had gotten behind the defensive backs. It was a style of attack preferred by many AFL teams, including the Oakland Raiders and Houston Oilers. In the last game of the 1963 season those teams hooked up in a game that the Raiders won 52–49 on a late field goal. Houston's George Blanda threw for 342 yards and five touchdowns, while Oakland's Tom Flores did even better with 407 yards and six touchdowns. "As a player, that was probably my most pleasurable day," recalled Flores years later. "We threw the ball all day and scored from all areas of the field."[3] When Flores left the Raiders after the 1966 season, coach Al Davis traded for Daryle Lamonica, who came to be known as "The Mad Bomber." "They named him right," said Chiefs quarterback Len Dawson. "He was going after it. He was going for broke on *every* play."[4]

Gillman redefined the passing attack in several ways. Primarily, he began exploring unused space on the field, namely short horizontal areas. Ironically, it was Davis, the high priest of deep passing, who served as an assistant with Gillman in San Diego and credits him for developing the short passing game. "It had been thought of as vertical, but Sid also thought of it as horizontal," said Davis. "Sid used the width of the field."[5] Gillman noted that the field was 100 yards long and 53 yards wide, "and we're going to use every inch of it."[6]

To use that space, Gillman turned loose his running backs. Up until this time, running backs had primarily been used on screen passes or as a dump off receiver if the quarterback couldn't find anyone else open. No matter what their role, they stayed in the backfield. Gillman changed that, moving his backs to the line of scrimmage in a slot formation as a third wide receiver. Of course, it required a special kind of running back, like the one Gillman found in Keith Lincoln. "Sid was one of the first people to lengthen the field, and he worked hard at that," said Lincoln. "Against us, the defense couldn't have the damn safeties three or four yards off the line of scrimmage, like they could before, because we'd throw it over their butts."[7]

Finally, Gillman expanded the role of the tight end in his passing offense. Tight ends had always been considered brutish blockers and rarely went out on pass patterns. Even when the Bears Mike Ditka set records by catching 56 passes for 1,076 yards and 12 touchdowns in

1961, most of those were short safety-valve plays where Ditka caught the ball a few yards beyond the line of scrimmage and simply bulled over people on his way to the end zone. In a 1963 game against Pittsburgh, Ditka caught a short pass from Bill Wade and ran over almost the entire Steelers defense on a 63-yard gain. "It was the greatest run I've ever seen," said Bears assistant Sid Luckman. "It wasn't speed that got him down the field. It wasn't his moves. It was just sheer determination. He literally carried defensive players on his back."[8]

Gillman envisioned a more athletic tight end, one that could run patterns downfield and force mismatches with smaller defensive backs. His concepts led to the development of the modern tight end, whose evolution traced through San Diego with Kellen Winslow and later Antonio Gates. Tony Gonzalez, who smashed every tight end record for yards, catches and touchdowns, would be at the top of Gillman's evolutionary chain.

A football lifer, Gillman stayed in the game almost until the day he died at age 91. He coached, advised and gave input to almost any program that asked for it, impressing people decades younger with his never-flagging enthusiasm and encyclopedic mind. "With some of them," he once said of other coaches, "football is a vocation. With some, it's an avocation. You know what football is to me? It's blood."[9]

For all of these achievements, Gillman was enshrined in the Pro Football Hall of Fame and has been called "The Father of the Modern Passing Game." But he might not even have had the most innovative passing mind in his own city.

The same year Vince Lombardi won the first of his championships in Green Bay, Don Coryell became the head coach at San Diego State University. He came from Whittier College (where a scrub named Richard Nixon once sat on the bench), where he used the power-I running attack to win three conference championships. He made an intermediate stop at USC, where as an assistant he worked with John McKay to refine the power-I that was to become the staple of the Trojan attack for the next two decades. Don Coryell was very much a believer in running the football.

Coryell inherited a San Diego State team that had won just one game in 1960 and he won seven games 1961. That was followed by records of 8–2, 7–2, 8–2 and 8–2 over the next four seasons. For a school playing small college football with little history of success, it was a tremendous accomplishment. But those two losses every year bothered Coryell a great deal. Every year, it seemed, his Aztecs would face a bigger, stronger team that would physically wear them down. He realized his teams couldn't stand in and slug it out toe-to-toe and expect to win. "I just decided, hell, you can't just go out and run the ball against better teams," he said. "You've got to throw the damn ball if you're going to beat better teams. So we started throwing the ball."[10]

Throwing it a lot. In 1961, Coryell's first season, his quarterback Harry Korsmeier threw only 72 passes for 547 yards. In 1966, Aztecs quarterback Don Horn passed for 2,234 yards and 18 touchdowns. Three years later, Dennis Shaw shattered those records with 3,185 yards and 39 touchdowns, and he was followed by Brian Sipe, who threw 41 touchdown passes in his two seasons. All three players quarterbacked in the NFL; Shaw was Rookie of the Year in 1970 and Sipe was MVP in 1980.

The 1966 Aztecs team, which finished unbeaten and won a bowl game, had eight players drafted by NFL teams, the same number as national champion Notre Dame. Nebraska had five picks in that draft, Alabama four and Ohio State three. A 10–1 record the following season helped San Diego State transition to big time college football by 1969. Don Coryell's willingness to try something new had put the San Diego State program on the football map. "Don was a killer running coach," said Joe Gibbs, later a Super Bowl winner in his own right and then an assistant under Coryell. "I formation, power running. But then it's amazing the transition that took place. Don switched to throwing it like mad, and he was very creative. He was not afraid to try anything."[11]

Still, the skeptics and critics remained at almost every level of football. At the same time Coryell was developing his passing offense at San Diego State, Darrell Royal revived the program at the University of Texas by introducing the wishbone. The wishbone was a three-back set that featured the triple option run game, and with it the Longhorns stampeded 30 straight opponents and won two national championships. At Ohio State, Woody Hayes was so dedicated to the ground game that he named his formations after the famous World War II tank general George Patton, and even reverted to the hoary old straight T-formation. As a result, "he took the best array of offensive talent in the country and stuffed it into a meat grinder. The Buckeyes ran one running play after another, each more boring and predictable than the last."[12]

Depending on the source, it was either Royal or Hayes who famously said, "There are three things that can happen when you pass, and two of them are bad."[13] Oklahoma's Barry Switzer never said it, but certainly agreed with it. Using the wishbone, the Sooners set rushing records in 1971 that still stand today—469 yards per game on the ground and 7.0 yards per rush—while throwing only about four passes a game. Switzer won three national titles at Oklahoma and even when he had passer Troy Aikman in the backfield, he stuck with the wishbone. Aikman transferred to UCLA and became the number-one player picked in the 1989 draft.

There were just as many critics of Gillman's passing offense and AFL offenses in general. NFL partisans looked at the gaudy numbers put up by the Chargers, Oilers and Raiders and scoffed. "The feeling," said NFL player turned broadcaster Pat Summerall, "was that it was the Major Leagues against the Triple A's."[14] The 1968 AFL title game matched Joe Namath and the Jets against Daryle "The Mad Bomber" Lamonica and the Raiders. As NFL executives and newspapermen watched the game on television prior to the Browns–Colts NFL championship game, Namath and Lamonica began trading deep passes early in the first quarter. Harry McClelland of the *Cleveland Press* said out loud what everyone was thinking. "What you are watching," said McClelland, "is known as Mickey Mouse football."[15]

"Another thing I've learned," said Coryell, "is not to believe what other people say,"[16] and indeed, he would go on to have the last laugh. Figuring he had gone about as far as he could go in the college ranks, in 1973 Coryell accepted the head coaching job of the moribund St. Louis Cardinals. The Cardinals had not qualified for the post-season in 25 years, and critics started chirping when he finished his first season at 4–9–1. But his passing offense, the same concepts and terminology used at San Diego State, began to take hold, and in 1974 the Cardinals won the NFC East and Coryell was named Coach of the Year. St. Louis won two division titles in Coryell's five seasons before he moved back to San Diego.

Taking over the Chargers in 1978, there was an abundance of talent to turn Coryell's system into "Air Coryell," one of the deadliest passing offenses in NFL history. Quarterback Dan Fouts threw for more than 4,000 yards in three straight seasons, tight end Kellen Winslow led the league in catches twice and three times surpassed 1,000 yards, and receiver Charlie Joiner had four 1,000-yard seasons. All three made the NFL Hall of Fame. During the heyday of Air Coryell, when the Chargers were routinely throwing the ball nearly 50 times a game, someone asked the coach why he liked to pass the ball so much, Coryell simply shrugged and said in a great moment of understatement, "It's the thing we think we do best."[17]

Coryell's system depended on spacing, timing and simplicity. Simplicity was borne of necessity at San Diego State, as Coryell relied heavily on junior college players who would only have two years in the system. Horn was one of those junior college players and in 1967 became the top draft pick of the Green Bay Packers. Timing was also essential. A quarterback had to take a quick drop and release the ball fast to avoid sacks. In St. Louis, the Cardinals routinely led the league in fewest sacks allowed during the Coryell era, and in 1975 allowed just eight sacks, a record that stood for more than a decade. "The key is quick drop and delivery," wrote Paul Zimmerman of *Sports Illustrated*, "and quick patterns, slants, square-outs, short posts. When the Chargers do it right, their opponents are slashed to pieces, like someone being put to death with a saber."[18]

Coryell probably never got the full credit he deserved, including inclusion in the Hall of Fame, because of his lack of success in the postseason. He never won a playoff game in St. Louis, and even with all that firepower in San Diego never made it to a Super Bowl, and usually the culprit was defense. The ultimate frustration came in the 1980 AFC Championship game, when the Chargers lost at home to the Raiders, 34–27. Trailing by a touchdown in the fourth quarter and needing the ball back to try and tie the score, the Chargers, football's ultimate passing machine, watched the Raiders grind out the last 6:43 of the game by pounding San Diego on the ground.

While San Diego was certainly the epicenter of the NFL's passing revolution, there were also rumblings elsewhere in California, particularly the Bay Area. In 1966, a young assistant coach was in his first year with the Oakland Raiders after similar jobs at Stanford and the University of California. Watching television in his hotel room the night before the Raiders would play in San Diego, he came across *The Sid Gillman Show* on a local channel and sat transfixed as Gillman began diagramming plays with receiver Lance Alworth. "Sid was describing the slant pattern," said Bill Walsh. "He ran the film back and forth, breaking down the play. That had a major influence on me. The attention to detail the man took with this one play was unbelievable."[19]

While Gillman undoubtedly deserves credit, Walsh took his offense even further and envisioned a system that relied more on the short pass than the long one. Both Gillman's and Coryell's offenses were deep-first approaches in which the quarterback's first read was long. Only if the deep receiver was covered did the quarterback look intermediate and then short. "Sid Gillman threw it down the field," said Coryell, "and I've probably watched Sid's teams. But this is *our* stuff."[20]

Walsh took some of Gillman and some of Coryell and came up with his own stuff. Moving to Cincinnati in 1967 as an assistant under Paul Brown, Walsh spent eight years running the Bengals offense. In 1969, he helped quarterback Greg Cook become a star in the making, as Cook threw 15 touchdown passes and led the league in quarterback rating. "Greg Cook was, I believe," said Walsh, "the greatest talent to play the position. He was Steve Young, but bigger. What a great, great talent."[21]

But Cook had suffered a major shoulder injury in a game against the Chiefs, and the injury never healed properly. After his sensational 1969 season, he played in only one game and completed one more pass in his career. Left with a hole at quarterback, Cincinnati traded for retread Virgil Carter, a capable player, but one with a weak throwing arm, especially compared to Cook. "The only choice we had," said Walsh, "was to build our offense around what Virgil could do. And believe me, the short pass was all he could [do]. He was a great competitor, and a great team leader, so we just played into his strength."[22]

Walsh devised a short passing game designed to control the ball through the air much like offenses controlled the ball by running. The emphasis was on short and intermediate throws that were relatively safe, with an occasional long one to keep defenses honest. Like Gillman, he used the horizontal areas of the field as well as the vertical. "Walsh didn't care if a play made only two yards," said Bengals tight end Bob Trumpy, "because it made the defense defend the entire field."[23]

Born in Cincinnati, the system later became known as the West Coast offense.

"Its core philosophy is that a team can keep possession and move the ball down the field with a multidimensional passing game," wrote former Brigham Young University coach Lavell Edwards, who won a college national championship with it in 1984. "Spread the defense out, present the defense with different looks, make more receivers available than can be covered, and get the ball to the open receiver."[24] "It really isn't a complicated philosophy," Walsh added. "We try to control the ball and build up a number of first downs. It's a systematic ball-control style of offense."[25]

Led by Carter, who "couldn't throw the ball 20 yards,"[26] according to his tight end Bruce Coslet, the 1970 Bengals won the AFC Central in only their third year of existence. In 1971, Cincinnati drafted small college quarterback Ken Anderson. In his five years working with Walsh, Anderson led the NFL in passing yards twice, passer rating twice, completion percentage once, and was twice named to the Pro Bowl. With an array of young talent in Cincinnati (including Isaac Curtis, a receiver at San Diego State under Coryell), there's no telling how far Walsh could have taken the Bengals. But when Paul Brown retired after the 1975 season, he named assistant Bill "Tiger" Johnson to replace him. Walsh felt insulted and left. He went so far as to say he believed Brown campaigned against him in getting an NFL head coaching job.

Walsh went to Stanford where he tutored quarterbacks Guy Benjamin and Steve Dils to NCAA passing titles. He finally got a coveted NFL head coaching job in 1979, taking over a terrible 49ers team that won

Eleven. Heir Coryell

only two games in his first season. "We really weren't that bad a team," said receiver Dwight Clark, "we just didn't have any talent. We could tell what he was trying to do was right, it's just that we didn't have the people to pull it off."[27]

As brilliant as he was as an offensive mind, Bill Walsh was every bit as good as a talent evaluator and developer. He started bringing in talent that first year, drafting Joe Montana in the third round, and then in 1980 finding running back Earl Cooper, Jim Stuckey and Keena Turner.

Walsh followed up in 1981 with Hall of Fame safety Ronnie Lott as well as defensive backfield starters Eric Wright and Carlton Williamson. Drafted in 1983, running back Roger Craig added yet another dimension to Walsh's attack at running back, and in 1985 became the first player to have both a thousand yards rushing and receiving in the same season. That same year, Walsh drafted transcendent receiver Jerry Rice, who would end his 20-year career as the NFL's all-time leader in catches, yards and touchdowns.

All of those players would play significant roles in a 49ers dynasty that won four Super Bowl titles in the 1980s. Walsh's best team may have been in 1984 when the 49ers went 15–1 and destroyed Miami in the Super Bowl, 38–19. The incredibly balanced 49ers finished third in the league in rushing offense, fourth in passing, and second overall in total offense. *The Sporting News* named the team the greatest in NFL history. When Walsh retired after a Super Bowl victory over the Bengals in 1988, George Seifert took over and the offense kept rolling. San Francisco set an all-time scoring record in routing Denver in the following Super Bowl, 55–10.

The impact of Walsh, Gillman and Coryell continues in the NFL to this day. Most significantly, their approaches represented a shift away from the running offenses that defined the first 50 years of the league. Early league rules required a player to be at least five yards behind the line of scrimmage to throw a pass, and there were penalties for throwing more than one pass in a series of downs. More often than not, NFL games became brutal, slogging, low-scoring affairs.

The success of these passing pioneers convinced skeptical players, coaches and executives that you could not only entertain with the forward pass, but win with it as well. Fans responded to the higher-scoring games and the rules changed to help open up the game further. When the NFL outlawed downfield harassment of receivers in 1978, the passing game really took off. It took until 1967 for a quarterback (Joe Namath of the Jets) to surpass 4,000 passing yards in a season. As of 2020, 184 quarterbacks have done it, while twelve have passed for more than 5,000—all but one since 2011. In 1963, Y.A. Tittle set an NFL record with

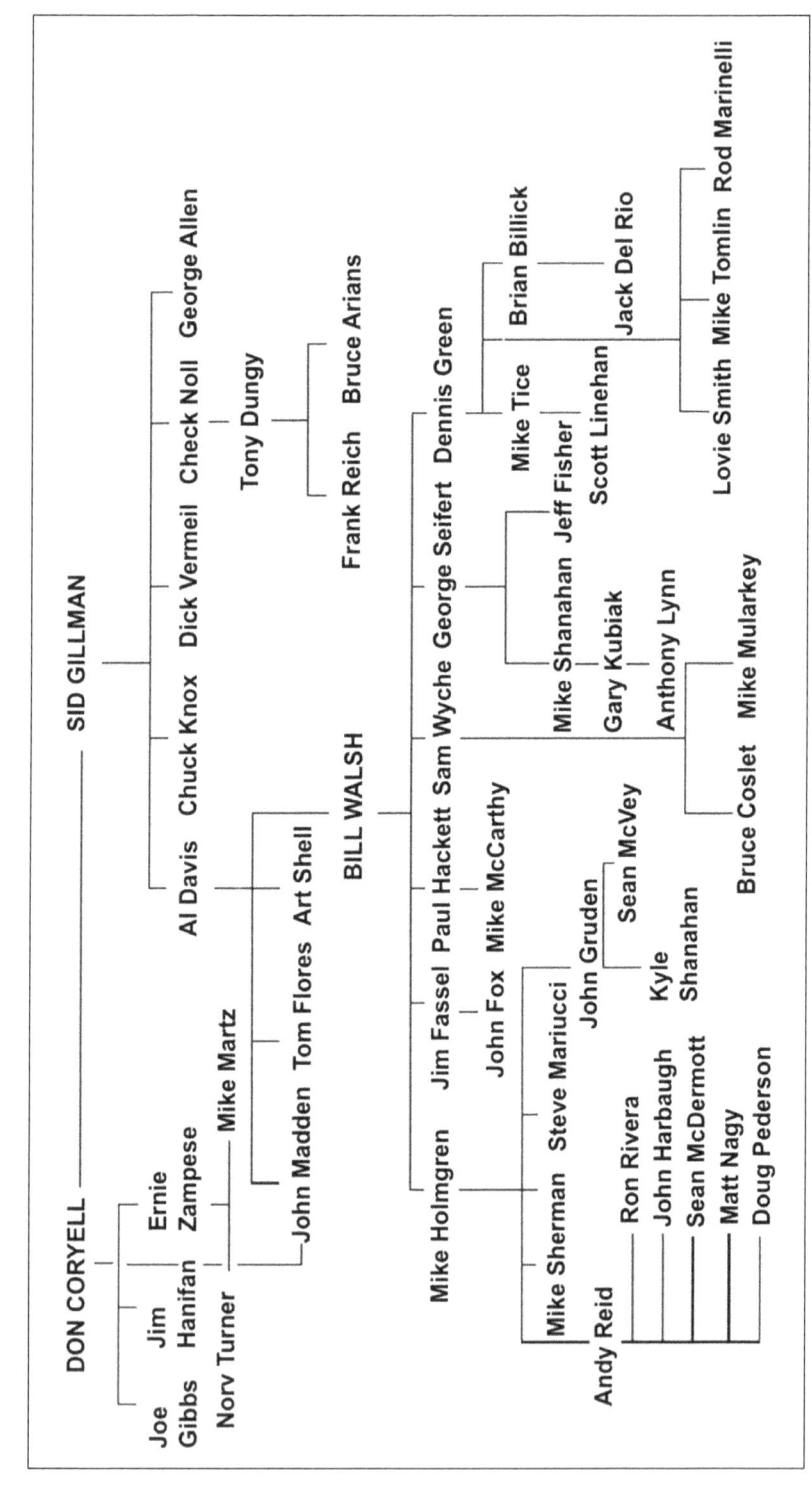

Eleven. Heir Coryell

what seemed like an astronomical total of 36 touchdown passes in a single season. Today, the record is Peyton Manning with 55, and 13 quarterbacks have thrown for more than 40.

Modern offenses have taken the work of Gillman, Walsh and Coryell and taken it into some new areas. The spread offense, often operated out of the shotgun formation, has put as many as six receivers out on a single play, many of them bunched together in groups of three or even four. But the basic concept remains the same—control the ball with short, safe throws to move up the field, such as with bubble screens. A quick throw to a receiver hiding behind a convoy of blockers is considered today nothing more dangerous than a long handoff from the quarterback.

Even these new offenses, especially in a copycat league, are grounded in the work of the three old masters. "The reality is that in today's NFL, every offense has elements of these three schemes incorporated into their playbooks, but there are distinct differences in verbiage and philosophy."[28] When Jason Garrett left as head coach of the Cowboys in 2020 to become offensive coordinator of the New York Giants, he took with him a variation of the Air Coryell passing attack. Garrett leaned it as a backup quarterback with the Cowboys in the 1990s, as it was taught by Norv Turner and Ernie Zampese. Zampese learned it directly from Don Coryell as an assistant at San Diego State in the late 1960s. Don Coryell's offense—perhaps it should be called "Heir Coryell"—is still alive and well in the NFL more than 50 years after it was born in San Diego.

Garrett, Turner, Zampese and so many more are a part of Coryell's coaching tree, which remains a living, breathing testament to the legacy of not only Coryell, but also Walsh and Gillman. While extensive trees can be developed for each man, it's probably better to think of them as coming from Gillman. As the oldest, he undoubtedly influenced both Coryell and Walsh. "All our terminology—and the terminology Bill Walsh took with him when he left here—came from Sid," said the Raiders Al Davis. At the height of his success in San Francisco, Walsh admitted, "Much of what I did I got from Sid Gillman 20 years ago."[29]

Sid Gillman coached his first game in 1955 and several coaches from his tree are still coaching today. It's not just longevity, but also success. Although Gillman won but the one AFL title in 1963, those who have come under his influence have accounted for 28 Super Bowl championships as of 2020, with more possibly to follow.

Opposite: **A coaching tree of the NFL passing revolution should start with Sid Gillman, but leads prominently through Don Coryell and Bill Walsh.**

These offensive philosophies have also trickled down to the college and high school levels. College players, who once wanted to go into programs to run the ball and win championships, now want to play at schools that can "get them ready for the pros." That means places that throw the ball a lot and feature modern ideas and systems. High school kids, too, want to be able to play in college, so they need development in passing offenses. The spread, West Coast, and Coryell offenses have all become commonplace on high school fields across the country.

But just as critics called these offenses "Mickey Mouse" and no more than a passing fancy when they first came out, there are still detractors today. The chief complaint seems to be that such offenses are creating "system" players that can only succeed under certain conditions. In the late 1980s and early 1990s, John Jenkins at the University of Houston created a seemingly unstoppable run-and-shoot offense first popularized by Darrel "Mouse" Davis at Portland State University. The run-and-shoot was like a spread attack on steroids—passing almost every down, receivers running all over the field, and plays run to a fast tempo.

In 1989, Andre Ware triggered Jenkins' offense to the tune of 4,699 yards, 44 touchdowns and 26 NCAA records to win the Heisman Trophy. Ware's replacement, David Klingler, passed for 716 yards in one game and eleven touchdowns in another. His career totals included 91 touchdown passes. Houston beat teams by scores of 60–0, 82–28 and 69–0, and an unapologetic Jenkins took delight in running up the score. Jenkins claimed his refinements to Mouse's system was "like NASA discovering some new solar system. Other teams are crawling, we're flying."[30]

But when Ware and Klingler got to the NFL they were grounded more often than not. Ware threw only five touchdown passes in four seasons with the Lions, while Klingler got hurt in Cincinnati and lost his starting job. Both threw more interceptions than touchdowns in their careers. After a 10–1 season in 1990, Jenkins went 8–14 the next two seasons and lost his job.

In a similar way, Vince Young was considered to be a transformational player that would change the NFL. The focal point of a run-pass option offense at the University of Texas, Young led the Longhorns to a national title in 2005 and set a Rose Bowl record with 467 yards of total offense in the title win over USC. Drafted in the first round by the Tennessee Titans, Young was considered to be the player who would bring the run-pass option to the NFL. But after a successful start that included a Pro Bowl selection in his rookie season, Young regressed and was out of the league for good after six years.

Perhaps Young was the bridge that led to Lamar Jackson, Patrick Mahomes and Deshaun Watson. All are run-pass quarterback in the same way as Young, but even more successful and dangerous. Jackson and Mahomes have won league MVP honors, and Mahomes led the Chiefs to a Super Bowl title. They are the prototypes of the new quarterback in the NFL—fast, mobile and unafraid to throw the ball or take-off running any time. When Fran Tarkenton first popularized the style in the 1960s, he was considered an outlier who would likely get killed when defenses caught up with him.[31] While critics laughed at Tarkenton, no one is laughing at Watson, Mahomes or Jackson. Today, the future of the NFL appears to be in the hands of this new group of quarterbacks, who seem to be reinventing the game.

But even if the league does reinvent itself, as it does every so often, the roots of that reinvention can be found with Sid Gillman, Don Coryell and Bill Walsh. They are the true pioneers who took a game grounded in the run and pointed it to the sky.

TWELVE

Time and Place

In 1994, longtime reporter and political analyst James Cannon wrote a biography of former U.S. President Gerald Ford entitled *Time and Chance*. The book only nominally touched on Ford's early years and focused more on his unlikely ascendancy to the presidency—the only Vice President and President never elected to office. In 1972, Ford had just been elected to a 13th term as a U.S. Representative from Grand Rapids, Michigan, but the election left him disappointed. Because the Democrats retained control of Congress, Ford would likely not achieve his lifelong ambition of becoming Speaker of the House. He made the decision to leave politics after Richard Nixon finished his second term as President.

Nixon was at the height of his powers on election night 1972 as he and Vice President Spiro Agnew had just been returned to office in the greatest landslide in presidential electoral history. Who could have guessed that less than two years later both Nixon and Agnew would be forced to resign in humiliation, and that Ford, who never sought or wanted the office, would become the unlikeliest President in U.S. history? In Cannon's view, Ford was the right man in the right place at the right time. "Fate or destiny or kind Providence," he wrote, "would replace Nixon with the one man uniquely qualified to become President in a unique moment in the life of the Republic."[1]

Cannon based the title of his book on a verse from the Biblical book of Ecclesiastes in the Old Testament:

> The race is not to the swift
> or the battle to the strong,
> nor does food come to the wise
> or wealth to the brilliant
> or favor to the learned;
> but time and chance happen to them all.[2]

Time and chance. The entire NFL landscape has been shaped by unique people coming together in unique moments.

Consider one of the most famous games in league history. On December 28, 1975, the Dallas Cowboys and Minnesota Vikings met in the first round of the NFC playoffs in Bloomington, Minnesota. The game was a tight defensive struggle that saw the Vikings take a 14–10 lead with less than two minutes to go on a short touchdown run by Brent McClanahan.

The rest of the story is quite familiar to NFL fans. Dallas quarterback Roger Staubach completed two improbable passes to Drew Pearson: a 25-yarder on fourth and 17 and then a 50-yard scoring throw that created an enduring term for desperation touchdown passes in the final seconds. "I just closed my eyes and said a Hail Mary,"[3] Staubach said after the game, which Dallas ended up winning, 17–14.

But consider the sequence of events that had to take place in order for the Cowboys to stage their miraculous rally:

- Dallas center John Fitzgerald had been having trouble getting the shotgun snap back to Staubach and was replaced by rookie Kyle Davis. If Fitzgerald stays in the game, Staubach might not even get off the winning pass.
- On fourth and 17 from the Dallas 25, Staubach threw a deep sideline pass to Pearson, who did not get both feet in bounds. Pearson was in the air when defender Nate Wright pushed him out of bounds, which at the time was a legal catch. The rule has since been changed and a receiver must now come down with both feet in bounds and on the ground. Under today's rules, the pass would have been incomplete and Minnesota would have taken over on downs and won the game.
- On first down from the 50 and with 37 seconds remaining, Staubach threw short over the middle to running back Preston Pearson. Pearson already had the reputation as a clutch third-down back with great hands, but this time he somehow dropped the ball. Had Pearson made the catch, it is unlikely he would have been able to get out of bounds to stop the clock. Time could have run out, giving Minnesota the win.
- On second down with 32 seconds left, Staubach dropped back and pump faked a deep pass to his left in order to get safety Paul Krause away from his intended target Drew Pearson, who was running deep down the right side. Staubach let fly a pass for Pearson, who collided briefly with Wright at the five-yard line but caught the ball between his right hand and his hip, and he walked into the end zone for a touchdown. Officials threw a penalty flag on the play, but it was on Wright for defensive

pass interference and the touchdown stood. Offensive pass interference could have easily been called as replays suggested that Pearson may have pushed off on Wright, who had the receiver well covered. Obviously, a call of offensive pass interference would have negated the touchdown and made it much more likely that Minnesota would have won the game.

The final minute of the Dallas–Minnesota game was surreal, especially for Vikings fans. After Pearson's fourth down catch, a frustrated security guard (and apparent Vikings fan) kicked the receiver while he was still on the ground. Fans were so frustrated after Pearson's winning catch that one threw a whiskey bottle on the field, hitting field judge Armen Terzian in the head. The blow momentarily stunned Terzian, who finished the afternoon wrapped in bandages. All of this was apparently too much for the father of Vikings quarterback Fran Tarkenton, who had a heart attack during the game and passed away.

Think of how much history would have been changed if Minnesota had somehow been able to hold on and win the game. Such speculation is not that far-fetched considering the unlikely series of events that eventually led to the Vikings' defeat. Had any single link in the chain of events failed, the chain itself would have broken.

Time and chance.

Many football researchers, writers and authors have subscribed to a Darwinian theory of NFL growth; namely, that the league has gone through a continual evolution, thanks mainly to the presence, power and ultimate cooperation of its founding fathers. They were the ones who lifted the league from obscurity to omnipotence. "Over time the pro game was able to climb out of this hole because these owners—the Redskins' Marshall, the Steelers' Art Rooney, the Chicago Bears' George Halas, the New York Giants' Tim Mara, and the Philadelphia Eagles' Bert Bell—embraced a strategy grounded in a subtle blend of competition and cooperation."[4]

If indeed the NFL goes through cycles of evolution, its Big Bang took place from 1957 to 1962. That was a unique time in NFL history filled with unique moments and unique people that combined to form the most important time period in league history. Just as "fate or destiny or kind Providence" worked in the success of Gerald Ford, so too did they come together for athletes and sports organizations, including the man who created the Ruthian Moment.

Babe Ruth became Babe Ruth because of the unique combination of circumstances that placed him in the right place at the right time.

Twelve. Time and Place 189

The country had to move from the Puritanism of the Victorian Era to the relaxed standards of the Jazz Age. Ruth himself had to move from a relatively smaller stage in Boston to the media capital of the country in New York. His new team had to allow him to essentially give up a successful pitching career and let him play in the outfield, where his talent could shine every day. As a result, according to Eric Jentsch at the Smithsonian Museum, Ruth "was adopted as part of the new media landscape, becoming a towering figure"[5] who lives on in popular culture while many of his contemporaries are forgotten.

Just as Babe Ruth could only happen in the culture of the 1920s, so too could the major changes taking place in the NFL only happen in that narrow slice of time, 1957–1962.

Consider the empowerment of the players that began with the Radovich decision in 1957. It came about in part because of a cultural acceptance of unionization that began in the early 20th century and culminated in the mid–1950s when "unions in the U.S. had successfully organized approximately one out of every three non-farm workers. This period represented the peak of labor's power, as the ranks of unionized workers shrank in subsequent decades."[6] Labor has fallen from its heyday of 35 percent of the workforce in the 1950s to less than 7 percent today.

The birth of NFL unionization in the 1950s, and its subsequent growth in the following decades, empowered the players beyond their wildest expectations. It was the NFL Players Association that was instrumental in creating minimum salaries and working conditions, collective bargaining with league owners, and laying the groundwork for free agency. But just as unionization has fallen out of favor in most industrialized countries across the world, there is now a sense that perhaps the NFLPA has outlived its usefulness. Former player Domonique Foxworth believes the NFLPA helps the top stars in the league get extremely rich, but doesn't do anything to help the lower tier players. "The players have no practical response to the owners taking a bigger and bigger share as the leagues get more profitable," says Foxworth. "And the trend will only get worse for current and future players until they abandon the counterproductive construct of unions in sports."[7] Foxworth believes the union should decertify and become more of a trade association as it was in the late 1950s.

The 1950s were also a time of tremendous economic growth, another essential piece of timing that allowed the NFL to grow. The league constricted in the 1930s and 1940s due to the Great Depression and World War II, and by the time the recessions of the 1970s rolled around it was strong enough to weather the storm. Economic growth and success, for individuals as well as the country, opened up games to those who had previously been unable to attend. It also helped erase some of the social barriers that separated people outside the stadium. As personal incomes rose and ticket prices became affordable, fans in lower economic classes now found themselves able to go to the games, many times sitting next to upper class patricians from the townhouses or suburbs.

The modern NFL likes to believe it is an egalitarian melting pot, but just the opposite is true. As the money got bigger and the owners got richer, the social barriers went back up in the form of new stadiums. It began in 1968 when the Houston Oilers left tiny Jeppesen Stadium for the air-conditioned comfort of the fabulous new Astrodome (with a brief stop along the way at Rice Stadium). Soon, the intimacy of Franklin Field in Philadelphia, the Cotton Bowl in Dallas, and Wrigley Field in Chicago gave way to modern sports palaces with luxury boxes, personal seat licenses, and in effect, segregated seating.

When the Cowboys left the Cotton Bowl in 1971 a season ticket in the upper deck cost only $70. It would cost more than three times that much just to pay for a bond to build Texas Stadium and the right to buy tickets in the upper section. "It took the game away from the real fans and gave it to the people who had money," said defensive end George Andrie. "They had to do it, but it got to the point where we wanted to play on the road. Our fans had changed."[8] Some estimates suggested that less than 10,000 fans followed the team from the Cotton Bowl to Texas Stadium.

Economic growth also meant the NFL could attract and keep the talented players that fans would pay to see. Up until the 1950s, pro football was strictly a sideshow; something for young men to play as a hobby. Suddenly, it turned into a career. "In the old days, when a crack player had a choice between the pros and dental school, he often chose the latter," wrote Thomas Morgan in 1959. "Now the pro game competes, not only with dentistry, but with such a company as Warner Brothers."[9] Morgan was referring to halfback Frank Gifford, who chose to play with the New York Giants over a movie offer from Warner Brothers. In 1958, Gifford earned about $50,000 in salary, television commercials, endorsements and writing fees, which would translate to nearly half a million dollars today.

Gifford openly acknowledged the importance of the 1958 championship game in terms of making NFL players recognizable and more commercially viable. Once again the stars lined to produce another watershed moment that seemingly could only happen at that exact time and place. The 1958 game between the Colts and Giants took place in

Twelve. Time and Place 191

hallowed Yankee Stadium, giving it instant credibility. That the game was in New York, the media capital of the country, meant it would reach the greatest possible audience through television, radio and newspapers.

The most important of these media was television. By 1958, television was no fly-by-night operation, either in terms of the technology or its cultural significance. At the end of World War II only a few thousand wealthy Americans could even afford a television set. By 1957, there were 37 million sets and nearly two-thirds of every household had one. Advertising money spent on television rose from $128 million in 1951 to an astounding $1 billion in 1955.[10]

It could not have happened in the 1940s, as the development of television was put on hold for World War II. It could not have happened in the 1960s as the NFL was fighting a different kind of war with the AFL. In the late 1950s the NFL and the country were fat, happy and at peace—a rare confluence of culture, economics and technology.

In a similar way, the mythology of the NFL that grew out of the 1957–1962 time period, and specifically the 1958 title game, could not be replicated in other eras. The 1920s certainly contributed to the mythology of athletes such as Babe Ruth, Jack Dempsey and Bobby Jones. But the NFL was not developed enough as an organization to take advantage of the cultural opportunity. The 1960s and 70s contributed to the demythologization of culture through the Vietnam War, Watergate and various civil protests.

Technology contributed greatly to this process. As the probing eye of television reached farther into American life, it peeled back the veneer of mythology that surrounded institutions such as politics, government and sports. Americans saw the horrors of war and the excesses of government piped right into their living rooms. As they turned to sports to "get away from it all," they also saw Muhammad Ali refuse induction into the army, and Tommie Smith and John Carlos raised black-gloved fists at the 1968 Olympics. The very technology that made sports so popular in the first place now seemed to be destroying it in some way, leading author Joseph Campbell to declare in 1991, "What we have today is a demythologized world."[11]

The modern NFL is hugely successful, but it is success built on money, not mythology. As just one example, consider the growth of gambling. For decades, the league held firm to the mythology of the evils of gambling and its threat to the purity of sport. It's what got Frank Filchock and Merle Hapes suspended for the 1946 championship game, it's what got Paul Hornung and Alex Karras suspended for the entire 1963 season, and it's what drove Joe Namath to the brink of retirement with his New York bar Bachelor's III.

Today, as more and more states legalize sports betting in the wake of a U.S. Supreme Court decision, the NFL is waffling on its official position against gambling. The league has allowed fan betting sites FanDuel and DraftKings to advertise during games, and some teams even have sponsorship deals with the companies. At one time, both Cowboys owner Jerry Jones and Patriots owner Robert Kraft had ownership stakes in DraftKings. The combination of betting on games, fantasy leagues and other forms of gambling could add as much as $2.3 billion to the NFL's annual revenue. "Legal, regulated sports betting will create huge new revenue opportunities for sports leagues and the NFL could be the biggest winner of all," according to Sara Slane of the American Gaming Association.[12]

Well-publicized scandals involving steroids, concussions, drugs and the personal lives of NFL players have all combined to chip away at the mythology that began in 1958. Even the mythology of Vince Lombardi, who contributed more to the league's image than perhaps any single individual, has eroded over time. Modern critics have taken a more realistic look at Lombardi and his famous maxims, with one such essay declaring, "These lines are less a representation of the real Lombardi than a myth football men crafted in order to buttress their sport's image."[13]

Even before Lombardi died in 1970, the counter culture of the 1960s attempted to fight back against the mythology. Famous NFL "dropouts" such as Chip Oliver, George Sauer and Dave Meggyesy quit the league at young ages because of what they called the dehumanization of the game. "Football is an archaic ethos," Meggyesy wrote in 1971. "It's a game for yahoos, like the old Roman sports. If this society changes like I hope it will, football will be obsolete."[14]

Of course, Meggyesy and his disciples were in the minority, but their attitudes, coming just a decade after the Colts and Giants played for the 1958 championship, showed just how unique that game and that time period truly were.

Time and chance.

Another part of the demythologization of the game came with the growing corporate culture of the late 1950s. Just as the culture as a whole became more regimented and buttoned-down, so too did the NFL. The free-spirited days of "Crazylegs" Hirsch, "Night Train" Lane and "Slingin'" Sammy Baugh were giving way to a more sanitized era which would see the league evolve into what critics called the "No Fun League." "There was no single incident that was the catalyst, and there was no particular person or team campaigning to keep such things as button-down as possible" wrote Mark Maske. "The NFL never set out to be the 'No Fun League.' It just happened that way."[15]

Twelve. Time and Place

The transition from Bert Bell to Pete Rozelle in the commissioner's office played an important part of this evolution. While Bell did make important strides to modernize the NFL (see Chapter Eight), he was a holdover from the chaotic early days of the league and in many ways ran a growing corporate entity much like a corner drug store. He saw NFL ownership as a fraternity of like-minded pals, refused to move league offices out of his hometown of Philadelphia, and made it a habit to watch games from the stands so he could visit with fans.

It was in the stands that Bell died of a heart attack while watching a game at Franklin Field in 1959. While Maske was right in that "no single incident" was the catalyst in the changing NFL, Bell's death was a signal moment. Pete Rozelle—young, forward-thinking, image-conscious—took over as commissioner and immediately set the league on a path of corporatization. "From the day he took over as commissioner," reads his entry in the Sports Broadcasting Hall of Fame, "Rozelle began crafting what would become the business model for all professional sports, led by the revolutionary belief that professional sports belonged in the same light as big business."[16] As the NFL looked to find its identity after the death of Bert Bell, Pete Rozelle came along as the right man at the right place at the right time, even if his ascension came about through the unlikeliest of circumstances.

Time and chance.

Rozelle took over just in time to deal with the challenge of the new American Football League. Other leagues had tried and failed to take on the NFL and the failures were not entirely their own fault. The second AFL tried to begin play during the Great Depression and lasted only one year. The third AFL started in 1940, but the loss of players due to World War II forced it out of business after two seasons.

The fourth and final AFL came along at the precise moment when the American nation was ready for change. The growing baby boomer generation, now comprising the largest ever college enrollment in U.S. history, wanted to move past the Eisenhower conservatism of their parents. Thus in the 1960s, according to *U.S. News & World Report*, "America's cities had become powder kegs as African-Americans, despite historic gains toward legal equality, became more impatient than ever at being second-class citizens. Women began demanding their rights in unprecedented numbers. Young people and their parents felt a widening generation gap as seen in their differing perceptions of patriotism, drug use, sexuality, and the work ethic."[17]

Announced in 1959 and launched in 1960, the American Football League represented the promise and change of the times. "There was a sense of newness and freshness, and even mystery about [the AFL]," wrote Neil Longley, "that was somehow intriguing."[18] Young people gravitated to the new league and its new young stars like Lance Alworth, Mike Garrett and "Broadway" Joe Namath, creating a new kind of generation gap. Parents gravitated toward the stability and success of the NFL while their kids embraced the excitement and unpredictability of the AFL.

No player symbolized this divide more than Namath, who became a Pied Piper for a legion of young fans attracted by his rebellion, adventurous nightlife and smoldering good looks. "Namath, wearing low-cut white shoes in a sea of high-topped black-on-green, the catalytic figure in every game he played as a pro ... looked tradition in the eye and poked a finger in it. Why, said Namath, can't an athlete admit publicly to drinking alcohol, smoking tobacco, making love to beautiful women—if indeed he does?"[19]

The AFL, Joe Namath, Pete Rozelle, Johnny Unitas, Bill Radovich, Tom Landry, Vince Lombardi and A. Salam Qureishi all came together in a unique five-year slice of sports history. The people, places and personalities of 1957–1962 did nothing less that change the course of league history and create the modern NFL.

Time and chance.

* * *

Just as change is a fundamental part of life, individuals and organizations tend to resist that change. Almost by nature, organisms prefer the feelings of comfort and stability that come from stasis, or lack of change. Psychologists agree that "as creatures of habit, we often have difficulty incorporating new changes into our routines, no matter how beneficial they are for us, because we tend to do the things that make us feel good, secure and comfortable."[20] Rosabeth Moss Kanter of the Harvard Business School says that factors such as loss of control, excess uncertainty and lack of familiarity make people resistant to change.[21]

The same principles apply to organizations, which are in their own way living organisms. Organizations must continually adapt to changing circumstances and the National Football League is no exception. Like any organization, the NFL is subject to a constantly evolving life cycle. There are many models of the organizational life cycle in existence, but they all seem to refer to the same five stages of development: existence, survival, success, renewal and decline.

The existence stage is when the organization is just born and the focus is on "viability, or simply identifying a sufficient number of customers to support the existence of the organization."[22] For the NFL, this would be the rough-and-tumble period of the 1920s when franchises, administrators and players popped up and disappeared just as suddenly.

During the decade no less than 35 teams abandoned their franchises as "the early NFL was just a loose confederation of local club teams, [and] any organization with 11 warm bodies and a place to play had a good chance of being accepted for NFL membership."[23]

The existence stage is followed by survival, characterized by a desire for growth and formalization of structure. This corresponds to the NFL period of the 1930s and 1940s, which saw both growth and formalization despite the challenges of the Depression and World War II. It was during the 1930s that the league stabilized its rules regarding games, schedules and rosters, and also developed the first championship games. Coverage of the NFL by the media, and especially on radio, allowed the league to grow even in difficult circumstances.

The third stage of the organizational life cycle is success. This is when the group reaches a stage of maturity through organization and bureaucracy, and "such organizations have passed the survival test, growing to a point that they may seek to protect what they have gained instead of targeting new territory."[24] This was the NFL in the late 1940s and for most of the 1950s, as it sought to protect its turf in the face of challenges from the All-American Football Conference, growing player rights, and other external threats such as gambling issues. Starting in 1953, NFL Commissioner Bert Bell, the league's ultimate bureaucrat, began keeping tabs on gambling prices and point spreads to prevent another gambling scandal. "We have an ex–FBI man in every game city, visiting joints to make sure the players don't hang around where bettors are," Bell said. "Bettors would be happy just to be seen with a player, anything to fluctuate the price. Look, the bookies don't want to touch a horse bet any more—they'd rather handle football and baseball."[25]

The final two stages in the organizational life cycle are renewal and decline. After a business succeeds it must look for ways to renew itself and keep growing. Otherwise, it falls into a stasis that leads to decline and possible death. History is littered with organizations that failed to change and innovate and paid the ultimate price. As just one example, Blockbuster was incredibly popular and profitable in the 1990s as an in-store video rental chain. When technology made it possible to deliver content without going to a store, new firms like Netflix became pioneers in digital delivery. However, "Blockbuster failed to follow suit [and] continued to offer their in-store service for a number of reasons which, to many, may seem somewhat foolish."[26] In its heyday Blockbuster had more than 9,000 stores worldwide. As of 2020, there was exactly one left in Bend, Oregon.

Sports organizations and leagues are no different. Like the NFL, pro basketball was constantly in danger of collapse during its formative years, and several leagues folded between 1900 and 1950. In the 1949-50 National Basketball Association season, nine of the 17 teams in the league scored less than 80 points per game and the champion Minneapolis Lakers averaged only 84.1. The problem was stalling and freezing the ball, especially in close games. The NBA responded by implementing a 24-second clock in the 1954-55 season, a decision that was "so important, in fact, that many people believe it saved the league from going out of business."[27]

Competition often forces organizations to either renew or decline. When the American Basketball Association began play in 1967, the older and established NBA barely took notice until the ABA began raiding NBA rosters and signing top-end college talent. Much like the fight between the NFL and AFL, the battle became contentious and expensive. The ABA finally ran out of money in 1976 and its four most successful teams—Denver Nuggets, Indiana Pacers, New York Nets and San Antonio Spurs—were absorbed into the NBA.

But the ABA left an imprint on basketball that continues to this day. When it began, the ABA was considered a gimmick league for such innovations as a three-point line and a red, white and blue basketball. ABA games were high scoring as teams ran up and down the court, and its best players were the outside gunners who could hit the three pointers. The established NBA laughed, preferring its low-post, grind-it-out style that emphasized the importance of muscle and big men.

But the NBA began to decline in the late 1970s, falling into "an era of cocaine abuse, poor imaging and non-televised games,"[28] including NBA Finals series in 1979 and 1980 that were televised partially on tape delay. In 1979, the NBA benefited from rookies Larry Bird and Magic Johnson, but also borrowed from the ABA by creating a three-point shot. Like the adoption of a 24-second clock, the three-point line not only meant revival, it created transformation. "The whole NBA [today] is the ABA," said Walt Frazier, a Hall of Fame NBA player for the Knicks who now works on television for the team. "All the NBA [does now] is run and gun. Now all we have to do is color the ball red, white and blue. It's like the old AFL."[29]

Frazier's comparison is a good one. The AFL and ABA were flashy, offensive-minded and willing to take chances. Their attitudes ultimately forced their competitors to accept them as equals and adapt many of their new ideas. The two-point conversion after touchdown, part of the AFL from its beginnings and initially ridiculed by the NFL, was eventually adopted by the older league in 1994.

If one looks at the organizational life cycle in graphic form, it can be plainly seen how the NFL has progressed through the years. It is argued

Twelve. Time and Place

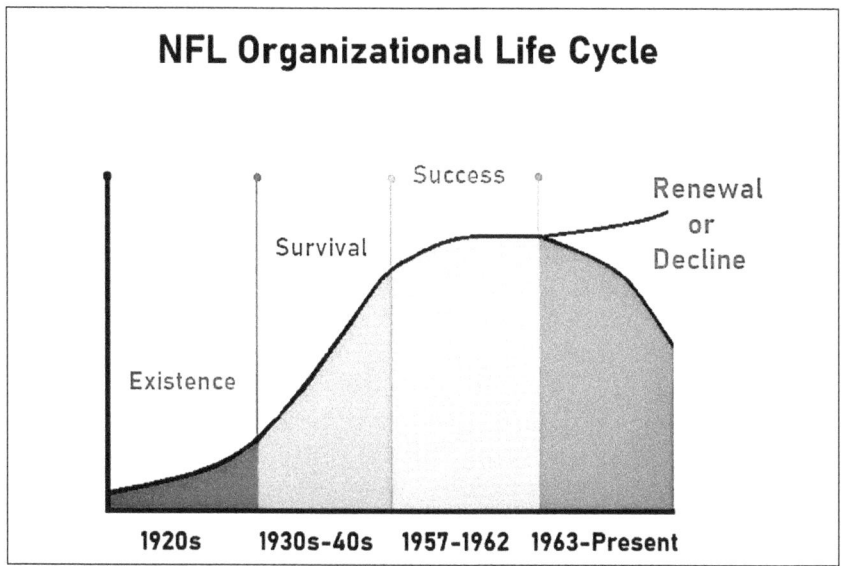

Like any business, the NFL continues to evolve as part of its organizational life cycle. As the league faces new challenges in the 2020s, it can either adapt and continue to grow or face the threat of decline.

that the key time period of success for the league was in 1957–1962. These were the years that set the NFL on a path of success and renewal instead of decline, which raises an important question—can the league replicate such success as it faces the challenges of the 2020s?

The NFL faced some of the same issues when it celebrated its 50th season in 1969. That's when *US News & World Report* conducted a special look at the game, acknowledging that while professional football clearly had not yet peaked, "How much longer can football's dominance continue?"[30]

The article mentioned several factors related to that dominance, including money, which primarily comes from television (and now digital) rights fees. In 1963, the NFL and AFL collected $6.5 million combined for the rights to televise games. Today, the NFL makes more than five billion dollars a year from broadcast rights, nearly double what the league earned in 2006, and there are talks of yet another increase when a new deal comes out in 2022. It should come as no surprise that "no other professional sports league generates the kind of cash off its broadcasting rights as the NFL."[31]

That money has filtered down to the players, who in 1969 had an average salary of $25,000 compared to about two million today. Team revenue has climbed from $3.8 million per team in 1967 to nearly $300 million today, while the main revenue stream has shifted from ticket sales to television.

The improvement of technology since 1969, both for television and emerging digital platforms, has also spurred interest. After a couple of years with down television ratings thanks to the Colin Kaepernick controversy (see Introduction), television ratings rebounded in both 2018 and 2019. While more fans are watching on television, they are also going to the games. League attendance has increased from a total of 8.9 million fans in 1969 to 16.7 million in 2019. When the AFL and NFL came together in 1970, stadiums were required to have at least 50,000 seats. Today's NFL teams have that and much more, and in 2019 all but two of the league's 32 teams averaged more than 50,000 in attendance.[32]

Add all of these things together and it looks like the NFL is as strong and as healthy as ever. In 1963, the Philadelphia Eagles were sold for $5.5 million. Five years later, the team was resold for $16.1 million. Today, the Eagles are worth $3.05 billion and every team in the league has a value of at least $1.9 billion.[33]

But as then–Commissioner Pete Rozelle observed in 1969, "I wouldn't say that the boom is over, but we can hardly continue to grow at the same percentage rates as we have in the past."[34] Rozelle's words are even more compelling today as costs continue to rise just as fast and in some cases faster than revenue.

The main driver of cost is player salaries, which have risen dramatically thanks to free agency and increased television revenues. In 1969, the average NFL player made about four times the salary of the average American; today, with NFL salaries in the multi-millions, an NFL player makes about 50 times what an average American does. In 2019, the salary of the average NFL player was about $2.7 million. Perhaps to save owners from themselves, the league does have a salary cap for each team, which in 2019 was $188.2 million. The cap has risen from $57.28 million in 1999 and from $123 million in 2009.

Those salaries are putting a squeeze on team operating costs. If not for revenue sharing, the philosophy that each team in the league equally shares the bountiful television revenue, several teams would be losing money. Of course, teams are still making money, not just as much as they did in years past. In 2017, the Green Bay Packers, the only community-owned team in the league, announced a profit of $34.1 million. A year later, the team saw profit fall 98 percent to just $724,000. During that same time expenses rose from $420.9 million to $477.2 million, due mainly to rising player salaries.[35] If not for the $255 million coming from television revenue, the Packers would have finished the year in the red.

Like any good business, NFL owners pass the increased cost off to their customers. In 2019, the average cost of a single ticket for an NFL game was $102.35, topped by the $165.77 charged for Los Angeles Chargers games. Add in the cost of personal seat licenses, concessions, parking and the like, and the cost for a family of four to go to a game now exceeds $500. Although is apparently has not been reached yet, at some point the high cost of going to games combined with the improved television viewing experience at home, will price many fans out attending the game in person. "It would be crazy for a family of four to go," said Vikings fan and Minneapolis resident Nathan Rice. "You have to have some serious coin to bring your whole family there."[36]

In 1969, Art Modell, who owned the Cleveland Browns, observed, "Pro football is not a prudent business investment. It is too unpredictable. Operating profits never justify your investment."[37] In 1953, the Browns sold for $600,000 and Modell bought the team for four million in 1963. By 1970, the team value was estimated at $14 million. In 2020, now owned by Dee and Jimmy Haslam, the Cleveland Browns are worth as estimated $2.2 billion. When Modell owned the team in 1969, operating income was $635,000. Today it is $32 million.[38]

So exactly where is the NFL headed? While the NFL is in no danger of becoming another Blockbuster, the league has several fundamental problems.

The pioneering spirit of the NFL's founding fathers—Halas, Marshall, Rooney and Bell—has been replaced with a cautious protectionism and desire to maintain the status quo. It's not survival of the league that's at stake so much as the billion-dollar investments of what author Mark Lebovich calls "The Membership," the team owners of today's NFL. "[They are] a considerably older, stodgier, and more entitled group than the founders," wrote Lebovich. "Say what you will about the merits of on-field protests; taking a knee in that setting takes guts. Bending the knee to [President] Trump, as the owners have done, takes none."[39]

Trump injecting himself into the Kaepernick controversy—"Wouldn't you love to see one of these NFL owners, when somebody disrespects the flag, to say, 'Get that son of a bitch off the field right now. Out! He's fired,'"[40] Trump said in 2017—polarized the country and dragged the divisiveness of politics into a sport that has always been regarded as something that brought the country together. "Liberals think it's dangerous, classist, totalitarian and cruel," wrote Will Leitch. "Conservatives think it's pandering [and] too 'politically correct.' The league that was once for everyone seems to be in crisis. Worse, it has no natural constituency."[41]

That constituency is now several splinter groups that have put the

NFL in a no-win situation. Whatever the league does on concussions, one group will complain that it's not enough and the game has become too dangerous, while another group rails that the game is becoming "soft" and getting away from its past. While the NFL stands by, trying to figure out what to do, participation in youth tackle football continues to decline, from 8.4 million in 2006 to 5.2 million in 2017. "Without that feeder system to provide fresh meat and fresh brains to the NFL meat grinder," says sportswriter John Kass, "the NFL as we know it is doomed. Without its connection to the middle class, the NFL loses what it can't afford—market share."[42]

No matter how the league handles the growing social issues surrounding Colin Kaepernick, one side will say that the league has waffled and has no interest in free speech, while the other side decries a lack of respect and claims they are done with the NFL until the protestors "stand their ass up."[43] Stuck between groups it cannot placate, no wonder the league is afraid to take bold action. "After attaining a certain amount of success," wrote *Sports Illustrated*, "[the NFL was] disincentivized from change, from just *trying* things more. When it comes to innovating, the NFL is frozen in time."[44]

In the organizational life cycle, frozen usually means dead. Businesses usually change and adapt or they simply go away. It's almost inconceivable to think that the most successful and profitable sports league in the country, with revenues at an all-time high of $14 billion, could be in danger, but the warning signs are clearly there. While almost all NFL success metrics—attendance, revenue, television ratings—are going up, they are not going up as fast as they did in years past. Game attendance, for example, has flattened out at between 16 and 17 million fans, and not moved much up or down in the past 20 years. Attendance in 2019 averaged 66,648, which represented the lowest mark since 2004. Television ratings rebounded in 2019 after two years of decline.

Some blame overexposure. Games on Sunday, Monday, Thursday and the occasional Saturday may be killing the game the same way television killed boxing in the 1950s. Gambling, once the bane of the NFL, has now been accepted and even encouraged in tangential ways, such as with fantasy football and now legalized sports betting in several states. "The NFL's overriding strategic goal should be getting people to watch on television," writes Jonathan Last. "That's the business they're in. So, again, why would you encourage side businesses that tell your audience they don't really need to consume the main product? It's madness."[45]

Perhaps more troubling, basketball has now surpassed football as the favorite sport of American youngsters, and while most adults still rank football as number-one, its popularity has steadily slipped since peaking in 2006. The NBA in particular has made successful inroads into American culture and seems to be everything the NFL is not: young, hip and forward thinking. "Whereas the NFL felt like the sport that best fit the cultural spirit of the past decades of American life, it's the NBA that reflects the future."[46]

But it's also important to remember that the NBA was once considered dead and buried; so dead, that before Magic Johnson and Larry Bird came along the television ratings were so microscopic that the league's signature event—the NBA Finals—was not even televised live but shown on tape delay. Johnson, Bird, Michael Jordan and now LeBron James have together saved the league and pushed it to unprecedented heights, but so did Oscar Robertson, Jerry West and Wilt Chamberlain in the 1960s before the league fell off a cliff in the 1970s.

Everything is cyclical including economic booms and busts, political fortunes, and the power and popularity of sports organizations. What triggers a boom is some sort of catalyzing event; a Ruthian Moment, if you will. That's what set the NFL on its way to unimaginable success following the critical years of 1957–1962. There's no reason that such an event could not happen again and propel the league even higher that it is now.

"The NFL will no doubt look different in a decade or two," wrote Nancy Armour of *USA Today* in 2019. "Players come and go, coaches innovate and rules change. But to think that the league will no longer exist, or be a shell of its current self, now seems as outlandish as the idea of Jerry Jones handing over the keys to the Dallas Cowboys to Johnny Manziel. Then again, we'd have watched that too."[47]

Time and chance.

Chapter Notes

Preface

1. A man named Troy Haupt owns the only existing broadcast copy of Super Bowl I, found in his mother's attic in Pennsylvania. Because of ongoing property rights issues with the NFL, the copy remains locked in a storage vault in New York.

Introduction

1. Bryan DeArdo, "Coronavirus: NFL's Chief Medical Officer Says for 2020 Season to Start on Time, Here's What Has to Happen," *CBS Sports*, 3 April 2020. From: https://www.cbssports.com/nfl/news/coronavirus-nfls-chief-medical-officer-says-for-2020-season-to-start-on-time-heres-what-has-to-happen/.
2. Don Van Natta, Jr., and Kevin Van Valkenburg, "Rice Case: Purposeful Misdirection by Team, Scant Investigation by NFL, *ESPN*, 19 September 2014. From: https://www.espn.com/espn/otl/story/_/id/11551518/how-ray-rice-scandal-unfolded-baltimore-ravens-roger-goodell-nfl.
3. "Colin Kaepernick Protests Anthem Over Treatment of Minorities," *The Undefeated*, 27 August 2016. From: https://thcundefeated.com/features/colin-kaepernick-protests-anthem-over-treatment-of-minorities/.
4. Dan Cancian, "Twitter Rages After NFL Commissioner Roger Goodell Explains Why Colin Kaepernick Is Still Out of Football," *Newsweek*, 31 January 2019. From: https://www.newsweek.com/colin-kaepernick-roger-goodell-super-bowl-liii-nfl-protests-colin-kaepernick-1312548.
5. Hal Bock, "Kaepernick Brings League to Its Knees," *Bock's Score*, 26 February 2019. From: http://sportsmediahistory.com/?p=380.
6. Juliet Macur, "For a Cowboys Star with Dementia, Time Is Running Out," *New York Times*, 26 January 2014. From: https://www.nytimes.com/2014/01/27/sports/football/for-a-cowboys-star-with-dementia-time-is-running-out.html.
7. "Correspondence," *Neurosurgery*, May 2006, vol. 58, no. 5: E1003.
8. Kevin Seifert, "Dr. Bennet Omalu: CTE Obsession Obscuring Truth About Brain Health of Football Players," *ESPN*, 4 August 2017. From: http://www.espn.com/nfl/story/_/id/20245394/dr-bennet-omalu-says-obsession-cte-obscuring-larger-truth-brain-health-football-players.
9. Lisa Rapaport, "Fewer U.S. High School Athletes Play Football Amid Concussion Fears," *Reuters*, 12 March 2018. From: https://www.reuters.com/article/us-health-kids-tackle-football/fewer-u-s-high-school-athletes-play-football-amid-concussion-fears-idUSKCN1GO2LY.
10. Mark Murray, "Poll: Nearly Half of Parents Would Discourage Football Due to Concussions," *NBC News*, 2 February 2018. From: https://www.nbcnews.com/politics/first-read/poll-nearly-half-parents-would-discourage-football-due-concussions-n843836.
11. Phil Mushnick, "NFL's Problems Run Much Deeper Than the Anthem Issue," *New York Post*, 9 September 2018.

From: https://nypost.com/2018/09/09/nfls-problems-run-much-deeper-than-the-anthem-issue/.

12. Michael Oriard, "Chronicle of a (Football) Death Foretold: The Imminent Demise of a National Pastime?" *The International Journal of the History of Sport*, Vol. 31, Issue 1–2 (2014): 120–133.

13. Roger Pielke, "The Decline of Football Is Real and It's Accelerating," *Forbes*, 28 January 2020. From: https://www.forbes.com/sites/rogerpielke/2020/01/28/the-decline-of-football-is-real-and-its-accelerating/#b21581f2f372.

14. "Hears Football Men," *Washington Post*, 10 October 1905. From: https://www.documentcloud.org/documents/1175005-144576144-1.html.

15. Europe's Premier League soccer would be the other contender for the revenue title.

16. Kurt Badenhausen, "The World's 50 Most Valuable Sports Teams, 2019," *Forbes*, 22 July 2019. From: https://www.forbes.com/sites/kurtbadenhausen/2019/07/22/the-worlds-50-most-valuable-sports-teams-2019/#70ef8af2283d.

17. Alison Kanski, "Why the NFL's Reputation Is Bulletproof," *PR Week*, 9 September 2016. From: https://www.prweek.com/article/1408484/why-nfls-reputation-bulletproof.

18. *Ibid.*

19. Joe Otterson, "World Series Ratings Fall 23% from 2017," *Variety*, 29 October 2018. From: https://variety.com/2018/tv/news/world-series-ratings-2018-1202994171/.

20. Larry Thornberry, "The Decline of the Sweet Science," *American Spectator*, 12 December 2016. From: https://spectator.org/the-decline-of-the-sweet-science/.

21. *Ibid.*

22. Harvey Frommer, *When It Was Just a Game: Remembering the First Super Bowl*. Lanham, MD: Taylor Trade Publishing, 2015, p. 140.

23. Kaelen Jones, "NFL Television Ratings Rose 5% in 2018," *Sports Illustrated*, 2 January 2019. From: https://www.si.com/nfl/2019/01/02/nfl-television-ratings-viewership-rise-five-percent-2018.

24. Jim Norman, "Football Still American's Favorite Sport to Watch," *Gallup*, 4 January 2018. From: https://news.gallup.com/poll/224864/football-americans-favorite-sport-watch.aspx.

25. Scott Roxborough, "Women's World Cup Smashes Global Ratings Records," *Hollywood Reporter*, 1 July 2019. From: https://www.hollywoodreporter.com/news/womens-2019-soccer-world-cup-smashes-global-ratings-records-1221957.

26. Joe Drape, "Youth Soccer Participation Has Fallen Significantly in America," *New York Times*, 14 July 2018. From: https://www.nytimes.com/2018/07/14/sports/world-cup-soccer-youth-decline.html.

27. Clyde Kuckhohn, *Mirror for Man: The Relation of Anthropology to Modern Life*. Tempe: University of Arizona Press, 1949, p. 27.

28. Thomas B. Morgan, "The Wham in Pro Football," *Esquire*, 1 November 1959, p. 97.

29. Paul Hornung and Billy Reed, *Lombardi and Me: Players, Coaches and Colleagues Talk About the Man and the Myth*. Chicago: Triumph Books, 2006, p. xx.

30. Jim Hunt, "Cards Tell Sad Grid Story," *Toronto Star*, 6 August 1959, p. B1.

31. Jeff David, *Rozelle: Czar of the NFL*. New York: McGraw-Hill, 2008, p. 127.

32. Rich Cohen, "They Taught America How to Watch Football," *The Atlantic*, October 2012. From: https://www.theatlantic.com/magazine/archive/2012/10/they-taught-america-to-watch-football/309083/.

33. Tex Maule, "Make No Mistakes About It," *Sports Illustrated*, 29 January 1968, p. 26.

34. *Ibid.*

Chapter One

1. "The Fabulous Fifties" (Vol. 1). *NFL Films*, 1987.

2. *Ibid.*

3. Robert Ringer, "The Age of Innocence," *RobertRinger.com*, 26 November 2015. From: https://robertringer.com/the-age-of-innocence/.

4. Stephen E. Ambrose, *Eisenhower, The President*. New York: Simon & Schuster, 1984, pp. 424–425.

Notes—Chapter One

5. "Wrote 22 Million Words About the Dauntless Frank Merriwell," *Delmarva Star*, 5 August 1923, p. 16.
6. Lawrence S. Ritter, *Lost Ballparks*. New York: Penguin Books, 1994, p. xii.
7. Peter Golenbock, *Bums*. New York: G.P. Putnam's Sons, 1984, pp. 87–88.
8. Harold Seymour, *Baseball, The Golden Age*. New York: Oxford University Press, 1971, p. 80.
9. *Ibid.*, p. 81.
10. Roger Kahn, *The Boys of Summer*. New York: Harper & Row, 1971, p. xvii.
11. "100 Figures Who Shaped the NFL's First Century," *Sports Illustrated*, 28 August 2019. From: https://www.si.com/nfl/2019/nfl-100-most-influential-figures-all-time.
12. Dan Daly, *The National Forgotten League*. Lincoln: University of Nebraska Press, 2012, p. 101.
13. Golenbock, *Bums*, 1984, pp. 561–562.
14. Ringer, "The Age of Innocence," 2015.
15. Stephen E. Ambrose, *Eisenhower, The President*. New York: Simon & Schuster, 1984, p. 257.
16. Shirley Povich, "Sportswriter Dick Young, Usually Aggressive and Always Fearless," *Washington Post*, 6 September 1987. From: https://www.washingtonpost.com/archive/sports/1987/09/06/sportswriter-dick-young-usually-aggressive-and-always-fearless/ec1e0c6c-8ab7-47dc-9484-24c27ecf87a7/.
17. Jim Bouton, *Ball Four Plus Ball Five*. New York: Stein & Day, 1980, p. vii.
18. Thomas B. Morgan, "The Wham in Pro Football," *Esquire*, 1 November 1959, p. 97.
19. *The First 50 Years*. New York: Ridge Press/Benjamin Company, 1969, p. 73.
20. *Ibid.*
21. "Gamblers' Itchy Fingers Reach Into Major Sports," *Pittsburgh Post-Gazette*, 18 January 1951, p. 16.
22. "Suspension Given Hapes and Filchock," *Eugene (OR) Register-Guard*, 4 April 1947, p. 8.
23. Eliot Asinof, *Eight Men Out*. New York: Henry Holt, 1963, p. 22.
24. "Milwaukee Heads for Another 2 Milllion Mark," *Prescott (AZ) Evening Courier*, 17 September 1957, p. 10.
25. Golenbock, *Bums*, 1984, p. 581.
26. Art Donovan, *Fatso*. New York: Avon Books, 1987, p. 130.
27. Bill Lubinger, "Remember When ... Off-Season Was Work Time for the Cleveland Browns?" *Cleveland Plain-Dealer*, 26 May 2010. From: https://www.cleveland.com/browns/2010/05/remember_when_offseason_was_wo.html.
28. "Income of Families and Persons in the United States: 1950," *U.S. Census Bureau*, 25 March 1952. From: https://www.census.gov/library/publications/1952/demo/p60-009.html.
29. Art Donovan, *Fatso*, pp. 119–121.
30. William Rhoden, "Sports of the Times: NFL's Labor Pioneer Remains Unknown," *New York Times*, 2 October 1994. From: https://www.nytimes.com/1994/10/02/sports/sports-of-the-times-nfl-s-labor-pioneer-remains-unknown.html.
31. *Radovich v. National Football League*, 352 U.S. 445 (1957).
32. William Rhoden, "Sports of the Times," 1994.
33. "Professional Gridders Form an Organization," *Milwaukee Journal*, 29 November 1956, Part 2, pp. 19–20.
34. David G. Surdam, *Run to Glory and Profits: The Economic Rise of the NFL During the 1950s*. Lincoln: University of Nebraska Press, 2013, p. 216.
35. Bernie Parrish, *They Call It a Game: Shoulders the NFL Stands On*. New York: Authors Choice Press, 2000.
36. *Ibid.*
37. Robert Lyons, *On Any Given Sunday: A Life of Bert Bell*. Philadelphia: Temple University Press, 2010, p. 263.
38. Surdam, *Run to Glory*, p. 216.
39. *Ibid.*, p. 264.
40. Lyons, *On Any Given Sunday*, p. 266.
41. "NFLPA Announces Plan for $4,200,000 Lawsuit," *St. Petersburg Times*, 22 November 1957, p. 4-C.
42. Lyons, *On Any Given Sunday*, p. 266.
43. *Ibid.*
44. "NFL Owners Meet Demands of Players," *Milwaukee Journal*, 3 December 1957, Part 2, p. 20.
45. Surdam, *Run to Glory*, p. 222.
46. Parrish, *They Call it a Game*, 2000.
47. *Ibid.*

48. "Federal Judge Rules Against Football Draft," *Charleston (SC) News and Courier*, 9 September 1976, p. C1.
49. "New Trouble Ahead for Grid Pact?" *Spokane (WA) Spokesman-Review*, 23 February 1977, p. 16.
50. Gene Wojciechowski, "NFL Strike, 1982: A History Lesson Not Learned," *Los Angeles Times*, 23 September 1987. From: https://www.latimes.com/archives/la-xpm-1987-09-23-sp-6303-story.html.
51. Dom Cosentino, "The 1987 NFL Players Strike Created the Modern NFL," *Deadspin*, 25 January 2018. From: https://deadspin.com/the-1987-nfl-players-strike-created-the-modern-nfl-1819152183.
52. Ibid.
53. Ibid.
54. Debra Bell, "U.S. News Questioned Football's Future Nearly 45 Years Ago," *U.S. News & World Report*, 1 February 2013. From: https://www.usnews.com/news/blogs/press-past/2013/02/01/us-news-questioned-pro-footballs-future-nearly-45-years-ago.
55. Terry Larimer, "Ringo Unable to Get Raise Out of Lombardi; Old Packers Coach Traded His Center Rather Than Giving Him $15,000 a Year," *Allentown (PA) Morning Call*, 14 November 1999. From: https://www.mcall.com/news/mc-xpm-1999-11-14-3276304-story.html.
56. Alex Rubenstein, "No, Russell Wilson's No-Trade Clause Is Most Certainly Not Proof of His Devotion to Seahawks," *SB Nation*, 18 April 2019. From: https://www.sbnation.com/nfl/2019/4/18/18430045/russell-wilson-seattle-seahawks-contract-no-trade-clause-mark-rodgers-agent-pete-carroll.
57. Tex Maule, "Players Are Not Just People," *Sports Illustrated*, 29 April 1963, p. 22.
58. Larry Schwartz, "Hornung, Karras Suspended for Betting on NFL," *ESPN*, 19 November 2003. From: http://www.espn.com/classic/s/moment010417hornung-karras-betting.html.
59. Harry Missildine, "Twice Over Lightly," *Spokane (WA) Spokesman-Review*, 18 April 1963, p. 12.
60. William J. Ryczek, *Crash of the Titans: The Early Years of the New York Jets and the AFL*. Jefferson, NC: McFarland, 2009, p. 161.
61. Andrew Brandt, "There'll Be No New CBA Without an 18-Game Season," *Sports Illustrated*, 23 July 2019. From: https://www.si.com/nfl/2019/07/23/nfl-nflpa-collective-bargaining-agreement-18-game-season.
62. Jill Martin and Steve Almasy, "Ray Rice Wins Suspension Appeal," *CNN*, 20 November 2014. From: https://www.cnn.com/2014/11/28/us/ray-rice-reinstated/index.html.
63. "A History of Football in 100 Objects," *Sports Illustrated*, 28 August 2019. From: https://www.si.com/nfl/2019/nfl-history-of-football-100-objects.
64. Michael Gee, "Crime and Punishment: Sheriff Roger Goodell Is Barney Fife Once More," *Boston Globe*, 18 November 2014. From: https://www.boston.com/sports/new-england-patriots/2014/11/18/crime-and-inept-punishment-sheriff-roger-goodell-is-barney-fife-once-more.
65. Ibid.
66. Barry Wilner, "NFL at 100: Finding Labor Peace Always a Tortured Process," *Associated Press*, 10 March 2019. From: https://www.apnews.com/271e005334fd481996212d2e25c5a647.
67. Ibid.
68. Mike Florio, "NFLPA Publishes 'Work Stoppage Guide' for Players," *NBC Sports*, 15 August 2019. From: https://profootballtalk.nbcsports.com/2019/08/15/nflpa-publishes-work-stoppage-guide-for-players/.
69. Martin and Almasy, "Ray Rice Wins," 2014.
70. "The Fabulous Fifties" (Vol. 1). *NFL Films*, 1987.

Chapter Two

1. *75 Seasons*, Atlanta: Turner Publishing, 1994. p. 25.
2. The fight to bring the championship back to Pottsville has raged for nearly 100 years. In 2003, Pottsville mayor John Reiley and Pennsylvania governor Ed Rendell petitioned NFL owners to have the Maroons and Cardinals declared co-champions. The petition was shot down by a vote of 30–2.

3. Gilbert King, "The Game That Put the NFL's Reputation on the Line," *Smithsonian*, 31 January 2012. From: https://www.smithsonianmag.com/history/the-game-that-put-the-nfls-reputation-on-the-line-84128969/.
4. *Ibid.*
5. It was the last game Rockne ever coached. He died in a plane crash, March 31, 1931.
6. Allen Barra, "The Sports Story That Changed America," *New York Times*, 17 October 1999. From: https://www.nytimes.com/1999/10/17/weekinreview/the-sports-story-that-changed-america.html.
7. "Red Grange, the Galloping Ghost," *New York Times*, 18 October 1924. From: http://archive.nytimes.com/www.nytimes.com/packages/html/sports/year_in_sports/10.18a.html.
8. Dan Daly, *The National Forgotten League*. Lincoln: University of Nebraska Press, 2012, p. 59.
9. Bob Carroll, "Giants on the Gridiron," *Pro Football Researchers Association*. From: http://www.footballresearch.com/articles/frpage_topic_01-1927-2.html.
10. "100 Figures Who Shaped the NFL's First Century," *Sports Illustrated*, 28 August 2019. From: https://www.si.com/nfl/2019/nfl-100-most-influential-figures-all-time.
11. Ron Grossman, "90 Years Ago: Red Grange's Amazing Game," *Chicago Tribune*, 10 October 1924. From: https://www.chicagotribune.com/history/ct-red-grange-flashback-1012-20141012-story.html.
12. *75 Seasons*, Atlanta: Turner Publishing, 1994, p. 37.
13. S.L. Price, "The Second World War Kicks Off," *Sports Illustrated*, 29 November 1999. From: https://www.si.com/vault/1999/11/29/270652/the-second-world-war-kicks-off-december-7-1941-redskins-versus-eagles-on-pearl-harbor-day.
14. 21 NFL players, ex-players or coaches were killed, including all-league tackle Al Blozis of the Giants. Those who survived included future Dallas Cowboys coach Tom Landry, who piloted 30 missions over Germany.

15. Ray Didinger, "The Stegles: An Unforgettable 1943 Season," *philadelphiaeagles.com*, 8 November 2018. From: https://www.philadelphiaeagles.com/news/the-steagles-an-unforgettable-1943-season.
16. Rick Reilly, "Browns Destroy Eagles, 35–10 in Huge Upset!" *Sports Illustrated*, 16 October 1991. From: https://www.si.com/vault/1991/10/16/125163/the-author-returns-to-yesteryear-to-report-on-a-history-making-football-game-browns-destroy-eagles-35-10-in-huge-upset-qb-graham-stars-nfl-champs-embarrassed.
17. *Ibid.*
18. Tex Maule, "The Browns' Jim Dandy," *Sports Illustrated*, 10 November 1958, p. 67.
19. Tex Maule, "The Curtain Falls on a Long Run," *Sports Illustrated*, 25 July 1966, p. 23.
20. Maule, "The Browns' Jim Dandy," p. 67.
21. Lulu Garcia-Navarro, "'Heroic, But He's No Hero,': Revisiting Football Great Jim Brown," *National Public Radio*, 13 May 2018. From: https://www.npr.org/2018/05/13/610396047/heroic-but-he-s-no-hero-revisiting-football-great-jim-brown.
22. "Johnny 'Blood' McNally, *Packerville*, 23 October 2008. From: http://packerville.blogspot.com/2008/10/johnny-blood-mcnally.html.
23. Art Donovan, *Fatso*. New York: Avon Books, 1987, pp. 1–2.
24. "Buddy Parker Quits as Detroit Grid Coach," *Pittsburgh Post-Gazette*, 13 August 1957, p. 16.
25. Dave Birkett, "When the Walls Talked: Inside Detroit Lions' Improbable 1957 Title Run," *Detroit Free Press*, 8 September 2017. From: https://www.freep.com/story/sports/nfl/lions/2017/09/08/when-walls-talked-inside-detroit-lions-improbable-1957-title-run/630599001/.
26. "As a Leader, Layne Passed All Marks," *Washington Post*, 3 December 1986. From: https://www.washingtonpost.com/archive/sports/1986/12/03/as-a-leader-layne-passed-all-marks/e0cf4cc4-e109-4820-afe1-40bc010a10d6/?utm_term=.4770e34a7a35.
27. *Ibid.*

28. Donovan, *Fatso*, 1987, p. 4.
29. Shawn Windsor, "1957 Detroit Lions: Reliving Tales from Franchise's Last Championship," *Detroit Free Press*, 4 September 2017. From: https://www.freep.com/story/sports/nfl/lions/2017/09/04/1957-detroit-lions-nfl-championship-joe-schmidt/631312001/.
30. "Morabito Rites Set," *Pittsburgh Post-Gazette*, 29 October 1957, p. 20.
31. Windsor, "1957 Detroit Lions," *Detroit Free Press*, 2017.
32. Jerry Crowe, "R.C. Owens' 'alley-oop' catches for 49ers were a hit right from the jump," *Los Angeles Times*, 12 December 2010. From: https://www.latimes.com/archives/la-xpm-2010-dec-12-la-sp-crowe-20101213-story.html.
33. Douglas Martin, "R.C. Owens, Receiver Who Made the Alley-Oop Famous, Dies at 77," *New York Times*, 19 June 2012. From: https://www.nytimes.com/2012/06/20/sports/football/r-c-owens-wide-receiver-behind-the-alley-oop-dies-at-77.html.
34. Elliott Harris and David Spada, "Talkzone: Sports and Torts," n.d. From: https://www.youtube.com/ watch?v=NYmIenNmJJg.
35. *75 Seasons*. Atlanta: Turner Publishing, 1994, p. 115.
36. Birkett, "When the Walls Talked," *Detroit Free Press*, 2017.
37. "Great Day for Rote," *Milwaukee Journal*, 23 December 1957, p. 8.
38. Ron Fimrite, "Mind You, This Time It's Not All Over," *Sports Illustrated*, 25 January 1982, p. 33.
39. "Great Day for Rote," *Milwaukee Journal*, 23 December 1957, Part 2, p. 11.
40. Larry Schwartz, "'Automatic Otto' Defined Versatility," *ESPN*, n.d. From: https://www.espn.com/sportscentury/features/00014210.html.
41. Rick Reilly, "Browns Destroy Eagles," *Sports Illustrated*, 16 October 1991.
42. Birkett, "When the Walls Talked," *Detroit Free Press*, 2017.
43. "Rote Ignored Play Sent In By Coach," *Pittsburgh-Post Gazette*, 30 December 1957, p. 18.
44. Phil Berger, "Paul Brown, One of Pro Football's Primary Architects, Dead at 82," *New York Times*, 6 August 1991. From: https://www.nytimes.com/1991/08/06/sports/paul-brown-one-of-pro-footballs-primary-architects-dead-at-82.htm.
45. "Everything Worked; Rote Called Fake Field Goal for Score," *Milwaukee Journal*, 30 December 1957, Part 2, p. 8.
46. Ibid.
47. "'57 Lions Discuss the Fords Crashing the After Party," *Detroit Free Press*, 3 September 2017. From: https://www.freep.com/videos/sports/nfl/lions/2017/09/03/57-lions-discuss-fords-crashing-after-party/105264270/.
48. "Lion Notes," *Detroit Free Press*, 22 August 1958, p. 35.
49. Bill Dow, "The Shocking Trade of Detroit Lions Legend Bobby Layne," *Vintage Detroit*, 29 November 2009. From: https://www.vintagedetroit.com/blog/2009/11/29/the-shocking-trade-of-detroit-lions-legend-bobby-layne/.
50. Carlos Monarrez, "Is Curse of Bobby Layne Real? 1957 Detroit Lions Say Team's Jinxed," *Detroit Free Press*, 6 September 1957. From: https://www.freep.com/story/sports/nfl/lions/2017/09/06/detroit-lions-curse-of-bobby-layne-1957-championship/629831001/.
51. Stephen E. Ambrose, *Eisenhower, The President*. New York: Simon & Schuster, 1984, p. 250.
52. "The Rise of American Consumerism," *Public Broadcasting Service*, n.d. From: https://www.pbs.org/wgbh/americanexperience/features/tupperware-consumer/.
53. Dennis R. Shaughnessy, "The Business of America Is Business!" *Northeastern University*, February 2017. From: https://www.northeastern.edu/sei/2017/02/the-business-of-america-is-business/.
54. Ibid.
55. Ambrose, *Eisenhower: The President*, p. 625.
56. Adam Schupak, "Dwight D. Eisenhower: Golf at the White House," *Golf Week*, 2 November 2009. From: https://golfweek.com/2009/11/02/dwight-d-eisenhower-golf-white-house/.
57. "Russians Claim Victory Over U.S. in Race," *Pittsburgh Post-Gazette*, 5 October 1957, p. 1.
58. Ambrose, *Eisenhower, The President*, p. 424.
59. Sloan Wilson, *The Man in the Gray*

Flannel Suit. Cambridge, MA: Da Capo Press, 2002, p. vi.
60. William I. Hitchcock, *The Age of Eisenhower: American and the World in the 1950s*. New York: Simon & Schuster, 2019, p. xiii.
61. William F. Buckley, *A Torch Kept Lit* (James Rosen, ed.), New York: Crown Forum, 2016, p. 15.
62. Thomas B. Morgan, "The Wham in Pro Football," *Esquire*, 1 November 1959, p. 97.
63. Donovan, *Fatso*, 1987, p. 2.

Chapter Three

1. Jess Mayhugh, "Colt Following," *Baltimore Magazine*, March 2014. From: https://www.baltimoremagazine.com//2014/3/20/is-baltimore-still-angry-about-the-colts.
2. John Steadman, "50 Years Ago Colts Had a Bizarre NFL Beginning," *Baltimore Sun*, 5 November 2000. From: https://www.baltimoresun.com/news/bs-xpm-2000-11-05-0011040041-story.html.
3. Art Donovan, *Fatso*. New York: Avon Books, 1987, p. 146.
4. *Ibid.*, p. 141.
5. "NFL Films Presents: Weeb Ewbank's Legacy," *NFL Films*, 2017.
6. Bob Carter, "Unitas Surprised Them All," *ESPN* (n.d.). From: https://www.espn.com/sportscentury/features/00016574.html.
7. Donovan, *Fatso*, p. 144.
8. "America's Game: 1968 Jets," *NFL Films*, 2012.
9. "1958: Baltimore Colts @ New York Giants," *Golden Football Magazine* (n.d.). From: http://goldenrankings.com/nflchampionshipgame1958.html.
10. Donovan, *Fatso*, p. 29.
11. Dave Maraniss, *When Pride Still Mattered: A Life of Vince Lombardi*. New York: Simon & Schuster, 1999, p. 152.
12. Robert M. Thomas, Jr. "Jim Lee Howell, Ex-Giants Coach, Dies at 80," *New York Times*, 6 January 1995. From: https://www.nytimes.com/1995/01/06/obituaries/jim-lee-howell-ex-giants-coach-dies-at-80.html.
13. Lawrence A. Pervin, *Football's New York Giants: A History*. Jefferson, NC: McFarland, 2009, p. 28.
14. "Giants Used Little Psychology— Just Got Inspired," *Milwaukee Journal*, 31 December 1956, Part 2, p. 9.
15. "Howell, Brown, Ewbank Laud Giants' Great Defensive Show," *Milwaukee Journal*, 22 December 1958, Part 2, p. 10.
16. Tex Maule, "The Best Football Game Ever Played," *Sports Illustrated*, 5 January 1959, p. 8.
17. Donovan, *Fatso*, p. 26.
18. *75 Seasons*. Atlanta: Turner Publishing, 1994, p. 118.
19. "Replay! The History of the NFL on Television," *NFL Films*, 1998.
20. "How JFK's Signature Changed the NFL, American Sports," *The Sports Digest*, 22 November 2013. From: http://thesportdigest.com/2013/11/how-jfks-signature-changed-the-nfl-american-sports/.
21. Tom Callahan, *Johnny U: The Life and Times of Johnny Unitas*. New York: Three Rivers Press, 2006, p. 152.
22. Donovan, *Fatso*, p. 35.
23. "1958: Baltimore Colts @ New York Giants," *Golden Football Magazine* (n.d.). From: http://goldenrankings.com/nflchampionshipgame1958.html.
24. Maule, "The Best Football Game Ever Played," p. 11.
25. "Ewbank Misjudged on Building Champ," *Milwaukee Journal*, 29 December 1958, Part 2, p. 11.
26. Donovan, *Fatso*, p. 38.
27. Callahan, *Johnny U*, p. 159.
28. Dave Klein, *The Game of Their Lives: The 1958 NFL Championship*. Lanham, MD: Rowman & Littlefield, 2008, p. 13.
29. Frank Gifford, "Everything Changed After the Glory Game of 1958," *ESPN*, 4 November 2008. From: http://www.espn.com/espn/page2/story?page=glorygame/081103.
30. *Ibid.*
31. Donovan, *Fatso*, p. 40.
32. Jonathan Rand, *Riddell Presents the Gridiron's Greatest Quarterbacks*. Champaign, IL: Sports Publishing, 2004, p. 32.
33. Maule, "The Best Football Game Ever Played," p. 60.
34. "'Too Much Unitas' Says Giants Coach," *Milwaukee Journal*, 29 December 1958, Part 2, p. 11.

35. George Bozeka (Ed.), *The 1958 Baltimore Colts: Profiles of the NFL's First Sudden Death Champions*. Jefferson, NC: McFarland, 2018, p. 246.
36. Donovan, *Fatso*, p. 41.
37. "1958 NFL Championship" *NBC Radio*, 28 December 1958. From: https://archive.org/details/1958NflChampionship.
38. "Who Died? Wife Wants to Know," *Milwaukee Journal*, 29 December 1958, Part 2, p. 11.
39. Callahan, *Johnny U*, p. 171.
40. "1958 NFL Championship" *NBC Radio*, 28 December 1958. From: https://archive.org/details/1958NflChampionship.
41. Perian Conerly and Frank Gifford, *Backseat Quarterback*. Jackson: University Press of Mississippi, 2003, p. 229.
42. "Ewbank Misjudged on Building Champ," *Milwaukee Journal*, 29 December 1958, Part 2, p. 11.
43. "'We Out-Gutted Them,' Cry Victorious Colts," *Pittsburgh Post-Gazette*, 29 December 1958, p. 24.
44. "30,000 Greet Team, Cause Near-Panic," *Pittsburgh Post-Gazette*, 29 December 1958, p. 24.
45. David J. Halberstam, "The '58 Overtime Thriller, 60 Years Ago Today, Is Still Ranked As The 'Greatest Game Ever Played," *Sports Broadcast Journal*, 28 December 2012. From: http://www.sportsbroadcastjournal.com/the-58-overtime-thriller-60-years-ago-today-is-still-ranked-as-the-greatest-game-ever-played/
46. Gifford, "Everything Changed," 2008.
47. Robert H. Boyle, "TV Wins on Points," *Sports Illustrated*, 2 November 1970, p. 14.
48. William Johnson, "After TV Accepted the Call Sunday Was Never the Same," *Sports Illustrated*, 5 January 1970, p. 23.
49. Ed Sherman and Steve Johnson, "He Changed the Face of Television," *Chicago Tribune*, 6 December 2002. From: https://www.chicagotribune.com/news/ct-xpm-2002-12-06-0212060373-story.html.
50. Boyle, "TV Wins on Points," p. 14.
51. Johnson, "After TV Accepted," p. 26.
52. Joe Reedy, "How Fox's 25 Seasons of Covering the NFL Changed the Game," *Associated Press*, 27 December 2018. From: https://apnews.com/9816ca0d0b3546ac92353c655d40cab8.
53. Pat Evans, "NFL Viewership Growth Throughout Europe Exposes Opportunities in the U.S.," *Front Office Sports*, 7 March 2019. From: https://frntoffice sport.com/two-circles-nfl/.
54. Bob Herzog, "Sudden Life Excerpt: Made for TV," *Press Box Online*, December, 2008. From: https://www.pressboxonline.com/story/4505/sudden-life-excerpt-made-for-tv.

Chapter Four

1. Eliot Asinof, *Eight Men Out: The Black Sox and the 1919 World Series* (2nd ed.). New York: Henry Holt and Company, 1987, p. 14.
2. Harold Seymour, *Baseball: The Golden Age*. New York: Oxford University Press, 1971, p. 288.
3. Asinof, *Eight Men Out*, p. 14.
4. Michael Kimmel & Amy Aronson, *Men and Masculinities: A Social, Cultural, and Historical Encyclopedia*. (Vol. 1). Santa Barbara, CA: ABC-CLIO, 2004, p. 55.
5. Jacob Pomrenke, "Two of a Kind," National Baseball Hall of Fame (n.d.). From: https://baseballhall.org/discover-more/stories/baseball-history/ruth-back-to-back-records.
6. Joseph Stromberg, "How Babe Ruth Changed Baseball," *The Smithsonian*, 16 August 2011. From: https://www.smithsonianmag.com/smithsonian-institution/how-babe-ruth-changed-baseball-51810018/.
7. Thomas Steissguth, *The Roaring Twenties*. New York: Infobase Publishing, 2007, pp. 44–45.
8. Edmund Wehrle, Babe Ruth Was No Babe in the Woods," *Baltimore Sun*, 17 April 2018. From: https://www.baltimoresun.com/opinion/op-ed/bs-ed-op-0418-babe-ruth-20180417-story.html.
9. *The Not So Great Moments in Sports*. [VHS]. New York: HBO Video, 1987.
10. Nack, "The Colossus," p. 64.
11. Harold Seymour, *Baseball, The*

Golden Age. New York: Oxford University Press, 1971, p. 80.
12. Thomas B. Morgan, "The Wham in Pro Football," *Esquire*, 1 November 1959, p. 101.
13. Mark Inabinett, *Grantland Rice and His Heroes, The Sportswriter as Mythmaker in the 1920s*. Knoxville: University of Tennessee Press, 1994, p. ix.
14. Hugh S. Fullerton, "Why Babe Ruth Is the Great Home-Run Hitter," *Popular Science*, 1921. From: https://www.popsci.com/scitech/article/2006-10/archive-why-babe-ruth-greatest-home-run-hitter/.
15. Ed Sherman and Steve Johnson, "He Changed the Face of Television," *Chicago Tribune*, 6 December 2002. From: https://www.chicagotribune.com/news/ct-xpm-2002-12-06-0212060373-story.html.
16. Robert Creamer, *Babe: The Legend Comes to Life*. New York: Simon & Schuster, 1974, p. 16.
17. Lawrence Ritter, *The Glory of Their Times*. New York: Macmillan, 1966.
18. Paul Henderson and Jim Prime, *How Hockey Explains Canada*. Chicago: Triumph Books, 2011.
19. Risto Pakarinen, "1980 Soviet Union Squad was History's Greatest International Hockey Team," *ABC News*, 15 September 2016. From: https://abcnews.go.com/Sports/1980-soviet-union-squad-historys-greatest-international-hockey/story?id=42117760.
20. E.M. Swift, "Run Over By the Big Red Machine," *Sports Illustrated*, 19 February 1979, p. 25.
21. Lawrie Mifflin, "Russian Hockey Team Annihilates Team USA 10–3 in Madison Square Garden Exhibition Before Start of 1980 Olympics in Lake Placid," *New York Daily News*, 10 February 1980. From: https://www.nydailynews.com/sports/hockey/russians-easy-u-s-olympians-fall-10-3-article-1.2023417.
22. Richard Sandomir, "TV Sports; 'Miracle on Ice' of 1980 Looks Different Today," *New York Times*, 22 February 2000. From: https://www.nytimes.com/2000/02/22/sports/tv-sports-miracle-on-ice-of-1980-looks-different-today.html.
23. Bob Herzog, "Sudden Life Excerpt: Made for TV," *Pressbox*, December 2008. From: https://www.pressboxonline.com/story/4505/sudden-life-excerpt-made-for-tv.
24. Frank Deford, "The Best There Ever Was," *Sports Illustrated*, 23 September 2002, p. 63.
25. Tom Callahan, *Johnny U: The Life and Times of John Unitas*. New York: Three Rivers Press, 2006, p. 23.
26. Charles Feeney, "Early Steeler Defeats Cut Rooney Deeply," *Pittsburgh Post-Gazette*, 22 December 1972, p. 15.
27. Lou Sahadi, *Johnny Unitas: America's Quarterback*. Chicago: Triumph Books, 2004, p. 50.
28. Art Donovan, *Fatso*. New York: Avon Books, 1987, pp. 158, 198.
29. "America's Game: 1970 Colts," *NFL Films*, 2007.
30. Ibid., p. 200.
31. "How Tough Was He?" *Sports Illustrated*, 23 September 2002, p. 62.
32. "1958 NFL Championship" *NBC Radio*, 28 December 1958. From: https://archive.org/details/1958NflChampionship.
33. Tex Maule, "The Best Football Game Ever Played," *Sports Illustrated*, 5 January 1959, p. 60.
34. David J. Halberstam, "The '58 Overtime Thriller, 60 Years Ago Today, Is Still Ranked as the 'Greatest Game Ever Played,'" *Sports Broadcast Journal*, 28 December 2018. From: http://www.sportsbroadcastjournal.com/the-58-overtime-thriller-60-years-ago-today-is-still-ranked-as-the-greatest-game-ever-played/.
35. Dave Zeitlin, "The Man Who Modernized Pro Football," *Pennsylvania Gazette*, September/October 2009. From: https://www.upenn.edu/gazette/0909/pro06.html.
36. Donovan, *Fatso*, p. 42.
37. Halberstam, "The '58 Overtime Thriller," *Sports Broadcast Journal*, 2018.
38. Morgan, "The Wham in Pro Football," *Esquire*, 1959.
39. Halberstam, "The '58 Overtime Thriller," *Sports Broadcast Journal*, 2018.
40. Marty Ralbovsky, *Super Bowl*. New York: Hawthorn Books, 1971, p. 109.
41. Herzog, "Sudden Life Excerpt," 2008.

42. Tex Maule, "A Stout Wall for Johnny," *Sports Illustrated*, 5 October 1959, pp. 36–37.
43. Dan Daly, *National Forgotten League: Entertaining Stories and Observations from Pro Football's First Fifty Years*. Lincoln: University of Nebraska Press, 2012, pp. 307–308.
44. Frank Gifford, "Everything Changed After the Glory Game of 1958," *ESPN*, 4 November 2008. From: http://www.espn.com/espn/page2/story?page=glorygame/081103.
45. "Sport: A Man's Game," *Time*, 30 November 1959. From: http://content.time.com/magazine/article/0,9171,825995,00.html.
46. Deford, "The Best There Ever Was," p. 65.
47. Gifford, "Everything Changed," 2008.
48. Deford, "The Best There Ever Was," p. 64.
49. Donovan, *Fatso*, p. 205.
50. Ralbovsky, *Super Bowl*, p. 74.
51. Donovan, *Fatso*, pp. 179–180.
52. Deford, "The Best There Ever Was," p. 65.

Chapter Five

1. Red Smith, "Lombardi Wears Two Grid 'Hats,'" *Oakland Tribune*, 5 August 1959, p. D45.
2. David Fleming, "Blaze of Glory," *ESPN*, 19 September 2013. From: https://www.espn.com/nfl/story/_/id/9669836/mysterious-fire-1950-saved-green-bay-packers-espn-magazine.
3. George Sauerberg, "Blackbourn Style Impressed Team," *Milwaukee Sentinel*, 15 June 1983, Part 2, p. 1.
4. LeRoy Butler and Rob Reischel, *Packers Pride: Green Bay Greats Share Their Favorite Memories*. Chicago: Triumph Books, 2013, p. 163.
5. Keith Dunnavant, *Bart Starr: America's Quarterback and the Rise of the National Football League*. New York: Thomas Dunne Books, 2011, p. 76.
6. Butler and Reischel, *Packers Pride*, p. 81.
7. Dunnavant, *Bart Starr*, p. 76.
8. Cliff Christl, "Bud Lea Saw it All During Lombardi Era," *packers.com*, 12 November 2015. From: https://www.packers.com/news/bud-lea-saw-it-all-during-lombardi-era-16277299.
9. Chuck Johnson, "Packers Name Vince Lombardi Head Coach, General Manager," *Milwaukee Journal*, 29 January 1959, Part 2, p. 11.
10. Ibid.
11. Ibid.
12. Mary Garber, "From Garber's Typewriter: Visit with a Legend," *Winston-Salem Journal*, 28 September 2008. From: https://www.journalnow.com/news/state/from-garber-s-typewriter-visit-with-a-legend/article_b8931a7a-53f0-5a53-9a81-b33fe4f683ef.html.
13. Dunnavant, *Bart Starr*, p. 81.
14. Red Smith, "Lombardi Wears," 1959.
15. Travis Vogan, *Keepers of the Flame: NFL Films and the Rise of Sports Media*. Champaign: University of Illinois Press, 2014.
16. Garber, "From Garber's Typewriter," 2008.
17. Ibid.
18. Jerry Kramer, "Winning Wasn't Everything," *New York Times*, 24 January 1997. From: https://archive.nytimes.com/www.nytimes.com/ref/opinion/06opclassic.html?pagewanted=all.
19. Jerry Kramer, *Instant Replay: The Green Bay Diary of Jerry Kramer* (Dick Schaap, ed.). New York: World Publishing Co., 1968, p. xvii.
20. Martin Hendricks, "McHan Once Held the Packer's Starting Job Over Starr," *Milwaukee Journal-Sentinel*, 18 March 2015. From: http://archive.jsonline.com/sports/packers/mchan-once-held-the-packers-starting-job-over-starr-b99459968z1-296680551.html/.
21. Ibid.
22. Garber, "From Garber's Typewriter," 2008.
23. Ian O'Connor, "For the First Time in 68 Years, Cherry Starr Will Watch Football Without the Love of Her Life," *ESPN*, 4 September 2019. From: https://www.espn.com/nfl/story/_/id/27535106/for-first-68-years-cherry-starr-watch-football-love-life.
24. "America's Game: 1966 Green Bay Packers," *NFL Films*, 2012.

25. Jerry Kramer, *Instant Replay*, p. 12.
26. Jerry Kramer, "Winning Wasn't Everything," 1997.
27. Tim Layden, *Blood, Sweat and Chalk, The Ultimate Football Playbook: How the Great Coaches Built Today's Game*. New York: Sports Illustrated Books, 2010, p. 107.
28. "A History of Football in 100 Objects," *Sports Illustrated*, 28 August 2019. From: https://www.si.com/nfl/2019/nfl-history-of-football-100-objects.
29. *Ibid.*
30. Butler and Reischel, *Packers Pride*, p. 137.
31. Cliff Christl, "Jerry Kramer Was Lineman at Forefront of Lombardi's Power Sweep," *Packers.com*, 1 February 2018. From: https://www.packers.com/news/jerry-kramer-was-lineman-at-forefront-of-lombardi-s-power-sweep-20326744.
32. Leyden, *Blood, Sweat and Chalk*, p. 113.
33. Phil Barber, "Lombardi Rules," *American Heritage*, Fall 2009, Vol. 59, Issue 3. From: https://www.americanheritage.com/lombardi-rules.
34. "America's Game," 2012.
35. *Ibid.*
36. Jerry Kramer, "Winning Wasn't Everything," 1997.
37. William Manchester, *American Caesar: Douglas MacArthur, 1880–1964*. Boston: Little, Brown and Company, 1978, p. 119.
38. Joseph Campbell and Bill Moyers, *The Power of Myth*. New York: Anchor Books, 1991, pp. 5–6.
39. Erin McCarthy, "Roosevelt's 'The Man in the Arena,'" *Mental Floss*, 23 April 2015. From: http://mentalfloss.com/article/63389/roosevelts-man-arena.
40. Dave Maraniss, *When Pride Still Mattered*. New York: Simon & Schuster, 1999, p. 366.
41. *Ibid.*, p. 359.
42. Jerry Kramer, "Winning Wasn't Everything," 1997.
43. Campbell and Moyers, *The Power of Myth*, p. 24.
44. *Ibid.*, p. xiii.
45. *Ibid.*, p. 4.
46. Gary D'Amato, "A Lombardi Revels in Green Bay Life Again," *Milwaukee Journal-Sentinel*, 8 December 2012.

From: http://archive.jsonline.com/sports/packers/a-lombardi-revels-in-green-bay-life-again-a67ugs8-182687361.html/.
47. "Faith Important to This Lombardi, Too," *Catholic Herald*, 21 March 2013. From: https://catholicherald.org/news/local/faith-important-to-this-lombardi-too/.
48. D'Amato, "A Lombardi Revels in Green Bay," 2012.
49. Graydon Royce, "Lombardi in the Spotlight," *Minneapolis Star-Tribune*, 29 September 2012. From: http://www.startribune.com/lombardi-in-the-spotlight/171627811/?refresh=true.
50. "Football Still Big with Mrs. Lombardi," *Lexington (NC) Dispatch*, 21 December 1972, p. 13.
51. Wright Thompson, "Vince Lombardi Lived Here," *ESPN*, 3 February 2011. From: https://www.espn.com/nfl/playoffs/2010/columns/story?id=6077292.
52. Campbell and Moyers, *The Power of Myth*, p. xvii.
53. Cliff Christl, "Bud Lea," 2015.
54. Maraniss, *When Pride Still Mattered*, p. 366.
55. Vogan, *Keepers of the Flame*, 2014.
56. "Lost Treasures of NFL Films: The Lost Sounds, 1966–1969," *NFL Films*, 2001.
57. "John Facenda Is Dead at 72; Narrator of N.F.L. Highlights," *New York Times*, 27 September 1984, Section B, p. 12.
58. Rich Cohen, "They Taught America to Watch Football," *The Atlantic*, October 2012. From: https://www.theatlantic.com/magazine/archive/2012/10/they-taught-america-to-watch-football/309083/.
59. *Ibid.*
60. Michael Oriard, *Brand NFL: Making and Selling America's Favorite Sport*. Chapel Hill: University of North Carolina, 2007, p. 16.
61. Cohen, "They Taught America," 2012.
62. "Sabol Files: Lombardi vs. Belichick," *NFL Films*, 18 September 2011. From: http://nflfilms.nfl.com/2011/09/18/sabol-files-lombardi-vs-belichick-2/.
63. "A History of Football in 100 Objects," *Sports Illustrated*, 2019.
64. Tex Maule, "The Old Pro Goes in

for Six," *Sports Illustrated*, 8 January 1968, p. 13.
65. Ibid., p. 15.
66. Warren Gerds, "CBS Special Focuses on Lombardi the Coach," *Green Bay Press-Gazette*, 15 September 1968, p. D-4.
67. Bill Glauber, "Lombardi's Legacy: It's Been 20 Years Since Coach's Death, But His Name Still Is Synonymous with Toughness, Winning," *Baltimore Sun*, 27 January 1991. From: https://www.baltimoresun.com/news/bs-xpm-1991-01-27-1991027150-story.html
68. Maraniss, *When Pride Mattered*, p. 14.
69. Bill Glauber, "Lombardi's Legacy," 1991.
70. Michael Oriard, *Brand NFL*, p. 18.
71. John Eisenberg, *That First Season: How Vince Lombardi Took the Worst Team in the NFL and Set It on Its Path to Glory*. Boston: Mariner Books, 2009, p. xii.

Chapter Six

1. Tex Maule, "The Shaky New League," *Sports Illustrated*, 25 January 1960, p. 49.
2. Jack Olsen, "Biggest Cheapskate in Big D," *Sports Illustrated*, 18 June 1972, p. 79.
3. Dave Anderson, "Sports of the Times: A New York-Baltimore Lesson for the N.F.L.," *New York Times*, 21 January 2001, Section 8, p. 2.
4. Michael MacCambridge, *Lamar Hunt: A Life in Sports*. Kansas City, MO: Andrews McNeel Publishing, 2012, p. 85.
5. Jack Olsen, "Biggest Cheapskate in Big D," p. 76.
6. "Super Bowl Is Forever Connected to Dallas," *Dallas Morning News*, 22 December 2010. From: https://www.dallasnews.com/news/2010/12/22/super-bowl-is-forever-connected-to-dallas/.
7. Jeff Miller, *Going Long: The Wild Ten Year Saga of the Renegade American Football League in the Words of Those Who Lived It*. Chicago: Contemporary Books, 2003, p. 6.
8. Maule, "The Shaky New League," p. 50.
9. Bill Althaus, *The Good, the Bad, & the Ugly: Kansas City Chiefs, Heart-Pounding, Jaw-Dropping, and Gut-Wrenching Moments from Kansas City Chiefs History*. Chicago: Triumph Books, 2007, p. 27.
10. Michael J. Mooney, "How Dallas Became a Football Town," *D Magazine*, November 2013. From: https://www.dmagazine.com/publications/d-magazine/2013/november/dallas-1963-how-dallas-became-a-football-town/.
11. Aimee Pass, "Football Pioneer Lamar Hunt Wouldn't Take 'No' for an Answer," *Park Cities People*, 14 October 2013. From: https://www.parkcitiespeople.com/2013/10/14/lamar-hunt-refused-to-take-no-for-an-answer/.
12. "Super Bowl Is Forever Connected to Dallas," 2010.
13. Chris Dufresne, "Vikings Are Far More Than Just a Hobby to Max Winter," *Los Angeles Times*, 3 October 1985. From: https://www.latimes.com/archives/la-xpm-1985-10-03-sp-789-story.html.
14. Harry Frommer, *When It Was Just a Game: Remembering the First Super Bowl*. Lanham, MD: Taylor Trade Publishing, 2015, p. 16.
15. Gary Cartwright, *The Best I Recall: A Memoir*. Austin: University of Texas Press, 2015, p. 46.
16. *Los Angeles Rams Football Clubs v. Cannon*, 185 F. Supp. 717 (S.D. Cal. 1960).
17. *Houston Oilers, Inc. v. Ralph Neely*, 361 F.2d 36 (10 Cir. 1966).
18. *American Football League v. National Football League*, 205 F. Supp. 60 (D. Md. 1962).
19. Harvey Frommer, "When It Was Just a Game," p. 20.
20. William J. Ryczek, *Crash of the Titans: The Early Years of the New York Jets and the AFL*. Jefferson, NC: McFarland, 2009, p. 169.
21. Ed Gruver, *The American Football League: A Year-by-Year History, 1960–1969*. Jefferson, NC: McFarland, 1997, p. 92.
22. Harvey Frommer, "When It Was Just a Game," p. 20.
23. Robert Boyle, "Show-Biz Sonny and His Quest for Stars," *Sports Illustrated*, 19 July 1965, p. 66.
24. Arthur Daley, "Jets Take Big Gamble on Namath," *Pittsburgh Post-Gazette*, 4 January 1965, p. 24.

Notes—Chapter Six

25. Robert Mcg. Thomas, Jr. "Sonny Werblin, an Impresario of New York's Sports Extravaganza, Is Dead at 81," *New York Times*, 23 November 1991, Section 1, p. 11.
26. *Sports Illustrated*, 19 July 1965.
27. Brian Murphy, "John Brodie: 49er Legend Relentlessly Positive After Stroke," *San Francisco Chronicle*, 4 January 2004. From: https://www.sfgate.com/health/article/PROFILE-JOHN-BRODIE-Spirited-comeback-49er-2833075.php.
28. Reid Laymance, "Texas, NFL Great Tommy Nobis Dies at 74," *Houston Chronicle*, 13 December 2017. From: https://www.chron.com/sports/longhorns/article/Texas-NFL-great-Tommy-Nobis-dies-at-74-12427738.php.
29. Matt Winkeljohn, "The First Falcon, Tommy Nobis, Was Epic, and Barely Made It to Atlanta," *Atlanta Journal-Constitution*, 13 December 2017. From: https://www.ajc.com/sports/the-first-falcon-tommy-nobis-was-epic-and-barely-made-atlanta/GtsnCfv64bKGBMtUJQX0QO/.
30. Ken Rappoport," The AFL-NFL Merger Was Almost Booted ... by a Kicker," *nfl.com*, 20 August 2009. From: http://www.nfl.com/news/story/09000d5d81206b90/article/the-aflnfl-merger-was-almost-booted-by-a-kicker.
31. "NFL, AFL Grid Loops in Merger," *Pittsburgh Post-Gazette*, 9 June 1966, p. 32.
32. Mike Vaccaro, "Birth of Giants-Jets Rivalry Still Carries Some Bitterness 50 Years Later," *New York Post*, 16 August 2019. From: https://nypost.com/2019/08/16/birth-of-giants-jets-rivalry-still-carries-some-bitterness-50-years-later/.
33. *Ibid.*
34. *Ibid.*
35. "Tarkenton Convinced by Chiefs," *Milwaukee Journal*, 12 January 1970, p. 13.
36. Jack Olsen, "Biggest Cheapskate in Big D," p. 81.
37. Rodger Sherman, "The AAF Failed Because All Minor-League Football Does," *The Ringer*, 4 April 2019. From: https://www.theringer.com/nfl/2019/4/4/18294528/american-alliance-football-aaf-collapse-suspend-xfl.
38. Edward J. Rielly, *Football: An Encyclopedia of Popular Culture*. Lincoln: University of Nebraska Press, 2009, p. 11.

39. Kenneth R. Crippen & Matt Reaser. *The All-America Football Conference: Players, Coaches, Records, Games and Awards, 1946–1949*. Jefferson, NC: McFarland, 2018, p. 8.
40. *Ibid.*, p. 4.
41. "The WFL: A League That Was Sacked Before It Dropped Back," *United Press International*, 18 August 1995. From: https://www.orlandosentinel.com/news/os-xpm-1985-08-18-0320230078-story.html.
42. Joe Marshall, "World Bowl in Crisis," *Sports Illustrated*, 16 December 1974, p. 23.
43. "WFL Stages Mercy-Killing; Closes Doors," *Pittsburgh Press*, 23 October 1975, p. 24.
44. "USFL vs. NFL, 1984 NFL Draft War," *NFL Films*, 1999.
45. Young collected about $4.8 million before the USFL went out of business.
46. Ben Terris, "And Then There Was the Time Donald Trump Bought a Football Team," *Washington Post*, 19 October 2015. From: https://www.washingtonpost.com/lifestyle/style/and-then-there-was-the-time-donald-trump-bought-a-football-team-/2015/10/19/35ae71ca-6dd6-11e5-aa5b-f78a98956699_story.html.
47. *Small Potatoes: Who Killed the USFL?* produced by ESPN in 2009.
48. Mike Piellucci, "Donald Trump and the Check That Should Have Changed Football Forever," *Vice*, 21 December 2015. From: https://www.vice.com/en_us/article/z4ae9w/donald-trump-and-the-check-that-should-have-changed-football-forever.
49. Drew Jubera, "How Donald Trump Destroyed a Football League," *Esquire*, 13 January 2016. From: https://www.esquire.com/news-politics/a41135/donald-trump-usfl/.
50. *Ibid.*
51. Jeff Perlman, "The Day Donald Trump's Narcissism Killed the USFL," *Manchester Guardian*, 11 September 2018. From: https://www.theguardian.com/sport/2018/sep/11/the-day-donald-trumps-narcissism-killed-the-usfl.
52. Hank Gola, "Donald Trump Defends USFL Past as He Readies Bid for Buffalo Bills," *New York Daily News*, 5 May

2014. From: https://www.nydailynews.com/sports/football/trump-defends-usfl-readies-bid-bills-article-1.1780131

53. Barry Werner, "Reasons to Believe in the Rebirth of the XFL," *USA Today*, 9 February 2020. From: https://touchdownwire.usatoday.com/2020/02/09/11-reasons-to-believe-in-the-rebirth-of-the-xfl/.

54. Justin Terranova, "Steve Levy: Why XFL Is 'Last Shot' for NFL Alternative," *New York Post*, 7 February 2020. From: https://nypost.com/2020/02/07/steve-levy-on-why-xfl-is-spring-footballs-best-last-shot/.

55. Gary Webster, *The League That Didn't Exist: A History of the All-American Football League, 1946–1949*. Jefferson, NC: McFarland, 2018. p. 163.

56. Allen Barra, "In a Lively League of its Own," *Wall Street Journal*, 16 September 2009. From: http://www.remembertheafl.com/WSJonTheAFL.htm.

57. Jim Thomas, "Ex-Football Stars Discuss 'Ugly Old Days' of 1960s Racism," *Canton (OH) Repository*, 10 February 2019. From: https://www.cantonrep.com/article/20100219/News/302199783.

58. William N. Wallace, "Sid Gillman, 91, Innovator of Passing Strategy in Football," *New York Times*, 4 January 2003. From: https://www.nytimes.com/2003/01/04/sports/sid-gillman-91-innovator-of-passing-strategy-in-football.html.

59. Kenny Moore, "To Baffle and Amaze," *Sports Illustrated* 26 July 1982, p. 68.

60. Pete Iacobelli, "Pass-happy Approach Reaches SEC," *Columbia (TN) Daily Herald*, 26 September 2019. From: https://www.columbiadailyherald.com/sports/20190926/pass-happy-approach-reaches-sec.

61. Rodger Sherman, "The AAF Failed Because All Minor-League Football Does," 2019.

62. "Lost Treasures of the NFL: The WFL," *NFL Films*, 2001.

Chapter Seven

1. "Who Is Canada's Team? We Asked Canadians That and More," *The Canada Project*, 1 June 2017. From: https://www.sportsnet.ca/more/canada-project-canadas-team-asked-canadians/.

2. Donnovan Bennett, "Why the CFL Is Integral to Canada's Sporting Identity," *Sportsnet Canada*, 23 June 2017. From: https://www.sportsnet.ca/football/cfl/cfl-integral-canadas-sporting-identity/.

3. This was not the AFL that eventually merged with the NFL in 1966, but one of four professional leagues named the American Football League. This iteration played during 1940-41 seasons before folding. See Chapter Six for more information.

4. Herb Manning, "One Man's Opinion," *Winnipeg Evening Tribune*, 26 August 1941, p. 10.

5. Herb Manning, "One Man's Opinion," *Winnipeg Evening Tribune*, 11 August 1941, p. 19.

6. Mark L. Ford, *A History of NFL Preseason and Exhibition Games, 1960 to 1985*. Lanham, MD: Rowman & Littlefield, 2014, p. 3.

7. Jack Koffman, "Show Scoring Power of Unlimited Interference," *Ottawa Citizen*, 13 August 1950. From: https://www.ottawaredblacks.com/2014/04/17/throwback-thursday-1950-ottawa-roughriders-vs-ny-giants/.

8. Robert Klemko, "'If Winning or Losing Is Going to Define You, You're on a Rough Road," *Sports Illustrated*, 1 February 2016. From: https://www.si.com/nfl/2016/02/01/nfl-mmqb-bud-grant-minnesota-vikings-super-bowl-losses-vince-lombardi-disklike.

9. *Ibid.*

10. James R. Wallen, *Gridiron Underground: Black American Journeys in Canadian Football*. Toronto: Dundurn Publishing, 2019, p. 98.

11. Dink Carroll, "Ealey's Success with 'Cats' May Change NFL's Attitude," *Montreal Gazette*, 19 December 1972, p. 32.

12. Kevin Mitchell, "Warren Moon: Breaking Down Barriers," *Canadian Football League*, 29 April 2010. From: https://www.cfl.ca/2010/04/29/warren-moon-breaking-down-barriers/.

13. George Johnson, "Stamps, Flutie Turn the Clock Back to 1992," *stampeders.com*, 27 June 2017. From: https://www.cfl.ca/2017/07/27/stamps-flutie-turn-clock-back-1992/.

Notes—Chapter Seven 217

14. "More Ushers at Army–Navy Game," *Ottawa Citizen*, 15 September 1958, p. 13.
15. Jack Kinsella, "Kinsella's Corner: Verdict Is Homicide and on Two Counts," *Ottawa Citizen*, 15 September 1958, p. 13.
16. Chris Willis, "1922 Cardinals vs. Bears: Fist Fight and Sleeveless T-Shirts," *Pro Football Journal*, 19 April 2016. From: http://nflfootballjournal.blogspot.com/2016/04/1922-cardinals-vs-bears-fist-fight-and.html.
17. Richard Rothschild, "Upsets of Bears Among Few High Spots of Cards' Dismal Last Decade Here," *Chicago Tribune*, 15 August 1997. From: https://www.chicagotribune.com/news/ct-xpm-1997-08-15-9708150013-story.html.
18. A.S. Young, "The Trading Game," *Ebony*, April 1971, p. 140.
19. Kevin Plummer, "Historicist: Mismatch of the Century or a Football Game?" *Torontoist*, 6 December 2008. From: https://torontoist.com/2008/12/historicist_mismatch_of_the_century/.
20. Jim Hunt, "Cards Tell Sad Grid Story," *Toronto Star*, 6 August 1959, p. 19.
21. Pat Livingston, "Steelers 'Confused" for Canada Opener," *Pittsburgh Press*, 3 August 1960, p. 40.
22. Bob Scott, "No Converts to NFL Game as Bears Beat Als 34–16," *Montreal Gazette*, 7 August 1961, p. 20.
23. Jim Hunt, "Steelers Buried Argos—Way Down Deep," *Toronto Star*, 4 August 1960, p. 21.
24. Marv Moss, "Game at Jarry Lays Football-Sized Egg," *Montreal Gazette*, 26 August 1969, p. 15.
25. Jack Sell, "Steelers Win Canadian-Style, 43–16," *Pittsburgh Post-Gazette*, 4 August 1960, p. 22.
26. Don Banks, "Adventures Abroad: Remembering NFL's 1976 Foray Into Japan," *nfl.com*, 15 November 2016. From: http://www.nfl.com/news/story/0ap3000000739785/article/adventures-abroad-remembering-nfls-1976-foray-into-japan.
27. Joe Zagorski, *The NFL in the 1970s: Pro Football's Most Important Decade*. Jefferson, NC: McFarland, 2016, p. 298.
28. Simon O'Hagan, "Monarchs Seek to Rule the World," *London (UK) Independent*, 26 March 1995. From: https://www.independent.co.uk/sport/monarchs-seek-to-rule-the-world-1612828.html

29. Rick Telander, "Go Downpitch Smartly, Mate," *Sports Illustrated*, 10 August 1986, p. 30.
30. Simon O'Hagan, "Monarchs Seek to Rule the World," 1995.
31. Sean Keeler, "'You Didn't Play to Get Rich': What Killed NFL Europe?" *Manchester (UK) Guardian*, 23 June 2016. From: https://www.theguardian.com/sport/2016/jun/23/you-didnt-play-to-get-rich-what-killed-nfl-europe.
32. Dean Smith, "New Book Chronicles Sudden Glory, Departure of Baltimore Stallions," *pressboxonline*, 15 November 2019. From: https://www.pressboxonline.com/2019/11/15/new-book-chronicles-sudden-glory-departure-of-baltimore-stallions.
33. Erik Malinowski, "Wild Stallions: How a Team from Baltimore Rocked Canadian Football," *Rolling Stone*, 18 November 2015. From: https://www.rollingstone.com/culture/culture-sports/wild-stallions-how-a-team-from-baltimore-rocked-canadian-football-42712/.
34. Ryan Baillargeon, "After 20 Years, Stallions Finally Celebrate Grey Cup Win," *Baltimore Sun*, 26 July 2015. From: https://www.baltimoresun.com/sports/bs-sp-baltimore-stallions-reunion-0727-20150726-story.html.
35. Erik Malinowski, "Wild Stallions," 2015.
36. Kyle Silagyi, "The Bills Toronto Series and Why Two-City Sports Teams Do Not Work," *USA Today*, 21 June 2019. From: https://billswire.usatoday.com/2019/06/21/buffalo-bills-toronto-series-two-city-sports-teams/.
37. Jenny Vrentas, "The NFL's Future in Europe," *Sports Illustrated*, 24 July 2015. From: https://www.si.com/nfl/2015/07/24/nfl-future-europe.
38. Ibid.
39. In the wake of the coronavirus pandemic, the NFL cancelled all international games and activities for the 2020 season.
40. Sean Keeler, "You Didn't Play to Get Rich," 2016.
41. Pat Evans, "NFL Viewership Growth Throughout Europe Exposed Opportunities in the U.S.," Front Office Sports, 7 March 2019. From: https://frntofficesport.com/two-circles-nfl/.

42. Simon O'Hagan, "Monarchs Seek to Rule the World," 1995.
43. Tom Hamilton, "How Close Is London to Getting an NFL Franchise?" *ESPN*, 30 October 2018. From: https://www.espn.com/nfl/story/_/id/25124631/how-close-london-getting-nfl-franchise.
44. Jeff Fedotin, "NFL Football Has Become Mexico's Second-Most-Popular Sport," *Forbes*, 19 November 2019. From: https://www.forbes.com/sites/jefffedotin/2019/11/19/football-has-become-mexicos-second-most-popular-sport/#30539efd638a.
45. Jenny Vrentas, "The NFL's Future in Europe," 2015.

Chapter Eight

1. Dan Daly, *National Forgotten League*. Lincoln: University of Nebraska Press, 2012, p. 13.
2. Jeff Davis, *Papa Bear: The Life and Legacy of George Halas*. New York: McGraw-Hill, 2006, p. 1.
3. *The First 50 Years: A Celebration of the National Football League in Its Fiftieth Season*, National Football League. New York: Ridge Press, 1969, p. 100.
4. Daly, *National Forgotten League*, p. 240.
5. Greg A. Bedard, "An Anniversary Note," *Boston Globe*, 24 April 2011. From: http://archive.boston.com/sports/football/articles/2011/04/24/bells_idea_nfl_draft_began_75_years_ago/.
6. Robert S. Lyons, *On Any Given Sunday: A Life of Bert Bell*. Philadelphia: Temple University Press, 2009, p. 57.
7. Bedard, "An Anniversary Note," 2011.
8. Michael MacCambridge, *America's Game: The Epic Story of How Pro Football Captured a Nation*. New York: Anchor Books, 2004, p. 38.
9. Gary Webster, *The League That Didn't Exist: A History of the All-America Football Conference, 1946–1949*. Jefferson, NC: McFarland, 2019, p. 28.
10. Ibid., p. 177.
11. "Bert Bell, NFL Czar, Dies at 65," *Milwaukee Sentinel*, 12 October 1959, p. B1.
12. Robert W. Peterson, *Pigskin: The Early Years of Pro Football*. New York: Oxford University Press, 1997, p. 197.
13. Richard O. Davies, *Sports in American Life: A History* (3rd Ed.). Hoboken, NJ: John Wiley & Sons, 2017, p. 225.
14. "Lion Notes," *Detroit Free Press*, 22 August 1958, p. 35.
15. Dave Zeitlin, "The Man Who Modernized Pro Football," *Pennsylvania Gazette*, September/October 2009. From: https://www.upenn.edu/gazette/0909/pro06.html.
16. "NFL Head Bert Bell Dies at 65," *Pittsburgh Post-Gazette*, 12 October 1959, Part 2, p. 1.
17. Zeitlin, "The Man Who Modernized Pro Football," 2009.
18. Michael MacCambridge, *Lamar Hunt: A Life in Sports*. Kansas City, MO: Andrews McNeel Publishing, 2012, p. 98.
19. Jerry Izenberg, *Rozelle: A Biography*. Lincoln: University of Nebraska Press, 2014, p. 44.
20. Kevin Cook, *The Last Headbangers*. New York: W.W. Norton, 2012, p. 22.
21. Harvey Frommer, *When It Was Just a Game: Remembering the First Super Bowl*. Lanham, MD: Taylor Trade Publishing, 2015, p. 19.
22. Michael Wilbon, "Rozelle Grew Into his Job, and NFL Grew Into a Giant," *Washington Post*, 26 March 1989. From: https://www.washingtonpost.com/archive/sports/1989/03/26/rozelle-grew-into-his-job-and-nfl-grew-into-a-giant/9c32914c-f8af-492e-b44e-fca5e7f0759a/.
23. Jerry Izenberg, *Rozelle: A Biography*, 2014, p. 44.
24. "Rams' Pete Rozelle, 33, Elected NFL Czar," *Pittsburgh Post-Gazette*, 27 January 1960, p. 16.
25. Jerry Izenberg, *Rozelle: A Biography*, 2014, p. 103.
26. Barry Wilner, "Rozelle: from Compromise Candidate to Commissioner Nonpareil," 2019.
27. Thomas G. Smith, "Civil Rights on the Gridiron," *ESPN*, 5 March 2002. From: http://www.espn.com/page2/wash/s/2002/0305/1346021.html.
28. William Gildea, "Integrating the Redskins: George Preston Marshall vs. the U.S. Government," *Washington Post*, 5 June 2002. From: https://www.washingtonpost.com/archive/politics/2002/06/05/

integrating-the-redskins-george-preston-marshall-vs-the-us-government/b8b8 2386-4cf0-498c-8a5a-e0498b8d5884/.
29. Ibid.
30. Ryan Basen, "Fifty Years Ago, Last Outpost of Segregation in N.F.L. Fell," *New York Times*, 6 October 2012. From: https://www.nytimes.com/2012/10/07/sports/football/50-years-ago-redskins-were-last-nfl-team-to-integrate.html?pagewanted=all&_r=0.
31. Jack Moore, "Throwback Thursday: The TV Deal That Created Modern Sports," *Vice*, 11 June 2015. From: https://www.vice.com/en_us/article/qkq7xq/throwback-thursday-the-tv-deal-that-created-modern-sports.
32. Barry Wilner, "Rozelle: from Compromise Candidate to Commissioner Nonpareil," 2019.
33. Jeff Duncan, "Remembering the Day 49 Years Ago When the New Orleans Saints Were Born," *New Orleans Times-Picayune*, 1 November 2015. From: https://www.nola.com/sports/saints/article_f62f72c0-726d-53bf-a711-d2c 17bcc3e17.html.
34. "NFL Relatively Clean—Rozelle," *Milwaukee Sentinel*, 18 April 1963, Part 1, p. 9.
35. "'Not Guilty' Karras Plans to Fight Ban," *Milwaukee Sentinel*, 18 April 1963, Part 2, p. 3.
36. John Underwood, "The True Crisis," *Sports Illustrated*, 19 May 1963, p. 18.
37. Jerry Izenberg, *Rozelle: A Biography*, 2014, p. 70.
38. Bud Lea, "Vince, Players Shocked, Hurt," *Milwaukee Sentinel*, 18 April 1963, Part 2, p. 2.
39. Lloyd Larson, "Sad Day for Pro Football, But There's Bright Side, Too," *Milwaukee Sentinel*, 18 April 1963, Part 2, p. 3.
40. Kenneth Rudeen, "Sportsman of the Year," *Sports Illustrated*, 6 January 1964, p. 29.
41. Ibid., p. 24.
42. Paresh Dave, "The NFL Carried on After JFK's Assassination, Even as Players Mourned," *Los Angeles Times*, 21 November 2013. From: https://www.latimes.com/sports/la-xpm-2013-nov-21-la-sp-nfl-jfk-assassination-20131122-story.html.
43. Hank Gola, "Hours After JFK was Assassinated, NFL Commish Pete Rozelle Made the Decision He Would Regret," *New York Daily News*, 23 November 2013. From: https://www.nydailynews.com/sports/football/days-jfk-assassination-nfl-played-article-1.1526740.
44. Dick Young, "They Came with Mixed Emotions," *New York Daily News*, 25 November 1963, p. 43.
45. Jerry Izenberg, *Rozelle: A Biography*, 2014, p. 81.
46. Bob Carter, "Rozelle Made NFL What It Is Today," *ESPN* (n.d.). From: http://www.espn.com/classic/biography/s/rozelle_pete.html.
47. E. Norman Gardiner, *Athletics in the Ancient World*. Oxford: Oxford University Press, 1955, p. 99.
48. Cooper Rollow, "He Made the NFL Into a Winner," *Chicago Tribune*, 23 March 1989. From: https://www.chicagotribune.com/news/ct-xpm-1989-03-23-89032 90629-story.html.
49. "Full Color Football: The History of the American Football League" (Episode 3, War and Peace), *NFL Films*, 2009.
50. Matt Bonesteel, "Deflategate Has Nothing on the Wars Waged Between Al Davis and Pete Rozelle," *Washington Post*, 31 January 2017. From: https://www.washingtonpost.com/news/early-lead/wp/2017/01/31/deflategate-has-nothing-on-the-wars-waged-between-al-davis-and-pete-rozelle/.
51. William N. Wallace, "Rozelle Denies Bias," *New York Times*, 24 January 1981, Section 1, p. 19.
52. Ibid.
53. Rich Tosches, "Rozelle Testifies at NFL Damage Trial," *United Press International*, 16 March 1983. From: https://www.upi.com/Archives/1983/03/16/Rozelle-testifies-at-NFL-damage-trial/4107416638800/.
54. Cooper Rollow, "He Made the NFL Into a Winner," 1989.
55. Ibid.
56. Barry Wilner, "Rozelle: from Compromise Candidate to Commissioner Nonpareil," 2019.

Chapter Nine

1. John Eisenberg, *Ten-Gallon War: The NFL's Cowboys, the AFL's Texans, and

the Feud for Dallas's Pro Football Future. New York: Houghton-Mifflin, 2012, p. 64.
2. Bob St. John, *Landry, the Legend and the Legacy.* Nashville: Word Publishing, 2000, p. 170.
3. Mark Ribowsky, *The Last Cowboy: A Life of Tom Landry.* New York: W.W. North & Company, 2014, p. 142.
4. "10 Things to Know About Tom Landry: From His Fedora to the Job He Almost Took Instead of the Cowboys," *Dallas Morning News,* 28 May 2019. From: https://www.dallasnews.com/sports/cowboys/2019/05/28/10-things-to-know-about-tom-landry-from-his-fedora-to-the-job-he-almost-took-instead-of-the-cowboys/.
5. "The Cowboys and the Indian," *ESPN Films,* 2014. From: https://fivethirtyeight.com/features/cowboys-and-indian-five thirtyeight-films-signals/.
6. Tex Maule, "Make No Mistakes About It," *Sports Illustrated,* 29 January 1968, p. 25.
7. Palash Ghosh, "Dallas Cowboys and the Indian: How a Computer Statistician from Uttar Pradesh Helped Create 'America's Team,'" *International Business Times,* 25 October 2013. From: https://www.ibtimes.com/dallas-cowboys-indian-how-computer-statistician-uttar-pradesh-helped-create-americas-team-1441358.
8. *Ibid.*
9. Peter Golenbock, *Cowboys Have Always Been My Heroes: The Definitive Oral History of America's Team.* New York: Warner Books, 1997, p. 168.
10. Gil Brandt, "1964 Draft Left Lasting Impact on Dallas Cowboys, NFL," *nfl.com,* 9 April 2014. From: http://www.nfl.com/news/story/0ap1000000340099/article/1964-draft-left-lasting-impact-on-dallas-cowboys-nfl.
11. *Ibid.*
12. Gary Cartwright, "Tom Landry: Melting the Plastic Man," *Texas Monthly,* November 1973. From: https://www.texasmonthly.com/articles/tom-landry-melting-the-plastic-man/.
13. Steve Perkins, *Winning the Big One.* New York: Grosset & Dunlap, 1972, p. 87.
14. Tex Maule, "The Day of Devastation," *Sports Illustrated,* 8 January 1962, p. 17.
15. Edwin Shrake, "Why Is This Man Laughing?" *Sports Illustrated,* 17 September 1972, p. 120.
16. "A Football Life: Tom Landry," *NFL Films,* 2014.
17. Bruce Tomaso, "NFL Network Presents—'Tom Landry, A Football Life,'" *Dallas Morning News,* 2 November 2011. From: http://thescoopblog.dallasnews.com/2011/11/nfl-network-presents-tom-landr.html/.
18. Cartwright, "Tom Landry: Melting the Plastic Man," 1973.
19. Gary Cartwright, "Turn Out the Lights," *Texas Monthly,* July 1997. From: https://www.texasmonthly.com/the-culture/turn-out-the-lights/.
20. Steve Perkins, *Winning the Big One.* New York: Grosset & Dunlap, 1972, p. 4.
21. Cartwright, "Turn Out the Lights," 1997.
22. Edwin Shrake, "Why Is This Man Laughing?" p. 123.
23. Gary D'Amato, "The Ice Bowl, 50 Years Later: An Oral History of the Packers-Cowboys 1967 NFL Championship Game," *Milwaukee Journal Sentinel,* 28 December 2017. From: https://www.jsonline.com/story/sports/nfl/packers/2017/12/28/ice-bowl-50-years-later-oral-history-packers-cowboys-1967-nfl-championship-game/962212001/.
24. Jim Murray, "Who Needs Emotion? Not Landry and His Cowboys," *St. Petersburg Times,* 16 August 1972, p. 3C.
25. Edwin Shrake, "Why Is This Man Laughing?" p. 120.
26. Peter Golenbock, *Cowboys Have Always Been My Heroes,* p. 262.
27. Thomas Henderson and Peter Knobler, *Out of Control: Confessions of an NFL Casualty.* New York: Pocket Books, 1987, p. 98.
28. Hutcherson briefly played for two other teams before beginning a 33-year career in pastoral ministry that ended with his death from cancer in 2013.
29. *Ibid.,* p. 93.
30. Golenbock, *Cowboys Have Always Been My Heroes,* p. 437.
31. *Ibid.*
32. Roger Staubach and Frank Luksa, *Time Enough to Win.* Waco, TX: Word Books, 1980, p. 33–34.

33. "Landry Undecided About Quarterback," *Wilmington (NC) Star-News*, 27 July 1973, p. 8C.
34. Perkins, *Winning the Big One*, p. 159.
35. Dan Daly, *The National Forgotten League*. Lincoln: University of Nebraska Press, 2012, p. 360.
36. Carlton Stowers, *Staubach: Portrait of the Brightest Star*. Chicago: Triumph Books, 2010, p. 2.
37. Tex Maule, "Wham, Bam, Stram!" *Sports Illustrated*, 19 January 1970, p. 10.
38. Mark Bullock, "What to Expect from Jon Gruden's Offense in His Return to the Raiders," *Washington Post*, 9 January 2018. From: https://www.washingtonpost.com/news/sports/wp/2018/01/09/what-to-expect-from-jon-grudens-offense-in-his-return-to-the-raiders/.
39. Steven Ruiz, "Tom Brady's Play-Call Wristband Is Proof NFL QBs Have the Hardest Job in Sports," *USA Today*, 9 June 2016. From: https://ftw.usatoday.com/2016/06/tom-brady-play-call-wristband-nfl-new-england-patriots.
40. Mark Ozanian, Kurt Badenhausen, and Christina Settimi, "The NFL's Most Valuable Teams 2019: Cowboys Lead League at $5.5 Billion," *Forbes*, 4 September 2019. From: https://www.forbes.com/sites/mikeozanian/2019/09/04/the-nfls-most-valuable-teams-2019-cowboys-lead-league-at-55-billion/#307d6a352f1b.
41. Golenbock, *Cowboys Have Always Been My Heroes*, p. 690.
42. Gary Myers, "1982 Draft Taught Cowboys a Lesson, *Chicago Tribune*, 27 April 1987. From: https://www.chicagotribune.com/news/ct-xpm-1987-04-27-8702010687-story.html.
43. Jim Lassiter, "Hot Rod Hill: Cowboys Man in 'One-Man Draft,'" *Daily Oklahoman*, 28, April 1982. From: https://oklahoman.com/article/1981813/hot-rod-hill-cowboys-man-in-one-man-draft.
44. Alex Nieves, "What Is the Wonderlic Test and Why Does the NFL Use It?" *Sports Illustrated*, 15 February 2016. From: https://www.si.com/nfl/nfl-combine-wonderlic-test-explained.
45. D. Orlando Ledbetter, "NFL's Success Using Wonderlic Test Subject to Interpretation," *Atlanta Journal-Constitution*, 6 March 2010. From: https://web.archive.org/web/20100527074021/https://www.ajc.com/sports/atlanta-falcons/nfls-success-using-wonderlic-352405.html.
46. Ibid.
47. Bob McGinn, "Peyton Manning Defied Some Predictions," *Milwaukee Journal Sentinel*, 25 January 2014. From: http://archive.jsonline.com/sports/packers/peyton-manning-defied-some-predictions-b99190928z1-241988471.html/#ixzz30m8VcCRe.
48. "NFL Next Gen Stats," *National Football League*, 2019. From: https://operations.nfl.com/the-game/technology/nfl-next-gen-stats/.
49. "Hangin' with the Boys: Long Hall," *dallascowboys.com*, 24 October 2019. From: https://www.dallascowboys.com/audio/hangin-with-the-boys-long-hall.
50. Mike Fisher, "Cowboys Coach McCarthy on Sports Analytics: 'I Used to Say Statistics Are for Losers,'" *Sports Illustrated*, 10 January 2020. From: https://www.si.com/nfl/cowboys/news/cowboys-coach-mccarthy-on-sports-analytics-i-used-to-say-statistics-are-for-losers.
51. Peter King, "FIMA Week 15: Mike McCarthy Gets Creative to Prepare for His Next Shot," *Pro Football Talk*, 16 December 2019. From: https://profootballtalk.nbcsports.com/2019/12/16/mike-mccarthy-coaching-nfl-fmia-week-15-peter-king/
52. Arnold J. Toynbee & David C. Somervell, *A Study of History, Volume 1*. London: Oxford University Press, 1946, p. 354.
53. Breer, "Analytics and the NFL," 2017.
54. "The Cowboys and the Indian," *ESPN Films*, 2014.
55. Ibid.

Chapter Ten

1. John Keim, "Washington NFL Team Says it Will Retire Redskins Name, Logo," *ESPN*, 13 July 2020. From: https://www.espn.com/nfl/story/_/id/29454868/washington-nfl-team-says-retire-redskins-name-logo.
2. Erik Brady, "Opinion: 'NEVER,' The Anatomy of Washington Team Owner

Daniel Synder's Most Famous Quote," *USA Today*, 4 July 2020. From: https://www.usatoday.com/story/sports/nfl/2020/07/04/washington-nfl-team-daniel-snyder-famous-never-quote/5374437002/.

3. Paul Gutierrez, "Hispanic Pioneer Tom Flores Still Waiting for Spot in Canton," *ESPN*, 3 January 2019. From: https://www.espn.com/blog/oakland-raiders/post/_/id/22162/tom-flores-a-profile-of-perseverence-for-raiders-in-wait-for-canton-call.

4. Scott Blair, "Rivera: Former Raiders Coach/QB Tom Flores Should Be in HOF," *NBC Sports*, 6 February 2016. From: https://www.nbcsports.com/bayarea/raiders/rivera-former-raiders-coachqb-tom-flores-should-be-hof.

5. Jarrett Bell, "L.A. Told NFL in 1946: Integrate or Play Elsewhere," *USA Today*, 14 February 2016. From: https://www.usatoday.com/story/sports/nfl/2016/02/14/coliseum-los-angeles-integration-national-football-league-nfl/77788824/.

6. Nathan Fenno, "How the Local Media Helped Overturn the NFL's Unwritten Ban on Black Players," *Los Angeles Times*, 28 January 2017. From: https://www.latimes.com/sports/sportsnow/la-sp-kenny-washington-rams-20170128-story.html.

7. 347 U.S. 483.

8. "JFK and Civil Rights," *Public Broadcasting Service* (n.d.). From: https://www.pbs.org/wgbh/americanexperience/features/jfk-domestic-politics/.

9. Peter Golenbock, *Cowboys Have Always Been My Heroes: A Definitive Oral History of America's Team*. New York: Warner Books, 1997, pp. 283–284.

10. Ryan Marshall, "Chiefs Great Willie Lanier Helped Pave the Way for Black Players in Football," *KSHB-TV*, 22 October 2019. From: https://www.kshb.com/sports/chiefs-great-willie-lanier-helped-pave-the-way-for-black-players-in-football.

11. Neil Jones, "Jim Lynch and Willie Lanier Are Reminder That Football Can Unite People," *KCTV-TV*, 17 December 2017. From: https://www.youtube.com/watch?v=VNSRlMXG9Yg.

12. Peter King, "The AFL," *Sports Illustrated*, 13 July 2009. From: https://www.si.com/vault/2009/07/13/105837113/the-afl.

13. B.J. Kissel, "Remembering the NFL's First Full-Time Black Scout, Lloyd Wells," *Kansas City Chiefs*, 19 February 2020. From: https://www.chiefs.com/news/remembering-the-nfl-s-first-full-time-black-scout-lloyd-wells-16867320.

14. Samuel G. Freeman, "The Last Time the Chiefs Were in the Super Bowl, They Won with HBCU Talent," *The Undefeated*, 29 January 2020. From: https://theundefeated.com/features/kansas-city-chiefs-superbowl-1969-hbcu-football/.

15. "Full Color Football: The New Frontier," *NFL Films*, 2009.

16. Edwin Shrake, "Wahoo! Wahoo! Wahoo!" *Sports Illustrated*, 26 October 1964, p. 66.

17. Gerald Eskenazi, "Wahoo McDaniel, 63, a Wrestler and Folk Hero for Fans of the Early Jets," *New York Times*, 25 April 2002. From: https://www.nytimes.com/2002/04/25/sports/wahoo-mcdaniel-63-a-wrestler-and-a-folk-hero-for-fans-of-the-early-jets.html.

18. Len Hayward, "Friends, Family Recall Wahoo's Legacy," *Midland (TX) Reporter-Telegram*, 20 October 2012. From: https://www.mrt.com/sports/article/Friends-family-recall-Wahoo-s-legacy-7446482.php.

19. "The Biggest Man in Pro Football," *Ebony*, January 1962, p. 63.

20. Marty Mul, "50 Years Ago: How New Orleans Lost the 1965 All-Star Game," *New Orleans Advocate*, 12 January 2015. From: https://www.nola.com/news/article_c98bfcea-af97-5b55-aa2e-c703ff8defb8.html.

21. Neil Graves, "When Racism Drove the AFL All-Star Game Out of New Orleans," *The Undefeated*, 27 January 2017. From: https://theundefeated.com/features/when-racism-drove-the-afl-all-star-game-out-of-new-orleans/.

22. Ibid.

23. Jon Kendle, "Players Boycott AFL All-Star Game," *Pro Football Hall of Fame*, 18 February 2010. From: https://www.profootballhof.com/news/players-boycott-afl-all-star-game/.

24. Jules Bentley, "The Big Cat and the Boycott: Remembering Ernie Ladd," *Anti Gravity Magazine* (n.d.). From: http://antigravitymagazine.com/feature/the-big-cat-and-the-boycott-remembering-ernie-ladd/.

25. Ibid.
26. Graves, "When Racism Drove the AFL All-Star Game Out of New Orleans," 2017.
27. Lonnae O'Neal, "Harry Edwards, a Giant of Sports Activism, Still Has People Shook," *The Undefeated*, 15 October 2018. From: https://theundefeated.com/features/harry-edwards-mexico-city-olympics-sports-activism-john-carlos-tommie-smith-1968/.
28. Bob Orkand, "I Ain't Got No Quarrel with Them Vietcong," *New York Times*, 27 June 2017. From: https://www.nytimes.com/2017/06/27/opinion/muhammad-ali-vietnam-war.html.
29. Mike Freeman, *Jim Brown: The Fierce Life of an American Hero*. New York: HarperCollins, 2006, p. 15.
30. Anthony Poisal, "Memories from Club 46: Jim Brown Looks Back at Importance of Illustrious Career with the Browns Both On and Off the Field," *Cleveland Browns*, 31 December 2019. From: https://www.clevelandbrowns.com/news/memories-from-club-46-jim-brown-looks-back-at-importance-of-illustrious-career-w.
31. Jonathan Eig, "The Cleveland Summit and Muhammad Ali: The True Story," *The Undefeated*, 1 June 2017. From: https://theundefeated.com/features/the-cleveland-summit-muhammad-ali/.
32. Marty Ralbovsky, *Super Bowl*. New York: Hawthorn Books, 1971, p. 14.
33. "Irate Black Athletes Stir Campus Tension," *New York Times*, 16 November 1969, p. 1.
34. Pat Putnam, "End of a Season at Syracuse," *Sports Illustrated*, 28 September 1970, p. 22.
35. John Underwood, "The Desperate Coach," *Sports Illustrated*, 25 August 1969, p. 66.
36. John Underwood, "Concessions—And Lies," *Sports Illustrated*, 8 September 1969, p. 31.
37. Golenbock, *Cowboys Have Always Been My Heroes*, p. 287.
38. Ibid., p. 289.
39. Jeff Merron, "Reel Life: 'North Dallas Forty,'" *ESPN*, 10 February 2001. From: https://www.espn.com/page2/s/closer/021101.html.
40. Charles Hughes, "Tell Them It's What Their Grandfathers Got," in *Performance and Professional Wrestling* (Broderick Chow, Eero Laine and Claire Warden, Eds.). New York: Routledge, 2017, p. 168.
41. "Adviser to Ali, Lloyd C.A. Wells, Dies at 81," *Plainview (TX) Daily Herald*, 14 September 2005. From: https://www.myplainview.com/news/article/Adviser-to-Ali-Lloyd-C-A-Wells-dies-at-81-8508288.php.
42. Maureen Smith, "New Orleans, New Football League, and New Attitudes: The American Football League All-Star Game Boycott, January 1965. From: *Sports and the Racial Divide: African American and Latino Experience in an Era of Change* (Michael Lomax, ed.). Jackson: University of Mississippi Press, 2008, pp. 16–17.
43. Jason Reid, "Marvin Briscoe Carved a Path for Black Quarterbacks to Follow," *The Undefeated*, 14 September 2017. From: https://theundefeated.com/features/former-denver-bronco-marlin-briscoe-carved-a-path-for-black-quarterbacks-to-follow/.
44. Jonathan Rand, *The Year that Changed the Game: The Memorable Months That Shaped Pro Football*. Washington, DC: Potomac Books, 2008, p. 178.
45. Michelle Kaufman, "Hispanic NFL Fan Base Is Exploding, So Why Are Only 16 of 1,696 Players Hispanic?" *Miami Herald*, 28 January 2020. From: https://www.miamiherald.com/sports/nfl/super-bowl/article239637573.html.
46. Ibid.
47. Joe Kapp and Jack Olsen, "A Man of Machismo," *Sports Illustrated*, 20 July 1970, pp. 26–31.
48. Tex Maule, "Kapping the Browns," *Sports Illustrated*, 12 January 1970, p. 12.
49. Martin Ralbovsky, *Super Bowl*. New York: Hawthorn Books, 1971, p. 117.
50. Adam Teicher, "'Why Are You Playing Football?' How Tony Gonzales Changed Perceptions," *ESPN*, 18 November 2019. From: https://www.espn.com/nfl/story/_/id/28082110/why-playing-football-how-tony-gonzalez-changed-perceptions.
51. Doug Tucker, "Obituary: Lamar Hunt/Chiefs Owner Helped Start AFL, Named Super Bowl," *Pittsburgh Post-Gazette*, 15 December 2006. From: https://

www.post-gazette.com/news/obituaries/2006/12/15/Obituary-Lamar-Hunt-Chiefs-owner-helped-start-AFL-named-Super-Bowl/stories/200612150175.

Chapter Eleven

1. "I Knew We'd Win Before Kickoff," *St. Petersburg Times*, 1 January 1962, p. 2-C.
2. It should have been eleven runners as Dave Hampton of Atlanta passed the 1,000-yard mark in the final game of the season against Kansas City. When he broke the mark, the game stopped and Hampton received the game ball. But later in the game, Hampton was thrown for a six-yard loss. Because Atlanta was behind and had to throw the ball, he never got another carry and finished the year with 995 yards. The following year he had a chance again in the final game to surpass 1,000 yards and finished with 997.
3. Michael Janofsky, "Motto of Raiders Is 'Throw Deep,'" *New York Times*, 14 December 1982, p. B19.
4. Ed Gruver, *The American Football League: A Year-By-Year History, 1960–1969*. Jefferson, NC: McFarland, 2011, p. 209.
5. William Wallace, "Sid Gillman, 91, Innovator of Passing Strategy in Football," *New York Times*, 4 January 2003. From: https://www.nytimes.com/2003/01/04/sports/sid-gillman-91-innovator-of-passing-strategy-in-football.html#:~:text=Sid%20Gillman%2C%20the%20longtime%20professional,He%20was%2091.
6. "War and Peace," *Full Color Football*, NFL Films, September 30, 2009.
7. Josh Katzowitz, *Sid Gillman: Father of the Passing Game*. Covington, KY: Clerisy Press, 2012, p. 6.
8. "Ditka Carried Bears to an NFL Title in Playing Days, Too," *Los Angeles Times*, 11 February 1988. From: https://www.latimes.com/archives/la-xpm-1988-02-11-sp-42167-story.html.
9. Paul Zimmerman, "Sid Gillman, Screen Gem," *Sports Illustrated*, 2 September 1991. From: https://www.si.com/nfl/2016/07/01/dr-z-paul-zimmerman-sid-gillman-sports-illustrated-nfl.
10. Tim Leyden, *Blood, Sweat and Chalk, The Ultimate Football Playbook: How the Great Coaches Built Today's Game*. New York: Sports Illustrated Books, 2010, p. 76.
11. Ibid.
12. Michael Rosenberg, *War As They Knew It: Woody Hayes, Bo Schembechler, and America in a Time of War*. New York: Grand Central Publishing, 2008, p. 70.
13. Hayes should have said *four* things could happen and three are bad. His career ended in the 1978 Gator Bowl after a Clemson player returned an intercepted pass and Hayes slugged him before a national television audience.
14. Harvey Frommer, *When It Was Just a Game: Remembering the First Super Bowl*. Lanham, MD: Taylor Trade Publishing, 2015, p. 20.
15. Marty Ralbovsky, Super Bowl. New York: *Hawthorn Books*, 1971, p. 81.
16. Dave Distel, "It's Tunnel Vision, but it Works for Coryell," *Playback*, 5 December 1982, p. 60.
17. Paul Zimmerman, "The Chargers' Fancy Is Passing," *Sports Illustrated*, 28 September 1981, p. 41.
18. Ibid., p. 42.
19. Katzowitz, *Sid Gillman: Father of the Passing Game*, p. 277.
20. Leyden, *Blood, Sweat and Chalk*, p. 77.
21. Chris Wesseling, "A Prince Who Never Became King," *nfl.com*, 21 May 2015. From: https://www.nfl.com/news/sidelines/the-ohio-river-offense.
22. Jack Sheppard, "Carter's Short Passes Provided Pattern for Walsh's 49er Success," *Los Angeles Times*, 31 August 1985. From: https://www.latimes.com/archives/la-xpm-1985-08-31-sp-24242-story.html.
23. "Things That Changed the Game," *NFL Top 10*, NFL Films, 13 May 2008.
24. Frank Henderson and Mel Olsen, *Football's West Coast Offense*. Champaign, IL: Human Kinetics, 1997, p. vii.
25. Sheppard, "Carter's Short Passes," 1985.
26. Leyden, *Blood, Sweat and Chalk*, p. 95.
27. Sheppard, "Carter's Short Passes," 1985.
28. David Howman, "Taking a Deep

Dive Into the Air Coryell Scheme the Cowboys Have Traditionally Used," *Blogging the Boys*, 12 May 2019. From: https://www.bloggingtheboys.com/2019/5/12/18240877/taking-a-deep-dive-into-the-cowboys-air-coryell-scheme-don-norv-turner-mike-martz-jason-garrett.

29. Paul Zimmerman, "Sid Gillman, Screen Gem," 1991.

30. Curry Kirkpatrick, "The Coach: Houston Coach John Jenkins Has No Apologies for His Wild Offense with the Wide-Open Throttle," *Sports Illustrated*, 26 August 1991. From: https://vault.si.com/vault/1991/08/26/the-coach-houston-coach-john-jenkins-has-no-apologies-for-his-wild-offense-with-the-wide-open-throttle.

31. Defenses never did catch up with Tarkenton, who ultimately made the Hall of Fame. When he retired in 1978 after an 18-year career, he was the NFL's all-time leader in touchdown passes.

Chapter Twelve

1. James Cannon, *Time and Chance: Gerald Ford's Appointment with History*. Ann Arbor: University of Michigan Press, 1994, p. xvi.

2. Ecclesiastes 9:11 (NIV).

3. Barry Wilner and Ken Rappoport, *Super Bowl Heroes: Fifty Years of the Greatest Players in Football's Greatest Game*. Lanham, MD: Lyons Press, 2016, p. 21.

4. Michael Nelson, "How Football Became the American Game," *Washington Examiner*, 16 September 2018. From: https://www.washingtonexaminer.com/weekly-standard/how-football-became-the-american-game.

5. Alice George, "When the Yankees Got the Larger-Than-Life Babe Ruth," *Smithsonian Magazine*, 23 December 2019. From: https://www.smithsonianmag.com/smithsonian-institution/when-yankees-larger-than-life-babe-ruth-180973795/.

6. "The Rise and Fall of U.S. Labor Unions, and Why They Still Matter," *The Conversation*, 27 March 2015. From: http://theconversation.com/the-rise-and-fall-of-us-labor-unions-and-why-they-still-matter-38263.

7. Domonique Foxworth, "All 22: Why Decertification of the NFLPA and Other Unions Could Pay Off Big," *The Undefeated*, 25 July 2017. From: https://theundefeated.com/features/all-22-why-decertification-of-the-nflpa-and-other-unions-could-pay-off-big/.

8. John Eisenberg, *Cotton Bowl Days: Growing Up with Dallas and the Cowboys in the 1960s*. New York: Simon & Schuster, 1997, p. 265.

9. Thomas B. Morgan, "The Wham in Pro Football," *Esquire*, 1 November 1959, p. 99.

10. "1950s TV Turns on America," *Advertising Age*, 28 March 2005. From: https://adage.com/article/75-years-of-ideas/1950s-tv-turns-america/102703.

11. Joseph Campbell and Bill Moyers, *The Power of Myth*. New York: Anchor Books, 1991, p. 9.

12. Chris Isidore, "NFL Could Pocket Billions from Boom in Sports Gambling," *CNN*, 5 September 2018. From: https://money.cnn.com/2018/09/05/news/companies/nfl-sports-gambling-revenue/index.html.

13. Jack Moore, "Vince Lombardi Isn't Who You Think He Is," *Vice*, 20 October 2014. From: https://www.vice.com/en_us/article/78yjq9/vince-lombardi-isnt-who-you-think-he-is.

14. Ben McGrath, "Does Football Have a Future?" *The New Yorker*, 24 January 2011. From: https://www.newyorker.com/magazine/2011/01/31/does-football-have-a-future.

15. Mark Maske, "The NFL Never Wanted to be the No Fun League. It Just Happened That Way—Until Now," *Washington Post*, 20 July 2017. From: https://www.washingtonpost.com/news/sports/wp/2017/07/20/the-nfl-never-wanted-to-be-the-no-fun-league-it-just-happened-that-way-until-now/.

16. "Pete Rozelle," *Sports Broadcasting Hall of Fame* (n.d.). From: https://www.sportsbroadcastinghalloffame.org/inductees/pete-rozelle/.

17. Kenneth T. Walsh, "The 1960s: A Decade of Promise and Heartbreak," *U.S. News & World Report*, 9 March 2010. From: https://www.usnews.com/news/articles/2010/03/09/the-1960s-a-decade-of-promise-and-heartbreak.

18. Neil Longley, *An Absence of Competition: The Sustained Competitive Advantage of the Monopoly Sports Leagues*. New York: Springer Publishing, 2013, p. v.
19. Marty Ralbovsky, *Super Bowl*. New York: Hawthorne Books, 1971, pp. 73–74.
20. Ralph Ryback, "Why We Resist Change," *Psychology Today*, 25 January 2017. From: https://www.psychologytoday.com/us/blog/the-truisms-wellness/201701/why-we-resist-change.
21. Rosabeth Moss Kanter, "Ten Reasons People Resist Change," *Harvard Business Review*, 25 September 2012. From: https://hbr.org/2012/09/ten-reasons-people-resist-chang.
22. Donald L. Lester, John A. Parnell & Shawn Carraher, "Organizational Life Cycle: A Five-Stage Empirical Scale," *International Journal of Organizational Analysis*, Vol. 11, No. 4, 2003, p. 342.
23. James Quirk and Rodney D. Fort, *Pay Dirt: The Business of Professional Team Sports*. Princeton: Princeton University Press, 1992, p. 34.
24. Lester, Parnell and Carraher, "Organizational Life Cycle," p. 343.
25. Thomas B. Morgan, "The Wham in Pro Football," *Esquire*, 1 November 1959. From: https://classic.esquire.com/article/1959/11/1/the-wham-in-pro-football.
26. Bianca Miller Cole, "Innovate or Die: How a Lack of Innovation Can Cause Business Failure," *Forbes*, 10 January 2019. From: https://www.forbes.com/sites/biancamillercole/2019/01/10/innovate-or-die-how-a-lack-of-innovation-can-cause-business-failure/#57272162fcb7.
27. Joe Jares, *Basketball: The American Game*. Chicago: Follett Publishing, 1971, p. 96.
28. Nick Gelso, "How the NBA Climbed Mountains Through an Era of Outlandish Proportions," *Bleacher Report*, 6 December 2009. From: https://bleacherreport.com/articles/303726-how-the-nba-climbed-mountains-through-an-era-of-outlandish-proportions.
29. Dwain Price, "NBA, ABA Merger Added Flavor to Pro Basketball," Ft. Worth Star-Telegram, 28 February 2017. From: https://www.star-telegram.com/sports/nba/dallas-mavericks/article135519293.html.
30. Debra Bell, "U.S. News Questioned Football's Future Nearly 45 Years Ago," *U.S. News & World Report*, 1 February 2013. From: https://www.usnews.com/news/blogs/press-past/2013/02/01/us-news-questioned-pro-footballs-future-nearly-45-years-ago.
31. Jabari Young, "With Football Ratings on the Rise, NFL Officials Look to Raise TV Broadcast Fees on Multiyear Media Deals," *CNBC*, 30 December 2019. From: https://www.cnbc.com/2019/12/30/nfl-ratings-recovering-new-media-deals-could-be-on-the-2020-agenda.html.
32. The Los Angeles Chargers finished last in attendance at 31,750 per game, but played in a stadium that seats only 27,000 fans. With standing room and other tickets counted, the Chargers actually averaged 117% of capacity. The team was allowed to use a smaller stadium while the new $4.9 billion SoFi Stadium, with a capacity of 70,240, finishes completion in 2020.
33. Mike Ozanian, "The NFL's Most Valuable Teams 2019: Cowboys Lead League at $5.5 Billion," *Forbes*, 4 September 2019. From: https://www.forbes.com/sites/mikeozanian/2019/09/04/the-nfls-most-valuable-teams-2019-cowboys-lead-league-at-55-billion/#6b20e3f22f1b.
34. Bell, "U.S. News Questioned," 2013.
35. "Packers Profit Drops 98 Percent to $724,000," *New York Post*, 13 July 2019. From: https://nypost.com/2019/07/13/packers-profit-drops-98-percent-to-724000/.
36. Melanie Hicken, "The High Cost of Being a Football Fan," *Money*, 7 September 2013. From: https://money.cnn.com/2013/09/07/pf/football-prices/index.html.
37. Bell, "U.S. News Questioned," 2013.
38. Ozanian, "The NFL's Most Valuable Teams," 2019.
39. Nelson, "How Football Became the American Game," 2018.
40. "President Trump Remarks at Senator Strange Campaign Rally," *C-SPAN*, 22 September 2017. From: https://www.c-span.org/video/?434480-1/president-trump-campaigns-alabama-senator-luther-strange.
41. Will Leitch, "Is This the End of the NFL?" *New York Magazine*, 25 November

2017. From: https://nymag.com/intelligencer/2017/11/leitch-is-this-the-end-of-the-nfl.html?utm_source=pocket&utm_medium=email&utm_campaign=pockethits.

42. John Kass, "Death of NFL Inevitable as Middle Class Abandons the Game," *Chicago Tribune*, 5 September 2017. From: https://www.chicagotribune.com/columns/john-kass/ct-football-concussions-youth-kass-met-0906-20170905-column.html.

43. Ibid.

44. Conor Orr, "Like a Rock, Stuck in a Hard Place," *Sports Illustrated*, 18–25 November 2019, p. 48.

45. Jonathan V. Last, "The NFL Is Dying; Here's Why," *Washington Examiner*, 20 November 2017. From: https://www.washingtonexaminer.com/weeklystandard/the-nfl-is-dying-heres-why.

46. Leitch, "Is This the End of the NFL?" 2017.

47. Nancy Armour, "Opinion: All Those Predictions of the NFL's Impending Demise Now Seem Quite Silly," *USA Today*, 13 November 2019. From: https://www.usatoday.com/story/sports/columnist/nancy-armour/2019/11/13/nfl-making-those-predictions-its-impending-demise-look-silly/2579279001/.

Bibliography

Ambrose, Stephen E. *Eisenhower, the President*. New York: Simon & Schuster, 1984.
American Football League v. National Football League, 205 F. Supp. 60 (D. Md. 1962).
Bell, Debra. "U.S. News Questioned Football's Future Nearly 45 Years Ago." *U.S. News & World Report*. 1 February 2013. From: https://www.usnews.com/news/blogs/press-past/2013/02/01/us-news-questioned-pro-footballs-future-nearly-45-years-ago.
"The Biggest Man in Pro Football." *Ebony*. January 1962.
Birkett, Dave. "When the Walls Talked: Inside Detroit Lions' Improbable 1957 Title Run." *Detroit Free Press*. 8 September 2017. From: https://www.freep.com/story/sports/nfl/lions/2017/09/08/when-walls-talked-inside-detroit-lions-improbable-1957-title-run/630599001/.
Bozeka, George (Ed.). *The 1958 Baltimore Colts: Profiles of the NFL's First Sudden Death Champions*. Jefferson, NC: McFarland, 2018.
Buckley, William F. *A Torch Kept Lit* (James Rosen, ed.). New York: Crown Forum, 2016.
Callahan, Tom. *Johnny U: The Life and Times of Johnny Unitas*. New York: Three Rivers, 2006.
Campbell, Joseph, and Bill Moyers. *The Power of Myth*. New York: Anchor, 1991.
Cannon, James. *Time and Chance: Gerald Ford's Appointment with History*. Ann Arbor: University of Michigan Press, 1994.

Cartwright, Gary. "Tom Landry: Melting the Plastic Man." *Texas Monthly*. November 1973. From: https://www.texasmonthly.com/articles/tom-landry-melting-the-plastic-man/.
"Colin Kaepernick Protests Anthem Over Treatment of Minorities." *The Undefeated*. 27 August 2016. From: https://theundefeated.com/features/colin-kaepernick-protests-anthem-over-treatment-of-minorities/.
Cook, Kevin. *The Last Headbangers*. New York: W.W. Norton, 2012.
"Correspondence." *Neurosurgery*. May 2006, vol. 58, no. 5: E1003.
"The Cowboys and the Indian." *ESPN Films*. 2014. From: https://fivethirtyeight.com/features/cowboys-and-indian-fivethirtyeight-films-signals/.
Creamer, Robert. *Babe: The Legend Comes to Life*. New York: Simon & Schuster, 1974.
Crippen, Kenneth R. & Reaser, Matt. *The All-America Football Conference: Players, Coaches, Records, Games and Awards, 1946–1949*. Jefferson, NC: McFarland, 2018.
Daly, Dan. *The National Forgotten League*. Lincoln: University of Nebraska Press, 2012.
David, Jeff. *Rozelle: Czar of the NFL*. New York: McGraw-Hill, 2008.
Davies, Richard O. *Sports in American Life: A History* (3rd Ed.). Hoboken, NJ: John Wiley & Sons, 2017.
Davis, Jeff. *Papa Bear: The Life and Legacy of George Halas*. New York: McGraw-Hill, 2006, p. 1.
Deford, Frank. "The Best There Ever Was." *Sports Illustrated*. 23 September 2002.

Donovan, Art. *Fatso*. New York: Avon, 1987.

Dunnavant, Keith. *Bart Starr: America's Quarterback and the Rise of the National Football League*. New York: Thomas Dunne, 2011.

Eisenberg, John. *Cotton Bowl Days: Growing Up with Dallas and the Cowboys in the 1960s*. New York: Simon & Schuster, 1997.

_____. *Ten-Gallon War: The NFL's Cowboys, the AFL's Texans, and the Feud for Dallas's Pro Football Future*. New York: Houghton-Mifflin, 2012.

Fenno, Nathan. "How the Local Media Helped Overturn the NFL's Unwritten Ban on Black Players." *Los Angeles Times*. 28 January 2017. From: https://www.latimes.com/sports/sportsnow/la-sp-kenny-washington-rams-20170128-story.html.

The First 50 Years: A Celebration of the National Football League in Its Fiftieth Season. National Football League. New York: Ridge Press, 1969.

"A Football Life: Tom Landry." *NFL Films*. 2014.

Ford, Mark L. *A History of NFL Preseason and Exhibition Games, 1960 to 1985*. Lanham, MD: Rowman & Littlefield, 2014.

Freeman, Mike. *Jim Brown: The Fierce Life of an American Hero*. New York: Harper Collins, 2006.

Frommer, Harry. *When It Was Just a Game: Remembering the First Super Bowl*. Lanham, MD: Taylor Trade, 2015.

"Full Color Football: The New Frontier." *NFL Films*. 2009.

Garcia-Navarro, Lulu. "'Heroic, but He's No Hero': Revisiting Football Great Jim Brown." *National Public Radio*. 13 May 2018. From: https://www.npr.org/2018/05/13/610396047/heroic-but-he-s-no-hero-revisiting-football-great-jim-brown.

Gardiner, E. Norman. *Athletics in the Ancient World*. Oxford: Oxford University Press, 1955.

Gifford, Frank. "Everything Changed After the Glory Game of 1958." *ESPN*. 4 November 2008. From: http://www.espn.com/espn/page2/story?page=glorygame/081103.

Gildea, William. "Integrating the Redskins: George Preston Marshall Vs. the U.S. Government." *Washington Post*. 5 June 2002. From: https://www.washingtonpost.com/archive/politics/2002/06/05/integrating-the-redskins-george-preston-marshall-vs-the-us-government/b8b82386-4cf0-498c-8a5a-e0498b8d5884/.

Golenbock, Peter. *Cowboys Have Always Been My Heroes: The Definitive Oral History of America's Team*. New York: Warner, 1997.

Graves, Neil. "When Racism Drove the AFL All-Star Game Out of New Orleans." *The Undefeated*. 27 January 2017. From: https://theundefeated.com/features/when-racism-drove-the-afl-all-star-game-out-of-new-orleans/.

Gruver, Ed. *The American Football League: A Year-by-Year History, 1960–1969*. Jefferson, NC: McFarland, 1997.

Henderson, Thomas & Knobler, Peter. *Out of Control: Confessions of an NFL Casualty*. New York: Pocket, 1987.

"A History of Football in 100 Objects." *Sports Illustrated*. 28 August 2019. From: https://www.si.com/nfl/2019/nfl-history-of-football-100-objects.

Hitchcock, William I. *The Age of Eisenhower: American and the World in the 1950s*. New York: Simon & Schuster, 2019.

Hornung, Paul, and Billy Reed. *Lombardi and Me: Players, Coaches and Colleagues Talk About the Man and the Myth*. Chicago: Triumph, 2006.

Houston Oilers, Inc. v. Ralph Neely, 361 F.2d 36 (10 Cir. 1966).

Inabinnet, Mark. *Grantland Rice and His Heroes, the Sportswriter as Mythmaker in the 1920s*. Knoxville: University Press of Tennessee, 1994.

Izenberg, Jerry. *Rozelle: A Biography*. Lincoln: University of Nebraska Press, 2014.

Jubera, Drew. "How Donald Trump Destroyed a Football League." *Esquire*. 13 January 2016. From: https://www.esquire.com/news-politics/a41135/donald-trump-usfl/.

Kass, John. "Death of NFL Inevitable as Middle Class Abandons the Game." *Chicago Tribune*. 5 September 2017. From: https://www.chicagotribune.com/columns/john-kass/ct-football-

concussions-youth-kass-met-0906-20170905-column.html.
Keeler, Sean. "'You Didn't Play to Get Rich': What Killed NFL Europe?" *Manchester (UK) Guardian*. 23 June 2016. From: https://www.theguardian.com/sport/2016/jun/23/you-didnt-play-to-get-rich-what-killed-nfl-europe.
Kimmel, Michael, and Amy Aronson. *Men and Masculinities: A Social, Cultural, and Historical Encyclopedia*. Vol. 1. Santa Barbara, CA: ABC-CLIO, 2004.
Klein, Dave. *The Game of Their Lives: The 1958 NFL Championship*. Lanham, MD: Rowman & Littlefield, 2008.
Kramer, Jerry. *Instant Replay: The Green Bay Diary of Jerry Kramer* (Dick Schaap, ed.). New York: World, 1968.
_____. "Winning Wasn't Everything." *New York Times*. 24 January 1997. From: https://archive.nytimes.com/www.nytimes.com/ref/opinion/06opclassic.html?pagewanted=all.
Kuckhohn, Clyde. *Mirror for Man: The Relation of Anthropology to Modern Life*. Tempe: University of Arizona Press, 1949.
Leitch, Will. "Is This the End of the NFL?" *New York Magazine*. 25 November 2017. From: https://nymag.com/intelligencer/2017/11/leitch-is-this-the-end-of-the-nfl.html?utm_source=pocket&utm_medium=email&utm_campaign=pockethits.
Lester, Donald L., Parnell, John A. & Carraher, Shawn. "Organizational Life Cycle: A Five-Stage Empirical Scale." *International Journal of Organizational Analysis*. Vol. 11, No. 4, 2003.
Longley, Neil. *An Absence of Competition: The Sustained Competitive Advantage of the Monopoly Sports Leagues*. New York: Springer, 2013.
Los Angeles Rams Football Clubs v. Cannon, 185 F. Supp. 717 (S.D. Cal. 1960).
"Lost Treasures of the NFL: The WFL." *NFL Films*. 2001.
Lyons, Robert. *On Any Given Sunday: A Life of Bert Bell*. Philadelphia: Temple University Press, 2010.
MacCambridge, Michael. *America's Game: The Epic Story of How Pro Football Captured a Nation*. New York: Anchor, 2004.

_____. *Lamar Hunt: A Life in Sports*. Kansas City, MO: Andrews McNeel, 2012.
Manchester, William. *American Caesar: Douglas MacArthur, 1880–1964*. Boston: Little, Brown, 1978.
Maraniss, Dave. *When Pride Still Mattered: A Life of Vince Lombardi*. New York: Simon & Schuster, 1999.
Maule, Tex. "The Best Football Game Ever Played." *Sports Illustrated*. 5 January 1959.
_____. "The Shaky New League." *Sports Illustrated*. 25 January 1960.
Mayhugh, Jess. "Colt Following." *Baltimore Magazine*. March 2014. From: https://www.baltimoremagazine.com//2014/3/20/is-baltimore-still-angry-about-the-colts.
Miller, Jeff. *Going Long: The Wild Ten Year Saga of the Renegade American Football League in the Words of Those Who Lived It*. Chicago: Contemporary, 2003.
Morgan, Thomas B. "The Wham in Pro Football." *Esquire*. 1 November 1959.
"1958: Baltimore Colts @ New York Giants." *Golden Football Magazine* (n.d.). From: http://goldenrankings.com/nflchampionshipgame1958.html.
"100 Figures Who Shaped the NFL's First Century." *Sports Illustrated*. 28 August 2019. From: https://www.si.com/nfl/2019/nfl-100-most-influential-figures-all-time.
Oriard, Michael. "Chronicle of a (Football) Death Foretold: The Imminent Demise of a National Pastime?" *The International Journal of the History of Sport*. Vol. 31, Issue 1–2, 2014.
Parrish, Bernie. *They Call It a Game: Shoulders the NFL Stands On*. New York: Authors Choice, 2000.
Perkins, Steve. *Winning the Big One*. New York: Grosset & Dunlap, 1972.
Pervin, Lawrence A. *Football's New York Giants: A History*. Jefferson, NC: McFarland, 2009.
Peterson, Robert W. *Pigskin: The Early Years of Pro Football*. New York: Oxford University Press, 1997.
Quirk, James & Fort, Rodney D. *Pay Dirt: The Business of Professional Team Sports*. Princeton: Princeton University Press, 1992.
Radovich v. National Football League, 352 U.S. 445 (1957).

Ralbovsky, Marty. *Super Bowl*. New York: Hawthorn, 1971.
Rand, Jonathan. *The Year That Changed the Game: The Memorable Months That Shaped Pro Football*. Washington, D.C.: Potomac, 2008.
Rapaport, Lisa. "Fewer U.S. High School Athletes Play Football Amid Concussion Fears." *Reuters*. 12 March 2018. From: https://www.reuters.com/article/us-health-kids-tackle-football/fewer-u-s-high-school-athletes-play-football-amid-concussion-fears-idUSKCN1GO2LY.
"Red Grange, the Galloping Ghost." *New York Times*. 18 October 1924. From: http://archive.nytimes.com/www.nytimes.com/packages/html/sports/year_in_sports/10.18a.html.
"Replay! the History of the NFL on Television." *NFL Films*. 1998.
Rhoden, William. "Sports of the Times: NFL's Labor Pioneer Remains Unknown." *New York Times*. 2 October 1994. From: https://www.nytimes.com/1994/10/02/sports/sports-of-the-times-nfl-s-labor-pioneer-remains-unknown.html.
Ribowsky, Mark. *The Last Cowboy: A Life of Tom Landry*. New York: W.W. North &, 2014.
Rielly, Edward J. *Football: An Encyclopedia of Popular Culture*. Lincoln: University of Nebraska Press, 2009.
"The Rise of American Consumerism." *Public Broadcasting Service*. n.d. From: https://www.pbs.org/wgbh/americanexperience/features/tupperware-consumer/.
Ritter, Lawrence. *The Glory of Their Times*. New York: Macmillan, 1966.
Rudeen, Kenneth. "Sportsman of the Year." *Sports Illustrated*. 6 January 1964.
Ryback, Ralph. "Why We Resist Change." *Psychology Today*. 25 January 2017. From: https://www.psychologytoday.com/us/blog/the-truisms-wellness/201701/why-we-resist-change.
Ryczek, William J. *Crash of the Titans: The Early Years of the New York Jets and the AFL*. Jefferson, NC: McFarland, 2009.
Sahadi, Lou. *Johnny Unitas: America's Quarterback*. Chicago: Triumph, 2004.
St. John, Bob. *Landry, the Legend and the Legacy*. Nashville: Word, 2000.
Seifert, Kevin. "Dr. Bennet Omalu: CTE Obsession Obscuring Truth About Brain Health of Football Players." *ESPN*. 4 August 2017. From: http://www.espn.com/nfl/story/_/id/20245394/dr-bennet-omalu-says-obsession-cte-obscuring-larger-truth-brain-health-football-players.
75 Seasons. Atlanta: Turner, 1994.
Shrake, Edwin. "Why Is This Man Laughing?" *Sports Illustrated*. 17 September 1972.
Smith, Maureen. "New Orleans, New Football League, and New Attitudes: The American Football League All-Star Game Boycott, January 1965. From: *Sports and the Racial Divide: African American and Latino Experience in an Era of Change* (Michael Lomax, ed.). Jackson: University Press of Mississippi, 2008.
Staubach, Roger, and Frank Luksa. *Time Enough to Win*. Waco, TX: Word, 1980.
Stowers, Carlton. *Staubach: Portrait of the Brightest Star*. Chicago: Triumph, 2010.
Thompson, Wright. "Vince Lombardi Lived Here." *ESPN*. 3 February 2011. From: https://www.espn.com/nfl/playoffs/2010/columns/story?id=6077292.
Thornberry, Larry. "The Decline of the Sweet Science." *American Spectator*. 12 December 2016. From: https://spectator.org/the-decline-of-the-sweet-science/.
Toynbee, Arnold J., and David C. Somervell. *A Study of History, Volume 1*. London: Oxford University Press, 1946.
Vogan, Travis. *Keepers of the Flame: NFL Films and the Rise of Sports Media*. Champaign: University of Illinois Press, 2014.
Vrentas, Jenny. "The NFL's Future in Europe." *Sports Illustrated*. 24 July 2015. From: https://www.si.com/nfl/2015/07/24/nfl-future-europe.
Wallen, James R. *Gridiron Underground: Black American Journeys in Canadian Football*. Toronto: Dundurn, 2019.
Walsh, Kenneth T. "The 1960s: A Decade of Promise and Heartbreak." *U.S. News & World Report*. 9 March 2010. From: https://www.usnews.com/news/

articles/2010/03/09/the-1960s-a-decade-of-promise-and-heartbreak.
Webster, Gary. *The League That Didn't Exist: A History of the All-American Football League, 1946–1949.* Jefferson, NC: McFarland, 2018.
Wilner, Barry. "NFL at 100: Finding Labor Peace Always a Tortured Process." *Associated Press.* 10 March 2019. From: https://www.apnews.com/271e005334fd481996212d2e25c5a647.
Wilner, Barry & Rappoport, Ken. *Super Bowl Heroes: Fifty Years of the Greatest Players in Football's Greatest Game.* Lanham, MD: Lyons Press, 2016.
Wilson, Sloan. *The Man in the Gray Flannel Suit.* Cambridge, MA: Da Capo, 2002.
Young, A.S. "The Trading Game." *Ebony.* April 1971.
Zagorski, Joe. *The NFL in the 1970s: Pro Football's Most Important Decade.* Jefferson, NC: McFarland, 2016.

Index

Aaron, Hank 67
Adams, K.S. "Bud" 95–98, 102, 105, 147
Agnew, Spiro 186
Aikman, Troy 177
Alcindor, Lew 167–168
Ali, Muhammad 167, 170, 192
Alworth, Lance 101, 174, 179, 194
Ambrose, Stephen 18–19, 44
Ameche, Alan 48, 50, 52, 54–55, 58–59, 72–74
Ameche, Don 103
Anderson, Donny 92
Anderson, Ken 180
Andrie, George 191
Argovitz, Jerry 107
Arledge, Roone 60, 62, 67
Armour, Nancy 201
Artoe, Lee 37
Asinof, Eliot 21
Atkins, Doug 72

Bassett, John 105, 107
Baugh, Sammy 36, 74, 193
Beane, Billy 158
Beatty, Ed 39
Bednarik, Chuck 25
Bell, Bert 3, 15, 43, 73, 114, 118, 134, 188, 195, 199; dealing with AAFC 24, 132; death of 2, 13–14, 133, 143, 193; as Eagles owner and early NFL 130–131; on gambling in the NFL 21, 133, 196; on players union and relations 25–27; on role of television in the NFL 54, 132–33
Bell, Bobby 101, 164
Bell, Upton 133
Benjamin, Guy 180

Bennett, Donnovan 114
Berle, Milton 17
Berry, Raymond 48, 55–58, 72, 94–95, 148
Berwanger, Jay 131
Bidwell, Charles 95
Biletnikoff, Fred 148
Bird, Larry 197, 201
Bisciotti, Steve 6
Blackbourn, Lisle 80–81
Blanda, George 101, 110, 175
Bock, Hal 6
Boeke, Jim 151
Bolan, Joe 57
Bonds, Barry 67
Borman, Frank 102
Bouton, Jim 20
Boyd, Bobby 146
Bradshaw, Terry 157
Brady, Tom 31, 77, 111, 155
Brandt, Andrew 31
Brandt, Gil 15, 147–149, 154, 156, 160
Brees, Drew 77, 111
Bright, Johnny 116
Briscoe, Marlin 116, 170–171
Brodie, John 102
Brooks, Herb 69
Brown, Jim 37, 42, 50, 137, 146, 168
Brown, Paul 23–25, 29, 36, 41–43, 48, 86–87, 134–135, 139, 179–180
Browne, Joe 31, 38, 41, 138
Bryant, Paul "Bear" 111
Bryant, William B. 28
Buchanan, Buck 110, 164, 170
Buckley, William F. 45
Burrow, Joe 111
Butkus, Dick 148–149, 159

Caesar, Sid 17
Caffey, Lee Roy 92

Calhoun, George 80
Campbell, Joseph 86–88, 192
Cannon, Billy 98–99
Cannon, James 186
Caraway, Don 120
Carlos, John 167, 192
Carr, Joe 34
Carroll, Dink 116
Carter, Virgil 180
Celler, Emanuel 25, 27, 138
Chamberlain, Wilt 70, 201
Chandler, Don 56, 58
Chase, Hal 63
Christiansen, Jack 40
Clark, Dwight 181
Clarke, Bobby 68
Clarke, Frank 147
Cohen, Lizabeth 44
Cole, Trent 159
Conerly, Charlie 51, 54–56, 58–59
Conerly, Perian 58
Conzelman, Jimmy 130
Cook, Greg 179–180
Coolidge, Calvin 44
Cooper, Earl 181
Cooper, Gary 76
Coryell, Don 111, 176–185
Cosell, Howard 60
Cosentino, Mike 125
Coslet, Bruce 180
Costas, Bob 110
Cothren, Paige 57
Creamer, Robert 18, 67
Crimmins, Bernie 71
Crippen, Ken 104
Cronin, Gene 39, 41, 43
Cronkite, Walter 76
Crosby, Bing 103
Csonka, Larry 105, 174
Culverhouse, Hugh 31
Cunningham, Bruce 124
Curran, Pat 122
Curry, Bill 84

235

Curtis, Isaac 180
Curtis, Mike 72

Dale, Carroll 20
Daley, Arthur 100
Daniels, Clem 166
Danielson, Gary 111
Davidson, Gary 104–105
Davis, Al 3, 101, 110–111, 142–143, 175, 183
Davis, Darrell "Mouse" 184
Davis, Kyle 187
Davis, Michael 171–172
Davis, Willie 168
Dawson, Len 101, 175
Deford, Frank 77–78
Del Bello, Jack 48
Dempsey, Jack 66, 191
Dibble, Dorne 39
Dichter, Ernest 60
Dickenson, Dave 117
Dils, Steve 180
Ditka, Mike 175–176
Dixon, David 106
Donovan, Art: on AAFC 23; on Baltimore Colts fans 48; on early years of NFL 38–39, 42, 46; on John Unitas 71, 77; on modern NFL 78; on 1958 NFL title game 52, 54–57, 74; on 1958 season 50; on Weeb Ewbank 49
Dubenion, Elbert 165
Duda, Antoinette 47
Dudley, Bud 117
Dupre, L.G. 54

Ealey, Chuck 116
Ebsersol, Dick 60
Edwards, Harry 167
Edwards, Lavell 180
Einhorn, Eddie 111
Eisenhower, Dwight D. 3, 44–45, 87, 194
Elway, John 77
Enke, Fred 48
Evans, Pat 126
Evers, Medgar 167
Ewbank, Wilbur "Weeb" 48, 50; on John Unitas 49, 71; on 1958 NFL title 54–55, 59

Facenda, John 90
Faison, Earl 166
Fears, Tom 162
Ferguson, Howie 82
Feudtner, Chris 8
Filchock, Frank 21, 133, 192
Fimrite, Ron 41

Fitzgerald, F. Scott 18
Fitzgerald, John 187
Flaherty, Joe 18
Flood, Curt 22
Flores, Tom 162, 170–171, 175
Flutie, Doug 106, 117, 125
Ford, Bill 43
Ford, Gerald 186
Ford, Mark 115
Foss, Joe 103, 145, 167
Foster, Bud 162
Fouts, Dan 111
Foxworth, Domonique 190
Francis, Joe 80, 83
Frazier, Walt 197
Frederickson, Tucker 149
Fullerton, Hugh 67

Gabriel, Roman 101
Gallup, George 10
Ganoe, William 86
Gardiner, E. Normal 142
Garrett, Jason 183
Garrett, Mike 164, 194
Garrison, Walt 149
Gates, Antonio 176
Gee, Michael 31
Gent, Pete 148, 169–170
Gholston, Vernon 157
Gibbs, Joe 177
Gibbs, Ron 56
Gibron, Abe 24
Gifford, Frank 56, 59, 76, 142, 191
Gillman, Sid 110, 174–176, 178–183, 185
Gogolak, Pete 101
Gonzalez, Tony 172, 176
Goodell, Roger 5–6, 30–31
Graham, Otto 37, 41–42, 87, 108
Gramatica, Bill 171
Gramatica, Martin 171
Grange, Red 35–37, 130
Grant, Bud 115, 117
Grantham, Larry 99, 103
Grayson, Dave 166
Green, Cornell 148
Gregg, Forrest 80
Grier, Rosey 51
Griese, Bob 174
Groza, Lou 23, 37, 108, 113, 146
Gruden, John 155
Gruver, Ed 74
Gunsel, Austin 134

Halas, George 25–26, 29, 33, 90, 95–96, 120, 129–131, 134–136, 188, 199

Halbritter, Ray 161
Haley, Martin 66
Hall, Chris 158
Hall, Jason 126
Hanner, Dave 80
Hapes, Merle 21, 133, 139, 192
Harding, Warren 17, 65
Harris, James 117, 171
Haslam, Dee 199
Haslam, Jimmy 199
Haupt, Troy 203
Havlicek, John 148
Hawkins, Alex 70, 82
Hayes, Bob 148–149, 153
Hayes, Woody 177, 224
Haynes, Abner 165
Heinrich, Don 54
Hemmetter, Chris 105
Henderson, Paul 68
Henderson, Thomas "Hollywood" 153
Herber, Arnie 79
Hewitt, Don 67
Hill, Rod 156
Hilton, Barron 96–97
Hilton, Conrad 96
Hirsch, Elroy "Crazy Legs" 174, 193
Holloway, Condredge 116–117
Hooper, Harry 67
Hope, Bob 103
Horn, Don 177–178
Hornung, Paul 13–14, 30, 43, 80, 84, 139–140, 173, 192
Houston, Jim 23
Howell, Jim Lee 51–52, 54, 56–57, 59
Howsam, Bob 96
Howton, Billy 27
Huber, Robert 125
Hudson, Lou 148
Huff, Sam 39, 51, 55, 76
Hunt, H.L. 94, 98, 100
Hunt, Jim 119–120
Hunt, Lamar: in college 94; on 1958 NFL championship game 94; role in AFL-NFL merger 102–103, 112, 134; role in formation of American Football League 2, 13, 95–100, 145, 147; role in integration of pro football 110, 163–164, 171–172; wealth of 105
Hurd, Michael 164
Hutcherson, Ken 152–153, 220
Hutson, Don 79

Ibarra, Alejandro 172
Irsay, Robert 47
Izenberg, Jerry 135
Jackson, Lamar 185
James, LeBron 201
Jaworski, Ron 122
Jenkins, John 184
Jessup, Roger 163
Jeter, Gary 28
Johnson, Bill "Tiger" 180
Johnson, Butch 154
Johnson, Earvin "Magic" 197, 201
Johnson, Stuart H. 28
Johnson, William 60
Joiner, Charlie 178
Jones, Barbara 31
Jones, Bobby 66, 191
Jones, Ed "Too Tall" 149
Jones, Jerry 29, 154, 192, 201
Jordan, Cameron 29
Jordan, Henry 82, 84
Jordan, Lee Roy 153
Jordan, Michael 201
Junker, Steve 42
Jurgensen, Sonny 101

Kaepernick, Colin 3, 6, 198, 200
Kanski, Alison 9
Kanter, Rosabeth Moss 195
Kapp, Joe 28, 171–172
Karras, Alex 14, 30, 139–140, 192
Kass, John 200
Kassulke, Karl 172
Katcavage, Jim 51
Kellet, Don 48, 50, 134
Kelly, Jim 71, 157
Kemble, Ed 96
Kemp, Jack 144
Kemp, Ray 19
Kennedy, John F. 3, 140–142, 163
Kerkorian, Gary 48
Khan, Tony 159
Kiesling, Walt 71
Kiick, Jim 105
Kilory, Bucko 37
King, Martin Luther 19, 163, 167
Kinsella, Jack 118
Klingler, David 184
Knafelc, Gary 80, 83
Koffman, Jack 115
Kraft, Robert 192
Kramer, Jerry 80, 82–85, 87, 92
Kramer, Ron 85

Krause, Paul 187
Krieger, Zanvyl 48
Kuckhohn, Clyde 11
Kuechle, Oliver 81

Ladd, Ernie 166–167, 170–171
Lambeau, Earl "Curly" 79–81, 91
Lamonica, Daryle 101, 175, 178
Landis, Kenneth "Kenesaw Mountain" 21, 64, 143
Landry, Tom: as coach of Dallas Cowboys 2, 90, 141, 147, 169, 194; coaching reputation of 146, 150; comparison to Vince Lombardi 15; as New York Giants assistant 15, 51; in 1958 NFL title game 56; "system" of 150–154; use of computerization 15, 147, 149–150, 155–157, 160
Lane, Dick "Night Train" 193
Lanier, Willie 110, 163–164, 170
Larscheid, Jack 162
Larson, Lloyd 140
Lassiter, Jim 156
Last, Jonathan 200
Lavelli, Dante 24, 37
Layden, Elmer 35, 131–132
Layne, Bobby 38–44, 46, 165
Lea, Bud 88
Leaf, Ryan 158
Leahy, Marshall 134–135
Lebovitch, Mark 199
Leitch, Will 199
Leiser, Bill 40
Levy, Daniel 127
Levy, Steve 108
Lewin, Dennis 69
Lilly, Bob 152
Lincoln, Keith 174–175
Lindbergh, Charles 66
Lipscomb, Gene "Big Daddy" 56, 166
Lombardi, Marie 87
Lombardi, Susan 87
Lombardi, Vince: authoritarian style of 30, 81–83, 88, 168–169, 173; comparison to Tom Landry 15, 149; as football strategist 84–85; hired as Packers coach 2–3, 12; in Ice Bowl 91–92, 152;

mythology of 86–88, 92–93, 159, 192; as New York Giants assistant 51, 56; as Packers coach/general manager 81–83, 115–116, 138, 140, 147, 149–150, 174, 176, 194; relationship with NFL Films 89–90, 92–93; reputation of 13–14, 29, 84, 86
Lombardi, Vince, Jr. 88
Long, Russell 138
Longley, Neil 194
Lott, Ronnie 181
Lowe, Paul 174
Luck, Andrew 47
Luckman, Sid 90, 176
Lynch, Jim 164
Lyons, Brian 157
Lyons, Richard 133

MacArthur, Douglas 86
MacCambridge, Michael 131, 143, 164
Mack, Connie 64
Mackey, John 7
Madden, John 85–86, 143
Madel, Fred 23–24
Mahomes, Patrick 185
Mailer, Norman 45
Malinowski, Erik 124
Manning, Herb 114
Manning, Peyton 47, 77, 158, 183
Manziel, Johnny 111, 201
Mara, Tim 188
Mara, Wellington 36, 53, 134
March, Harry 34–35
Marchetti, Gino 50, 56
Marino, Dan 71, 77, 157
Maris, Roger 67
Marshall, George Preston 25–26, 37, 110, 134–137, 162, 188, 199
Martin, Harvey 149
Martinkovic, John 80
Maske, Mark 193
Matson, Ollie 119, 174
Maynard, Don 49–50, 101, 103
McBride, Shawn 9
McCarthy, Mike 159
McClanahan, Brent 187
McClelland, Harry 178
McClinton, Curtis 171
McColgan, Bill 57–58, 73
McDaniel, Ed "Wahoo" 165–166
McElhenny, Hugh 41
McFadin, Bud 99

McGee, Max 80, 84
McGraw, John 64
McHan, Lamar 83
McKay, Jim 69
McKay, John 176
McLean, Ray "Scooter" 80–81
McMahon, Vince 107
McNally, Johnny "Blood" 38, 46
McNamee, Frank 136, 141
McNeil, Clifton 20
Meggyesy, Dave 193
Meredith, Don 60, 150–151, 153, 170
Michaels, Al 69
Miller, Connell 22
Miller, Creighton 24–27, 32
Miller, Giles 22
Mingo, Barkevious 160
Mingo, Gene 170
Mix, Ron 98, 110, 167
Modell, Art 102, 199
Modzelewski, Dick 51
Molinet, Iganacio Saturnino "Lou" 162
Montana, Joe 71, 77, 122, 181
Moon, Warren 117, 125
Moore, Lenny 48
Morabito, Tony 50, 54, 72
Morgan, Thomas 20, 191
Morrall, Earl 43
Morris, Mercury 174
Morton, Craig 151, 153–154
Motley, Marion 37, 108, 163
Munoz, Anthony 171–172
Murchison, Clint, Jr. 96, 145, 155
Murdoch, Rupert 123
Murray, Jim 152
Mushnick, Phil 8
Mutscheller, Jim 55, 58
Myhra, Steve 54, 57–58

Namath, Joe 30, 49–50, 71, 74, 77, 100–101, 103, 111, 148–149, 172–173, 178, 181, 192, 194
Nave, Doyle 147
Neely, Ralph 98, 154
Newton, Cam 111
Nitschke, Ray 80
Nixon, Richard 176, 186
Nobis, Tommy 102
Nolan, Dick 146, 150

O'Connell, Tommy 42–43
Olejniczak, Dominic 81
Olive, Arturo 127
Oliver, Chip 193
O'Malley, Walter 22
Omalu, Bennett 7
Oriard, Michael 8, 93
Oswald, Lee Harvey 141
Owen, Steve 50–51, 146
Owens, Jeff 157
Owens, R.C. 40

Parilli, Babe 42, 80, 83
Parker, Buddy 38, 43, 165
Parker, Jim 74
Parks, Rosa 19, 163
Parrish, Bernie 27
Patoski, Joe 148, 160
Pearson, Drew 150, 154, 156, 187–188
Pearson, Preston 187–188
Perkins, Steve 151
Perry, William "Refrigerator" 122–123
Pielke, Roger 8
Pilson, Neil 61
Plum, Milt 42–43
Plunkett, Jim 162, 171–172
Pollard, Fritz 19
Pope, Edwin 142
Poussaint, Renee 69
Povich, Shirley 20, 137
Pugh, Jethro 92, 149

Radovich, Bill 3, 12, 15, 23–24, 26, 29, 32, 189, 194
Ralbovsky, Marty 74
Ratterman, George 24, 42
Reaser, Matt 104
Rechichar, Bert 57
Reddy, Bill 22
Reeves, Dan 25
Reichow, Jerry 38, 42
Renfro, Mel 149, 153
Rice, Grantland 34, 66
Rice, Jerry 181
Rice, Nathan 199
Rice, Ray 5–6, 31–32
Riley, Pat 148
Ringer, Robert 17, 19
Ringo, Jim 29–30
Rivera, Ron 162
Robertston, Oscar 201
Robinson, Jackie 18–19, 162
Robinson, Johnny 98
Robustelli, Andy 51, 146
Rockne, Knute 34, 149
Rollow, Cooper 143
Rooney, Art 26, 130, 134, 188, 199

Roosevelt, Theodore 8, 86
Rosenbloom, Carroll 25, 59, 135
Ross, Herb 19
Rote, Kyle 55, 58
Rote, Tobin 40–42
Rotkiewicz, Stan 73
Royal, Darrell 177
Rozelle, Pete: becomes NFL commissioner 2, 14, 134–136; on gambling in the NFL 14, 30, 139–140; on integrating the NFL 137; on Kennedy assassination 140–142; on NFL Films 89–90; relations with NFL union 31–32, 142; relationship with AFL 96, 98, 102, 135, 194; relationship with Al Davis 3, 143; success as NFL commissioner 15, 135–144, 193, 198; on television and the NFL 10, 61, 137–138
Rozier, Mike 106
Rubenstein, Alex 30
Russell, Bill 70, 168
Ruth, Babe 12, 34, 64–67, 74, 188–189, 191
Ryan, Buddy 155
Ryan, Frank 174

Saban, Nick 111
Sabol, Ed 3, 14–15, 89–90
Sabol, Steve 14, 89–90, 92
Salata, Paul 77
Salinger, Pierre 141
Sample, Johnny 74–75
Sauer, George 193
Sayers, Gale 148
Schenkel, Chris 72
Schmidt, Joe 43–44
Schnelker, Ray 55
Schramm, Tex 15, 28–29, 31, 52, 102, 135–136, 140, 145–149, 156, 160
Schwarzkopf, Norman 85
Scott, Harry 66
Scott, Ray 53
Seifert, George 181
Septien, Rafael 171
Seymour, Harold 18, 66
Shaw, Dennis 177
Shaw, George 57, 71
Sherman, Rodger 103, 111
Shofner, Del 174
Shula, Don 29, 86
Sills, Allan 5
Simmons, Chet 106
Simpson, O.J. 174

Index 239

Sipe, Brian 177
Skoronski, Bob 85, 92
Slane, Sara 192
Smith, James "Yazoo" 28
Smith, Maureen 170
Smith, Red 79, 141
Smith, Tommie 167, 192
Snell, Matt 103, 173
Snyder, Daniel 161
Spagnola, John 28
Spavital, Jim 48
Speros, Jim 125
Spinney, Art 59
Stabler, Kenny 7
Stafford, Matthew 111
Starr, Bart 80–85, 87, 91–92, 110, 151, 173
Starr, Cherry 83
Staubach, Roger 90, 149, 153–154, 187
Steadman, John 47
Steiner, Charley 106
Steissguth, Thomas 65
Stout, Steve 49
Stram, Hank 155, 164
Strode, Woody 19, 163
Stuckey, Jim 181
Suhonen, Alpo 68
Summerall, Pat 51–52, 54, 99, 178
Svoboda, Bill 58
Switzer, Barry 177

Tagliabue, Paul 32
Tarkenton, Fran 185, 188
Tassef, Carl 56
Tate, James 141
Taylor, Jim 80, 173
Taylor, Otis 101, 110, 164
Teresa, Tony 162
Terzian, Armen 188
Theismann, Joe 117
Thomas, Duane 149
Thomas, Joe 49

Thompson, Chuck 72, 74
Thornberry, Larry 10
Thorpe, Jim 129–130
Tittle, Y.A. 40, 173, 181
Tollin, Mike 106–107
Tomsula, Jim 127
Topping, Dan 103
Toynbee, Arnold 159
Trimble, Joe 59
Triplett, Mel 55–56
Trump, Donald 106–108, 199
Trumpy, Bob 180
Tubbs, Jerry 147
Turner, Keena 181
Turner, Norv 183

Underwood, John 140
Unitas, Dorothy 58
Unitas, Johnny: early life and career 48, 70–71; importance to NFL 12, 15, 76–78, 194; in NFL title games 54–58, 72–74, 146; personality of 72; relationship with Weeb Ewbank 49–50

Vaccaro, Mike 103
Valley, Wayne 96
Van Brocklin, Norm 25, 174
Van Buren, Steve 162
Ventner, Mel 162
Villanueva, Danny 163

Wade, Bill 174, 176
Walker, Herschel 106, 111
Wallace, George 163
Walsh, Bill 110, 155, 179–181, 183, 185
Ware, Andre 184
Warfield, Paul 23, 105
Washington, Kenny 19, 163

Waterfield, Bob 174
Watson, Deshaun 185
Webster, Alex 55
Webster, Mike 7
Wells, Lloyd 101, 110, 164, 170
Werblin, David "Sonny" 100
West, Jerry 201
White, Randy 149
White, Reggie 106, 159
Wilbur, John 163
Willard, Ken 149
Williams, Cy 64
Williams, Doug 117
Williamson, Carlton 181
Williamson, Fred "The Hammer" 168
Willis, Bill 163
Wilson, George 41–43
Wilson, Ralph 100
Wilson, Russell 8
Wilson, Sloan 45
Winslow, Kellen 176, 178
Winter, Max 96–97
Wismer, Harry 96–97, 99–100
Wistert, Al 36
Wolff, Bob 70
Wolfner, Walter 95, 135–136
Wright, Eric 181
Wright, Mike 115
Wright, Nate 187–188
Wright, Rayfield 7, 148

Young, Dick 20, 141
Young, Steve 106, 179, 215
Young, Vince 184–185
Younger, Paul "Tank" 17

Zampese, Ernie 183
Zimmerman, Paul 100, 179
Zirin, Dave 38

www.ingramcontent.com/pod-product-compliance
Ingram Content Group UK Ltd.
Pitfield, Milton Keynes, MK11 3LW, UK
UKHW041942140426
5217IPUK00014B/618